IN DEFENCE OF PRINCIPLES

Law and Society Series
W. Wesley Pue, General Editor

The Law and Society Series explores law as a socially embedded phenomenon. It is premised on the understanding that the conventional division of law from society creates false dichotomies in thinking, scholarship, educational practice, and social life. Books in the series treat law and society as mutually constitutive and seek to bridge scholarship emerging from interdisciplinary engagement of law with disciplines such as politics, social theory, history, political economy, and gender studies.

A list of titles in the series appears at the end of the book.

IN DEFENCE OF PRINCIPLES
NGOs and Human Rights in Canada

Andrew S. Thompson

UBCPress · Vancouver · Toronto

© UBC Press 2010

All rights reserved. No part of this publication may be reproduced, stored in a retrieval system, or transmitted, in any form or by any means, without prior written permission of the publisher, or, in Canada, in the case of photocopying or other reprographic copying, a licence from Access Copyright, www.accesscopyright.ca.

20 19 18 17 16 15 14 13 12 11 10   5 4 3 2 1

Printed in Canada on FSC-certified ancient-forest-free paper (100% post-consumer recycled) that is processed chlorine- and acid-free.

Library and Archives Canada Cataloguing in Publication

Thompson, Andrew S. (Andrew Stuart), 1975-
    In defense of principles: NGOs and human rights in Canada / Andrew S. Thompson.

(Law and society, ISSN 1496-4953)
Includes bibliographical references and index.
ISBN 978-0-7748-1861-2

    1. Civil rights – Canada – Cases. 2. Canada. Canadian Charter of Rights and Freedoms – Cases. 3. Non-governmental organizations – Canada – Case studies. I. Title. II. Series: Law and society series (Vancouver, B.C.)

KE4381.5.T46 2010   342.7108'5   C2010-904777-X
KF4483.C5T46 2010

Canada

UBC Press gratefully acknowledges the financial support for our publishing program of the Government of Canada (through the Canada Book Fund), the Canada Council for the Arts, and the British Columbia Arts Council.

This book has been published with the help of a grant from the Canadian Federation for the Humanities and Social Sciences, through the Aid to Scholarly Publications Programme, using funds provided by the Social Sciences and Humanities Research Council of Canada.

Printed and bound in Canada by Friesens
Set in Futura Condensed and Warnock Pro by Artegraphica Design Co. Ltd.
Copy editor: Dallas Harrison
Proofreader: Lesley Erickson

UBC Press
The University of British Columbia
2029 West Mall
Vancouver, BC V6T 1Z2
www.ubcpress.ca

TO ALISON, ELISE, AND AMY ...
BUT ESPECIALLY ALISON

Contents

Preface and Acknowledgments / ix

Abbreviations / xiii

Introduction: In Defence of Principles / 1

1 My Brother's Keeper: The Canadian Council of Churches and the Rights of Refugees / 15

2 The "Misuse" of Freedom? The Canadian Jewish Congress, the Canadian Civil Liberties Association, and the Limits of Expression / 54

3 Shocking the Conscience? Amnesty International Canada and Abolition of the Death Penalty / 88

Conclusion: Principles in the Age of Rights / 117

Notes / 121

Selected Bibliography / 179

Index / 194

Preface and Acknowledgments

This book began in the summer of 2000, although I didn't know it at the time. From 1999 to 2000, I was briefly on staff at Amnesty International Canada, serving as its interim media officer while the full-time occupant of that position was on secondment to the organization's international secretariat in London, England. In July 2000, I was asked to attend hearings at the Supreme Court of Canada in *United States v. Burns,* a case involving the potential extradition of two Canadians to the United States to face the death penalty (see Chapter 3). There, I witnessed some of Canada's finest legal minds – including David Matas, who was representing the organization – attempt to convince the court that the section of Canada's extradition treaty with the United States that allowed the minister of justice the discretion to decide whether to place conditions on an individual's surrender was unconstitutional. Although at the time I did not fully appreciate the significance of what I was witnessing, those events at the country's highest court sparked my interest in both the emergence of ideas or norms about rights and the role of non-state actors and institutions in championing and ultimately codifying those same ideas or norms into law.

Like many projects, this book began as one thing and ended up as another. My original intention was to analyze the influence of four human rights organizations at the Supreme Court of Canada that intervened in three precedent-setting *Charter* cases involving the rights of refugee claimants to due process and procedural fairness; free expression and protection of vulnerable minorities from messages of hate; and the rights to life, security of the person, and freedom from cruel and unusual treatment and punishment as they related to capital punishment and Canada's extradition treaty with the United States. But the book soon came to be about more than this. As it progressed, my focus shifted. What emerged was a broader study of what scholars in Canada and elsewhere have come to call the "age of rights" or "rights revolution."

Abstract human rights principles, because of their ethical character, are often spoken of in absolute terms. In practice, however, they are anything but. When they are tested by real, often difficult cases involving moral ambiguity and tremendous material considerations, even respect for claims considered to encompass fundamental or "first order" rights is far from assured. In each of the three case studies featured in this book, acceptance and adoption of a claim were context specific and subject to backsliding, inherent tensions, contradictory pulls, and even unintended consequences. Cumulatively, they reveal the capriciousness of ideas about human rights, even in countries such as Canada that have a strong tradition of the rule of law, a judiciary that possesses the constitutional authority to engage in judicial review, and a vibrant civil society.

In this sense, the book is a product of the post-9/11 period. In the first decade since that fateful day, advanced liberal democracies around the world, including Canada, have responded to the threat posed by transnational terrorism with a systematic weakening of human rights standards, including the ones mentioned above. And though this book was written at a time when seemingly well-established rights were contested and disregarded, its purpose is not to be dismissive of Canada's rights revolution. The three case studies also reveal the resilience of these ideas that define the ways in which governments treat their citizens, a resilience that is due in no small measure to the advocacy of non-governmental organizations prepared to defend principles, often at a considerable cost.

This book would not have been possible without the help, guidance, and support of a number of people and organizations. I would like to thank the Osgoode Society for Canadian Legal History, the Social Sciences and Humanities Research Council of Canada, and the Ontario Graduate Scholarship for the financial support that each gave to this project. I would also like to thank the staff at Library and Archives Canada (LAC) in Ottawa and the International Institute for Social History in Amsterdam for their assistance in tracking down documents necessary for my research. The book also could not have been written without the assistance of the organizations featured in its pages. I would like to express sincere appreciation to Amnesty International Canada, B'nai Brith, the Canadian Civil Liberties Association, and the Canadian Council of Churches for granting me permission to review their files. I would like to especially mention Bob Goodfellow, the executive director of Amnesty International's office in Ottawa, for arranging a number of the interviews that I conducted throughout the research and Gina Hill, the former president of the organization, for reading drafts of some of the chapters.

I would also like to extend my gratitude to Andrew F. Cooper for including me in so many of his projects, all of which taught me a great deal about the work of NGOs; James Walker, whose own pioneering work has influenced so much of my thinking, for helping me to articulate my ideas and see "the forest through the trees"; Brian Orend and Irving Abella for their constructive feedback; and, most of all, John English, who has given me and my family so much. He has mentored me, inspired me, challenged me, and shown me the world. For this, I am truly humbled and forever grateful.

To the entire Department of History at the University of Waterloo, I would like to say thank you. There is a saying that it takes a village to raise a child. The same holds true for graduate students: it takes an entire department to raise them. That I have been raised so well is a testament to the calibre of the professors who walk the hallways of Hagey Hall. I would like to mention especially P. Whitney Lackenbauer, who not only read early drafts of several of the chapters but also has come to be one of my closest friends during the few years that I have known him.

I would also like to thank the many colleagues who have supported and encouraged this and other projects over the years. They are Stephanie Bangarth, James Blight, Gerard Boychuk, Kelly Brown, Alison Brysk, Jennifer Clapp, Ken Coates, William Coleman, Patricia Goff, Jorge Heine, Eric Helleiner, Kathryn Hochstetler, Thomas Homer-Dixon, Susan Horton, Rhoda Howard-Hassmann, Sherry Howse, Janet Lang, Terrence Levesque, Bessma Momani, Richard Nutbrown, Daniel Schwanen, Yasmine Shamsie, Brian Tanguay, Ramesh Thakur, Debora VanNijnatten, Heather Vogel, David Welch, April Wettig, Randy Wigle, and Lena Yost.

I would like to thank UBC Press for all of the time and energy that it has invested in the production of this book. Special thanks go to Randy Schmidt, who, from the first day I contacted him, always saw potential in this manuscript, Holly Keller for all of her help in getting it ready for the printers, and

David Drummond for designing the cover. I would also like to thank the three anonymous peer reviewers, whose collective criticisms have had such a positive influence on my thinking and the final product.

Finally, I would like to thank my family. To my parents, Mary and Carl, thank you for all of your support and advice. To my younger brother Alan, thank you for making me laugh throughout the trials and tribulations of writing this book. To my older brother Simon, thank you for all of your help with the research for Chapter 2; your insights have been invaluable. And I would like to thank my wife, Alison. You have been a tireless partner who has seen me at my best and through my worst. Without your love, I would not be where I am today.

Abbreviations

ACLU	American Civil Liberties Union
AI	Amnesty International
CARDP	Coalition against the Return of the Death Penalty
CCC	Canadian Council of Churches
CCLA	Canadian Civil Liberties Association
CCP	Court Challenges Program
CCR	Canadian Council for Refugees
CJC	Canadian Jewish Congress
CSIS	Canadian Security Intelligence Service
CUSO	Canadian University Students Overseas
FCSS	Federation of Canadian Sikh Societies
IAB	Immigration Appeal Board
IACHR	Inter-American Commission on Human Rights
ICCHRLA	Inter-Church Committee on Human Rights in Latin America
ICCPR	*International Covenant on Civil and Political Rights*
ICCR	Inter-Church Committee for Refugees
ICEFRD	*International Convention on the Elimination of All Forms of Racial Discrimination*

ICESCR	International Covenant on Economic, Social, and Cultural Rights
ICRC	International Committee of the Red Cross
IISH	International Institute for Social History
IRB	Immigration Refugee Board
IRO	International Refugee Organization
IRPA	Immigration and Refugee Protection Act
JCRC	Joint Community Relations Committee
LAC	Library and Archives Canada
LEAF	Women's Legal Education and Action Fund
LTTE	Liberation Tigers of Tamil Eelam
NJPRC	National Joint Public Relations Committee
NGOs	non-governmental organizations
NPD	National Democratic Party
OAS	Organization of American States
POC	prisoner of conscience
RSAC	Refugee Status Advisory Committee
SIO	senior immigration officer
UDHR	Universal Declaration of Human Rights
UNRRA	United Nations Relief and Rehabilitation Agency
VOV	Victims of Violence Society
WCC	World Council of Churches

IN DEFENCE OF PRINCIPLES

Introduction
In Defence of Principles

We live, to quote the philosopher Norberto Bobbio, in an "age of rights," a time in history characterized by the emergence of norms that define the entitlements and protections that all individuals, by virtue of being human beings, are guaranteed in their pursuit of self-fulfillment.[1] And, as Micheline Ishay argues in her aptly titled book *The History of Human Rights: From Ancient Times to the Globalization Era,* human rights norms are "part of a cumulative historical process."[2] This is a book about the age of rights and the cumulative historical process. More specifically, it is a history of the emergence, advancement, and defence of three human rights norms in Canada in the post–Second World War era – procedural rights for refugees, parameters on free expression for the purpose of confronting hate propaganda, and abolition of the death penalty – and the public interest groups (or non-governmental organizations [NGOs] as they are also known) that championed them, including as "*Charter* rights" at the Supreme Court of Canada, all in the hopes of securing and strengthening a human rights jurisprudence in Canada. Although the focus is on events that took place in Canada, this book's significance is broader. At its core, it is about unavoidable tensions. It is about the inherent dilemmas that all liberal parliamentary democracies encounter when governments attempt to reconcile the seemingly irreconcilable demands of individual rights and freedoms with the rights and protection of the collective, when judiciaries struggle to find a balance between the two, and when rights groups lobby to ensure that the latter, even in times of real or perceived emergency, are not permitted to overshadow the former.

Although the roots of modern human rights norms date back centuries,[3] it was the rise of fascism in Europe and the Second World War with all its horrors that truly ushered in the modern era of human rights. Historians point to events such as US president Franklin Delano Roosevelt's famous "Four Freedoms" speech to Congress on 6 January 1941, which marked the US entry into the war, the drafting of the UN *Charter*, which made the link between the protection of human rights and international peace and security, and the respective adoptions of the UN *Genocide Convention* and *Universal Declaration of Human Rights* (*UDHR*) on 9 and 10 December 1948 as the beginning of a new era in modern history. What emerged was a new way of thinking about the relationship between the state and its citizenry, especially, though not exclusively, in liberal democracies around the world. The purpose of this "rights" dialogue was simultaneously to limit the state's authority to encroach on political and civil freedoms and to compel it to play a positive role in supporting and protecting its citizenry.[4]

Canadian historians have begun, in recent years, to chart the emergence and internalization of this international rights consciousness in Canada, identifying three stages to Canada's age of rights. The first stage began sometime during the first few decades of the twentieth century and coincided with advances at the international level. For much of this period, English Canadians tended to see rights as an American phenomenon that interfered with British conceptions of parliamentary supremacy and utilitarianism, while in Catholic Quebec conceptions of individual liberal rights were considered to be at odds with the anti-democratic political culture that went hand in hand with the province's social and religious conservatism. Ross Lambertson, Stephanie Bangarth, and Dominique Clément argue separately that it was during the 1930s and 1940s that a nascent human rights movement began to emerge in Canada. It consisted of *ad hoc* civil libertarian and egalitarian organizations founded in response to specific incidents of repressive and discriminatory state practices. Increasingly, these groups came to rely on the international discourse of rights as a strategy to secure greater legal protections against arbitrary government authority.[5] Moreover, as James Walker and Constance Backhouse both show, it was also during this early period that significant advances were made in the struggle for greater racial equality. Gradually, the scientific racism of the late nineteenth century and early twentieth century slowly gave way to more progressive views. Equally significant was the emergence of a trend whereby aggrieved individuals and groups began to turn to the nation's courts, including the Supreme Court of Canada, to challenge discriminatory laws and policies and to secure greater minority rights and protections.[6]

According to Lambertson, the second stage began with the passing of the 1960 *Bill of Rights* and ended with the patriation of the Constitution in 1982.[7] The 1960s and 1970s were a time marked, paradoxically, by both rapid change and stifling inertia, great promise and dashed hope. Scholars such as Michael Ignatieff and Alan C. Cairns look back on the 1960s as the beginning of a "rights revolution," a movement whereby citizens in the democratic West, including Canadians, began increasingly to see themselves as "rights bearers" and employed rights discourse to challenge systemic inequities within societies.[8]

Again, this new awareness was bolstered by events at the international level. In 1966, the United Nations opened for signature the two covenants that make up the *International Bill of Rights* – the *International Covenant on Civil and Political Rights* (*ICCPR*) and the *International Covenant on Economic, Social, and Cultural Rights* (*ICESCR*) – which, along with other key treaties, defined both the scope and the legal status of the international human rights regime. These documents, in the words of the famous scholar of human rights Jack Donnelly, "recaptured, in a substantially purified form, the morally appealing idea of adherence to shared standards of justice as a condition for full membership in international society."[9] This was also the era in which NGOs came to be seen as legitimate, and at times even influential, actors within the international system, taking up the mantle as the natural champions and defenders of the ideals codified in international human rights law.[10]

In Canada, Pierre Elliott Trudeau's arrival in Ottawa captured the imagination of the country at a time of great social upheaval characterized by the Quiet Revolution and nationalist movement in Quebec, the proliferation of identity-based social movements, and the baby boom generation's growing disenchantment with political authority.[11] A civil libertarian who had witnessed the heavy-handedness of Maurice Duplessis, Trudeau, first as justice minister and then as prime minister, believed that the state should not "infringe on the conscience of the individual" and that this relationship should be reflected and codified in Canadian law.[12] The liberalization of Canada's divorce laws to include the concept of "marriage breakdown" in

1967 and subsequent reforms to the *Criminal Code* of 1969 relating to the legalization of contraceptives and family-planning materials, the decriminalization of homosexual intercourse between consenting adults, and the legalization of therapeutic abortions in cases where pregnancy threatened the "life or health" of the woman (all of which were embodied in his famous quotation "the state has no place in the bedrooms of the nation") marked a stark break from the past. Together, they represented a new, more inclusive and equitable vision of Canada, one in which the country's laws not only distinguished between "sin and crime" but also were founded on the primacy of the individual and equality of opportunity and reflective of a modern, pluralistic, and increasingly secular nation.[13]

This growing rights culture slowly began to be reflected in the judicial branch of government, specifically the Supreme Court of Canada. From its founding in 1875, the Supreme Court had been a relatively minor institution, its rulings, according to historians James Snell and Frederick Vaughan, unimaginative, conservative, and, above all, overly deferential to the tradition of parliamentary supremacy.[14] But the 1970s marked the beginning of a "coming of age" of sorts for the court. Signs began to appear that it was willing to become a significant player in the rights revolution and use its authority as a check on the laws and policies of the executive and legislative branches of government. In *R. v. Drybones* (1970), the Supreme Court boldly, and uncharacteristically, struck down section 94 of the *Indian Act*, which prohibited Aboriginal people from being intoxicated off reserve lands. It ruled that the act infringed on sections 1(b) and 2 of the 1960 *Bill of Rights*, which protected "the right of the individual to equality before the law and the protection of the law" and stipulated that all laws, unless otherwise stated by Parliament, must conform to the legal rights codified in the bill.[15] According to Snell and Vaughan, the turning point for the court was Trudeau's controversial decision in December 1973 to promote Bora Laskin to the position of chief justice. They contend that, despite being the court's second most puisne justice at the time, Laskin "provided much-needed intellectual vigour [to the court] and ... a philosophical position in constitutional law and civil liberties much akin to the prime minister's."[16] Two years later the court was given control of its docket, thereby giving it the ability to decide which cases it would hear and, by extension, which rights it would choose to advance.

Still, change at Canada's highest court came slowly. Much to the dismay of civil libertarians and equality-seeking groups who hoped that the court would be an instrument of progressive change, *Drybones* proved to be the exception, not the rule. In three high-profile cases in the mid- to late 1970s

– *Lavell v. A.-G. Canada* (1973), *Morgentaler v. The Queen* (1975), and *Bliss v. A.-G. Canada* (1979) – the court reverted back to its traditional conservatism, refusing to use the *Bill of Rights* to strike down statutes considered discriminatory toward women. According to political scientist Christopher Manfredi, the decisions had the cumulative effect of galvanizing the women's movement in Canada, prompting it to become more and more engaged with the activities of the courts.[17] The decisions also dashed any hope that the 1960 *Bill of Rights* might take on a quasi-constitutional status.[18]

As noted above, the coming into force of the *Charter of Rights and Freedoms* on 17 April 1982 marked the third stage in the age of rights for Canadians. A long-standing priority of Trudeau's, the constitutionally entrenched *Charter* was both a product of the emergence of a rights consciousness in Canada and an assertion of Canadian sovereignty.[19] As Cairns first observed, Canadians' sense of self had changed dramatically in the decades after the Second World War. At least in English Canada, the sense of identity and community that came with being part of the British Empire no longer resonated with the majority of the Canadian public. Britain's decline in world influence following the collapse of the Empire after the Suez Canal Crisis of 1956-57 and the decolonization movement of the 1960s, along with diminishing economic ties between Canada and the United Kingdom, meant that British traditions, notably the notion of parliamentary supremacy, were "no longer central to Canadian identity."[20] The vacuum left behind by the loss of "Britishness" was replaced by an ethos of "rights" legitimized by the emergence of an international human rights law regime at the United Nations, an ethos that Cairns argues not only "provided domestic groups with a powerful rights rhetoric" for advancing claims but also "suggested the criteria by which [the state's] performance could be judged." In essence, the *Charter* was Ottawa's answer to "the domestic effects of international forces."[21]

As John Saywell notes, through the *Charter* the Supreme Court was given "a clean slate on which to write its constitutional prescriptions,"[22] which in turn created a new opening for Canadian interest groups to advance their rights claims. Prior to 1982, the Supreme Court had been reluctant to grant interest groups intervener status, preferring instead to limit involvement to only the parties directly involved in the dispute.[23] Only in the 1970s, as its conservative culture was beginning to wane, did the court begin to allow third-party interveners, first in *Lavell* and then again in *Morgentaler*.[24] But after 1982, the Supreme Court revisited the rules governing third-party interventions. The change in thinking was in part a reflection of the court's unfamiliarity with the new Constitution, but it was also a response to growing calls to enlist the expertise of a wide range of voices to help give meaning to the *Charter*'s ambiguous language, the underlying rationale being that interest group interventions would help to ensure that the courts interpreted the Constitution and crafted their decisions in a manner reflective of the growing diversity within Canadian society. Concurrently, some of the more activist members of legal academe began to advocate "strategic litigation," an American phenomenon that involved the "long-term program of litigation in selected cases in order to influence the development of jurisprudence favourable to one's interests,"[25] the underlying premise being that the courts could be a viable vehicle for "righting the wrongs" of Canadian society.

Still, during the years immediately following introduction of the *Charter*, the Supreme Court wavered on the question of whether to allow third-party interventions at its proceedings. In 1983, interest groups that had participated in a case heard before a lower court were given an automatic right to participate in the appeal at the Supreme Court. This inclusiveness did not last long. Believing that hearings should remain between the principal parties involved in the dispute, the court rescinded the new rule the same year and began to turn away interest group applications for interventions in 1984.[26] Many NGOs were disappointed with the court's reversal. In the mid-1980s, A. Alan Borovoy, general counsel of the Canadian Civil Liberties Association, lobbied the Canadian Bar Association's Supreme Court Liaison Committee to permit interveners to "participate in important public interest litigation" on the grounds that NGOs could offer "nuanced alternatives" that would otherwise be unavailable to the court.[27]

The campaign for greater interest group participation spurred an internal debate among the justices of the Supreme Court. Madam Justice Bertha Wilson, Canada's first female Supreme Court justice, was supportive of the idea of opening the court up to a broad range of third-party interveners. Her position was not surprising given her views about the law and the role of judges in society. According to her biographer, Ellen Anderson, Wilson believed in a "sort of sociology of law," which advocated interpreting the law "contextually," meaning according to perceived realities.[28] But Wilson's enthusiasm for expanding the number of voices in the courtroom was not shared by all of her colleagues. Justices Jean Beetz and Willard Estey remained hesitant. Their concern was that interest groups would become "permanent fixtures of the Court," a prospect that they believed would undoubtedly add to the "length and complexity of the appeals."[29] As Robert Sharpe and Kent Roach note, Chief Justice Brian Dickson initially sided with

Beetz and Estey but gradually became more "receptive to a more liberal policy."[30]

By the mid-1980s, the pendulum had swung in favour of the Wilson and Dickson camp. In May 1987, the Supreme Court modified the rules governing intervention once again. This time it required that applicants demonstrate to the court their interest in the case as well as the usefulness and distinctiveness of their submissions. Factums were to be limited to twenty pages, and any intervener that wished to make an oral argument would have to seek special permission from the court to do so. In addition, the court interpreted the new rules in a fairly broad manner, adopting the position that any group with a history of involvement with the issue at stake would meet the criteria governing interventions. The result was not insignificant. By the late 1980s, the Supreme Court had effectively removed the barriers that had previously prevented interest groups from accessing the court for the purposes of social activism. Despite initial reservations, the stage had been set for NGOs to become "permanent fixtures" of the court.

The problem with revolutions – even bloodless rights revolutions – is that they are contentious and divisive. Throughout the 1980s, particularly around the time of the Meech Lake Accord, as Canadians seemed to be in an identity crisis and national unity was in jeopardy, critics began to question whether the *Charter* had been good for Canada. Although some viewed the Constitution as an important safeguard against government abuse,[31] others began to see it as an instrument for reframing political and moral questions into "legal" issues. They feared a shift in political power away from Parliament and into the hands of activist courts that used "rights" to justify judicial review. They warned against a reorientation in the way in which policy was made in Ottawa and saw evidence of a centralizing effect in which federal preferences trumped provincial autonomy.[32]

Nor did interest groups fare well in this backlash against the *Charter* and the courts, as the notion of strategic litigation came increasingly under fire. The prevailing view among observers of the courts was that the *Charter* had afforded a new "political commodity" to various groups, namely, the "ability to make a credible claim that some right, privilege or other entitlement is protected" by the Constitution.[33] Although many conceded that judicial oversight was one way to alert governments and the public to flaws in the "legislative calculus," there was a common perception among many scholars on the conservative end of the political spectrum that interest groups – predominantly civil libertarian and "equality-seeking" groups that engaged in "legal mobilization" – were using the courts to initiate "end-runs" around Parliament to further their particular political and social agendas, a practice that they viewed as elitist, irresponsible, and, above all, undemocratic.[34] Indeed, Cairns suggests that one of the most dramatic effects of the *Charter* on Canada's political culture has been that, in granting the courts exclusive jurisdiction over the Constitution's interpretation, it has encouraged the creation of "new groups of court watchers and interveners" whose narrow aim is to secure judicial decisions that are "sensitive to their constitutional interests" at the expense of the majority.[35]

University of Calgary political scientists F.L. Morton and Rainer Knopff have taken this idea a step further. They argue that the "Charter Revolution" has given rise to the "Court Party," a loose alliance of judges, lawyers, law schools, journalists, and "equality-seeking" and other interest groups with considerable resources at their disposal (much of which comes from state coffers), who together have sought to "reengineer society" through the judiciary rather than through the "traditional political party and bureaucratic channels" of government. According to this thesis, these actors have not only politicized the judiciary but also cultivated a highly divisive and fractious political climate that favours absolutist solutions over compromise and negotiation. Whether this is true remains the subject of considerable debate. Morton's and Knopf's ideas have been challenged, both directly and indirectly, by scholars on the left, notably Miriam Smith in her writings on the role of the courts in the struggle to advance the group rights of gays and lesbians in Canada.[36] Nevertheless, regardless of whether it has been used as an instrument of the right or the left, few would argue that the *Charter* has not fundamentally transformed the Canadian political landscape.

The purpose of this book is not to weigh in on the debate about the ideological leanings – or "value judgments," to quote Madam Justice Beverley McLachlin – of the Supreme Court in the *Charter* era.[37] Nor is it to comment on the privileged nature or legitimacy of these third-party interventions, whether their presence enhances or undermines Canadian democracy, federalism, or national unity. Nor for that matter is it to comment on *which* set of rights – libertarian or egalitarian – the court is more predisposed to favour (or reject) or whether the *Charter* has unduly transformed the processes of government or elevated the importance of the individual at the expense of the collective good. Rather, the purpose is to deepen understandings of the "age of rights" by charting the emergence, advancement, and defence of a particular standard of behaviour, principally through the advocacy of four "principled" and influential public interest organizations – the Canadian Council of Churches (CCC), the Canadian Jewish Congress (CJC), the Canadian Civil Liberties Association (CCLA), and Amnesty International (AI) Canada – including through their respective interventions in three precedent-setting cases at the Supreme Court – *Singh et al. v. MEI* (1985), *R. v. Keegstra* (1990), and *Kindler v. Canada (Minister of Justice)* (1991). At its core, this book is about the roles of principled ideas about rights, of the non-governmental actors that champion them, and of the state institutions that rule on their merit and apply them to real situations. It is about the process through which the parameters on the range of activities that governments can morally and legally engage in are defined as states attempt to further and protect individual liberties as well as the collective well-being. In sum, it is about the struggles associated with fulfilling the promise and ideals of the age of rights, struggles that confront not just Canada but also all liberal parliamentary democracies.

International relations theory offers a useful beginning point for understanding the process by which certain ideas about rights are adopted. In the 1990s, scholars of human rights and international relations grew dissatisfied with the realist framework that saw state behaviour and political change at the international level only as the calculus of power. They began to re-examine how and why international human rights were advanced in a world-system founded on the primacy and sovereignty of the nation-state. What emerged was the constructivist school of thought that attempted to provide an answer to the question of why states pursue policies that do little to advance their immediate material interests. Constructivists began to suggest that norms – collective moral expectations or social constructions that attempt to establish the parameters of appropriate conduct – matter when trying to understand state behaviour, because understandings of "oughtness," as Martha Finnemore and Kathryn Sikkink suggest, not only regulate state action but are central to state identity as well.[38] And as Ted Hopf observes, constructivism "assumes that the selves, or identities, of states are a variable; they likely depend on historical, cultural, political or social context," its advocates "believing in the power of knowledge, ideas, culture, ideology, and language, that is, discourse."[39] Constructivists such as Thomas Risse and Sikkink stress not only the importance of the "power of principle" and the "battleground of ideas" – the cumulative process by which norms about appropriate conduct are formed, debated, contested, and, in some cases, accepted – but also the non-state actors whose "principled commitment" has led them to become champions of particular norms.[40] Accordingly, the aim of these "norm entrepreneurs" is to *persuade* or *socialize* state actors for the purposes of, to quote Ignatieff, "rais[ing] the bar on the morally permissible."[41] "Human rights" – the "social expectations that have been codified to some degree in formal international legal instruments" – are the vehicle through which this process can occur.[42]

Finnemore and Sikkink have developed a theoretical framework, which they call the "norm life cycle," to explain the progression and adoption of certain ideas.[43] They identify three stages in the life cycle. The first stage involves the emergence of the norm and attempts on the part of norm entrepreneurs to convince state officials to conform to the norm by calling attention to key "issues by using language that names, interprets, and dramatizes them." This is followed by a second stage of "norm cascade" or general acceptance among a wide range of constituents. The third stage is realized only when the norm becomes "internalized," meaning that it becomes so well established that it acquires a "taken-for-granted quality and [is] no longer a matter of broad public debate."[44] Similarly, Ann Marie Clark suggests that this third stage is often realized when a norm is codified into law.[45] All three acknowledge that the process from emergence to codification is neither smooth nor inevitable. "Success" depends on a whole host of factors, including the receptiveness of the executive, legislative, and judicial branches of the state to "appeals of principle" by norm entrepreneurs in their deliberations about the scope and limits of rights.

The particular "rights" featured in this book were chosen for a variety of reasons. First, all of the rights involve political and civil rights, or first-generation rights as they are also known, that deal with questions of violence, specifically the protection from or the appropriate response to both the threat of violence and real acts of violence.[46] Second, in all three Supreme Court cases, the public interest groups felt compelled to intervene; indeed, to ignore the events at the court would have betrayed the values and ideals that were central to their respective identities. Their stands were principled and idealistic, at times uncompromising and even categorical. Yet they were not so doctrinaire that their positions were removed from the environments around them. All four had built up considerable expertise and experience with the issue being debated and in the process had struggled with their respective stances. Although none minimized the contentiousness of what they were saying, each paid a high price for participation that went well beyond the financial cost of intervention. And third, all three cases deal explicitly with the inherent dilemmas and governance challenges that free societies must come to terms with in order to remain free.

The chapters are organized chronologically according to the order in which the trials occurred and can be read in sequence or independently, as each is meant to stand on its own. Each chapter consists of a history of both the interest group and the law that would eventually be contested at the Supreme Court, the institution that, as the final arbiter and interpreter of the *Charter*, is central to the process of legitimizing norms.

Chapter 1 is an account of the Canadian Council of Churches' efforts to secure norms relating to the rights of refugees, a cause it first took up after the Second World War. In the late 1970s and early 1980s, the CCC attempted unsuccessfully to obtain reforms to the *Immigration Act, 1976*, that would have allowed for greater procedural protection for refugee claimants. Aligning themselves with a group of concerned immigration lawyers and human rights organizations, CCC member churches argued that the law was overly cumbersome and rigid and highly susceptible to inaccurate assessments. Among other concerns, they called on the federal government to provide claimants with an oral hearing before the body responsible for the final decision. They found little success. For its part, the Canadian government contended that the added financial costs and a growing backlog of claims would bankrupt the system.

Eventually, the CCC turned to the Supreme Court of Canada to resolve the matter in the *Singh* case of 1984-85. This was in many respects a last resort for the CCC and its allies. *Singh* was the culmination of a relationship gone sour, the product of the frustrations felt by a refugee advocacy community whose criticisms of the *Immigration Act, 1976*, had fallen on deaf ears. In *Singh*, the Supreme Court considered whether sections 45, 70, and 71 of the *Immigration Act, 1976*, were in contravention of section 2(e) of the *Canadian Bill of Rights* and section 7 of the *Charter*. At issue was whether claimants should be guaranteed the right to an oral hearing before those who were responsible for deciding their fate. Working alongside the counsel for the Federation of Canadian Sikh Societies (FCSS), the CCC was able to convince the court to award oral hearings not only to all seven appellants but also to all claimants who go through the system. The Mulroney government responded to *Singh* with a series of sweeping reforms (many of which remain in place), the aims of which were to limit access to the system and deter human smuggling. Consequently, for the CCC, as well as for the rest of Canada's refugee advocacy community, *Singh* was a short-lived victory. The case and the events that followed not only revealed the limits of Canadian tolerance toward refugees but also highlighted one of the central and most difficult tests facing liberal democracies that are destination points for those seeking a better life: how to resolve the seeming incompatibility of principles of fairness, compassion, and legal obligations to protect the security of the individual with the state's duty to maintain control of its sovereignty.

Chapter 2 charts the emergence of norms related to the protection of vulnerable minorities from pronouncements of hate through disputes between the Canadian Jewish Congress and the Canadian Civil Liberties Association relating to the controversial 1970 hate propaganda law. Of the two, the CJC's role was more pronounced; indeed, the law came about in large part at the behest of the organization, which had been calling for such legislation since the early 1950s. Its position rooted in the collective historical experiences of the Jewish community in Canada and abroad, the CJC adopted the argument that hate speech constituted a "misuse" of the principle of freedom of expression, one that undermined the very health and well-being of the democratic system, and as such was grounds for being restricted. In turn, the CCLA provided a strong counterweight to the CJC's arguments, its main positions being that ideas were the engine that drove social change and that it was better to confront hate through open public debate than through the courts. The result was a law that not only offered an uneasy balance between two competing rights but also codified the arguments that freedom of expression was accompanied by an obligation not to use speech to undermine the well-being of society and, in turn, that state intervention was justified in cases where this responsibility was ignored.

Both organizations defended their respective positions in *Keegstra*, a case that was deeply hurtful to Canada's Jewish community. At issue was whether Canada's hate propaganda law was constitutional, specifically whether section 281.2(2) of the *Criminal Code of Canada*, which prohibited the "wilful promotion of hatred" in situations in which there was no obvious call for violence, violated the right to freedom of expression found in section 2(b) of the *Charter* and whether section 281.3(a), which allowed for the "defence of truth," contravened James Keegstra's constitutional right to be innocent until proven guilty, as defined by section 11(d) of the Constitution. More generally, the court was asked to determine whether the limits on individual freedom of expression were reasonable in order to protect vulnerable minorities from group defamation. In a controversial four to three decision, the majority on the bench ruled that the law was unconstitutional but could be upheld because of section 1 of the *Charter*, which allows for reasonable limits on rights, provided that they are "demonstrably justified in a free and democratic society." The split reflected not only the two philosophical positions put forth by the two organizations but also the contentiousness that had surrounded the law from its inception. That the decision favoured the state was, in part, an expression of a period in which litigation in the name of a multicultural and pluralistic Canada was seen as a viable and acceptable avenue for redressing inequities within society and an emerging consensus that the effects caused by hate did not need to be physical to cause harm. Although the ruling reaffirmed the validity of the law, the case – the entire ordeal, for that matter – did little to resolve the larger question of at what point a free society can no longer in good conscience tolerate controversial and harmful expressions and must use coercive measures to limit the very democratic principles that it hopes to preserve.

Finally, Chapter 3 examines Amnesty International Canada's championing of the norm of abolition of the death penalty, including its relationship to Canada's extradition law.[47] Canada first became a *de facto* abolitionist country in the early 1960s. But in 1976, Minister of Justice Warren Allmand introduced Bill C-84, which called for the complete repeal of the death penalty from the *Criminal Code of Canada*. At the time, the legislation was highly divisive, sparking a heated debate about competing visions of Canadian justice. The bill passed in a free vote but only by a narrow margin of six votes; opponents of Bill C-84 put little stock in the outcome. Led by Tory back-bencher Bill Domm, the MP for Peterborough, Ontario, the formal campaign for reinstatement coincided with the Mulroney government's victory at the polls in 1984. On 13 February 1987, a motion for reinstatement was brought before Parliament. AI Canada and its supporters responded by launching a multi-pronged public awareness campaign, the aim of which was to discredit arguments in favour of the death penalty. The motion was eventually defeated, although the margin of victory remained narrow at twenty-one votes. Despite the victory, there remained little conclusive evidence that capital punishment offended Canadian sensibilities.

This ambivalence was the central issue in *Kindler*, a trial in which the constitutionality of Canada's 1976 extradition treaty with the United States was called into question. Wildly unpopular with Canadians, including Domm, the case involved the extradition to the United States of two violent fugitives, Charles Ng and Joseph Kindler, both of whom the Canadian government had agreed to extradite without first seeking assurances that neither would receive the death penalty if returned. Although extradition to stand trial was not in dispute, at issue was whether returning the two men to face potential execution was in violation of the *Charter of Rights and Freedoms*. *Kindler* dealt with the fundamental issue of how liberal states respond when confronted by those who pose a direct threat to their society and whether such situations ever warrant infringing upon the individual's rights to security and life in order to protect the public. Central to the case was the question of whether their extradition to face possible execution would "shock the conscience of Canadians." AI Canada contended that it would. It attempted to convince the court that unconditional extradition would contravene both domestic and international law. The court, however, was unpersuaded, ruling four to three in favour of the federal government. Indeed, the case was as much a reflection of the absence of clear norms about the merits of capital punishment at the time of the trial, either within Canada or the international community than it was about defining the limits of permissible state behaviour. It was an absence that checked the Supreme Court from using the *Charter* as an instrument that interfered unduly with the Canadian government's ability to conduct its bilateral relations with its neighbours.

Bobbio has written that the study of human rights "will not have any historical importance if it is not accompanied by the study of the conditions, the means and the situations in which a given right can be implemented."[48] This book – through an examination of the ideas, actors, and institutions through which human rights norms have been advanced in Canada – is an attempt to do just that. Its aim is to better understand the reasons why certain claims about the way in which individuals should be treated have been either respected or disregarded and the roles of judiciaries and civil society actors in liberal parliamentary democracies in influencing the long and tumultuous journey from "oughtness" to "is."

1

My Brother's Keeper
The Canadian Council of Churches and the Rights of Refugees

Individual human rights have always been at odds with traditional notions of state sovereignty. Perhaps nowhere is this tension more apparent than in the realm of rights for refugees. Norms related to rights of asylum for those individuals fleeing persecution challenge the state's claims to the absolute control of its borders. The question of how to balance efficiency and security with humanitarianism and compassion is one that every industrialized nation in the post-Second World War era has been forced to confront on a continual basis. Canada is no different. Forced to respond to the chaos and instability of the world around it, Canada, like other Western liberal parliamentary democracies, has often struggled with the question of how best to deal with those individuals who arrive at its doorsteps.

The Canadian Council of Churches (CCC), now a forum of Anglican, Evangelical, Eastern Orthodox and Oriental Orthodox, Protestant, Eastern Catholic and Roman Catholic churches, has played a seminal role in shaping the terms of this struggle. First drawn to issues involving the rights of refugees in the immediate years after the Second World War, the CCC had, by the mid-1970s, become one of the country's leading proponents of greater procedural rights for refugees. Although the rights of aliens in need of protection from political persecution and the principles of state sovereignty are not necessarily mutually exclusive, the Canadian experience in the post-Second World War era suggests that they have largely been conceived of and treated in this way by the state. In its efforts to advance and defend norms relating to the rights of those in need of protection from persecution, including at the Supreme Court of Canada, the CCC, along with other refugee advocates, has tried to ensure that the gap between the two – which is prone to considerable fluctuations depending on the political mood of the day – remains as narrow as possible.

The Canadian Council of Churches was founded as the Canadian arm of the global ecumenical movement. On 11 November 1942, the Reverend Dr. W.J. Gallagher of the United Church hosted a meeting in his Toronto office with delegates from a number of different Protestant churches and organizations for the purpose of establishing a council that would act as a coordinating body for issues of common concern. The idea was not entirely new. There had been earlier attempts to establish such a council, largely around issues of morality related to the ills of industrialization in Canada. But the war brought a new sense of urgency to Gallagher and his colleagues, who feared that the world was in desperate need of spiritual rejuvenation. Events moved rapidly from there. Six months after the initial meeting, a draft constitution was approved, and in September 1944 the CCC held its inaugural annual general meeting at Yorkminster Baptist Church in Toronto.[1] All in attendance shared the belief that the elusive answer to war could be found in the gospel. Indeed, the initial function of the organization was to condition "the mind of the world for peace" through Christ.[2]

The CCC was conscious of the failings of the state-centric Westphalian international system, specifically its inability to resolve disputes before they escalated into violence, and coming to the aid of refugees and displaced peoples was a key piece of the CCC's larger agenda for a more stable world. Although never a homogeneous group, particularly on issues concerning world affairs, the CCC's member churches generally subscribed to the idea that large refugee populations placed considerable strains on their host countries and that lasting peace between nations depended on the willingness of those states removed from the conflict to provide refuge to those displaced by war.[3]

In response to the displaced persons crisis in Europe, the World Council of Churches (WCC) in Geneva, the umbrella organization of the transnational ecumenical movement of which the CCC was the Canadian member, added a Refugee Division to its Commission on Reconstruction and Inter-Church Aid in 1946. In addition to providing material and spiritual relief to the refugees and displaced persons, the Refugee Division was responsible for finding sponsors willing to help resettle those individuals and families who were in the camps.

Despite some initial growing pains, the CCC quickly established itself as one of the leading contributors to the WCC's larger efforts to find new homes for Europe's displaced persons. Throughout the 1940s, it raised considerable funds for the WCC's Refugee Division, which at the time was operating inside the camps alongside the United Nations Relief and Rehabilitation Agency (UNRRA) and the International Refugee Organization (IRO). By 1949, the CCC had become a "linchpin," acting as the link between those whom the WCC tended to and potential sponsors in Canada through its network of denominational presses, its 6,000 ministers across the country, and its contacts outside the church. According to Gerald Dirks, during the latter half of the 1940s, ethnic and religious organizations were "especially energetic" in pressuring the Canadian government to "open Canada's doors to their ethnic and religious brethren."[4] The CCC was no exception. In 1953, it made the largest contribution of any of the church councils within the WCC, sponsoring 2,386 of the 5,645 refugees that were resettled that year. It was an accomplishment that was not lost on the Canadian government.[5]

Canada's contribution to resolving the Hungarian crisis of 1956-57 is rightly considered to be one of the most generous and impressive humanitarian responses to a refugee crisis in the nation's postwar history.[6] Orchestrated by Minister of Citizenship and Immigration Jack Pickersgill (who travelled to Europe to witness the emergency firsthand), the response was both expeditious and generous. Days after the Soviet invasion on 4 November 1956, Canadian officials reinforced the number of immigration officers at the Canadian Embassy in Vienna, Austria; loosened the normal requirements concerning proper travel documents, medical exams, and security clearances; and enlisted commercial airplanes to transport the refugees out of Austria. The effort produced impressive results. By the end of 1957, more than 37,000 Hungarians had been accepted in Canada, only slightly less than the number taken in by the United States. For Pickersgill, the government's handling of the situation was one of the most "useful" and "exciting" episodes of his career.[7] But his success was only possible because of the contributions of the many concerned voluntary organizations, including the CCC, that not only pressured Ottawa to accept a large number of refugees but also assisted in the process of integrating the new refugees into Canadian society.[8] Extending its full co-operation to the federal government, the CCC found sponsors for 5,172 of the Hungarian refugees that arrived in Canada that year. Increasingly, it came to view itself as a *de facto* partner in the implementation of Canada's refugee policy.[9]

The relationship worked well, in part because there were few risks and several benefits to both parties. The CCC's willingness to provide for many of the refugees' long-term needs relieved the Canadian government of much of the burden of looking after the newcomers. Moreover, throughout the 1940s and 1950s, Canada's Protestant churches were generally supportive of the government's policy toward refugees, finding little fault with either the ad hoc responses to the various crises in Europe or the larger aims of Canadian immigration policy. Indeed, the CCC not only recognized the importance of linking immigration to economic growth but also refrained from challenging the racialism central to the 1952 *Immigration Act*. As did much of Canadian society at the time, its member churches believed that greater efforts needed to be made to recruit immigrants from the British Isles, whose "understanding and appreciation of [Canadian] institutions" made them ideal candidates for life in Canada.[10]

The CCC benefited from the relationship considerably. In 1953, Ottawa established, with some reluctance, the Approved Church Program, which formally permitted the CCC (along with the Canadian Christian Council for the Resettlement of Refugees, the Rural Settlement Society of Canada, and the Canadian Jewish Congress) to be part of the overseas selection process.[11] Working with the Department of Citizenship and Immigration allowed the CCC to respond in a meaningful way to the WCC's calls for assistance. The program also permitted its members the opportunity to bolster their numbers. Not coincidentally, the immigrants and refugees whom the CCC helped to resettle were often of the same denominations as the churches that sponsored them.[12]

But, as Freda Hawkins notes, the relationship was often tenuous, even mistrustful.[13] Although there had been significant co-operation between the two during this period, particularly during moments of crisis, the federal government had often thought that the churches had been too preoccupied with the "hard cases," those individuals who would not easily be able to find employment in Canada. In turn, the churches believed that Ottawa, in its pursuit of the "productive" immigrants, was shirking its humanitarian obligations. Unfortunately for both sides (and for refugee claimants), the mistrust arising from competing priorities within the resettlement system would continue in the decades to come. Indeed, it would come to be the defining feature of the relationship after the 1950s.

The mid- to late 1960s saw a gradual shift in Canadian refugee policy away from a system "based exclusively upon ad hoc decisions and cabinet orders-in-council" and toward a program based on statutory procedures enforceable by the courts.[14] The shift took place in the context of a series of broader reforms to Canada's immigration policy intended to address growing labour deficits within the Canadian economy and a changing global environment in which new movements of peoples were emerging, not from Europe, but from Africa, Asia, and Latin America. These reforms were not insignificant. They were an acknowledgment that state sovereignty was not absolute on these matters. Still, even in an "age of rights," norms relating to the rights of states are not easily displaced. For governments, particularly in times of real and perceived crisis, commitments to the rights of refugees can often be fleeting.

In 1966, the newly created Department of Manpower and Immigration produced the seminal White Paper on Immigration, which would later become the blueprint for the 1976 reforms to the *Immigration Act*. The document is best remembered for advocating the removal of barriers based on "race, colour or religion" and the establishment of a points system based on the employability of the applicant (which the federal government later adopted on 1 October 1967). However, it also recommended that Canada become a signatory to both the 1957 *Hague Agreement on Refugee Seamen* and the 1951 UN *Convention Relating to the Status of Refugees* (the latter of which the Trudeau government eventually signed, on 15 April 1969, along with the treaty's 1967 *Protocol*).[15] A year later, Parliament established the Immigration Appeal Board (IAB), the independent body responsible for hearing appeals against deportation orders that effectively removed the decision to deport individuals who had violated the terms of the *Immigration Act* out of the hands of the minister of manpower and immigration.[16]

Shortly after the reforms of the late 1960s were implemented, Ottawa began having doubts about the desirability of a less restrictive immigration system.[17] The recommendations of the White Paper had been made at a time of relative prosperity. By the early 1970s, they seemed to be overly ambitious, ill suited for an economy that was faltering. Similarly, the IAB had been designed with procedural fairness in mind, but the new appeal process had become within a few short years, according to Christopher Wydrzynski, inefficient and "highly legalized," with the unintended consequence of steadily limiting "governmental discretion" within the immigration system.[18] Amid this growing sentiment of "buyer's remorse," Parliament amended the *IAB Act* in July 1973 because of growing backlogs in the system. Although it permitted the IAB to authorize admission based on humanitarian grounds, it limited appeals to permanent residents, persons seeking admission to Canada as an immigrant or non-immigrant, those claiming to be convention refugees, and those claiming to be Canadian citizens.[19]

Two months later (and coincidentally as a new refugee crisis was unfolding in Chile following the bloody military coup d'état of 11 September 1973 led by General Augusto Pinochet), Minister of Manpower and Immigration Robert Andras commissioned the Green Paper on Immigration on 17 September 1973 to conduct a comprehensive review of Canadian immigration policy in anticipation of future reforms. Released in 1974, and tabled in the House of Commons a year later, the Green Paper called for the creation of a formal refugee determination system based on the rights found in the UN *Convention and Protocol* but also recommended that there be a stronger correlation between admission levels and the economic needs of the country.[20]

As expected, the Trudeau government pressed ahead with sweeping reforms to Canada's immigration system. In 1976, Minister of Manpower and Immigration Bud Cullen introduced Bill C-24, *An Act Respecting Immigration to Canada (the Immigration Act, 1976)*, in the House of Commons. The intent of the bill was to construct an immigration policy reflective of a modern, pluralist nation, blending Canada's economic and social needs with its humanitarian obligations. As expected, Bill C-24 contained a number of provisions aimed specifically at refugees. The legislation was, in part, a response to what Dirks suggests was growing global support "for the idea of an automatic right to territorial asylum on request."[21]

Not surprisingly, any humanitarian impulses within Parliament were tempered by more pragmatic considerations. Much of the debate in the House of Commons focused on the related questions of "who qualified as a refugee?" and "how many?" Canada could – or should – absorb. The predominant fear in Parliament was that the new measures, if not carefully conceived, could, in the words of Cullen, have the unwanted effect of exposing the country to "literally millions" of claims.[22]

Still, the 1976 reforms represented a considerable improvement to the system. Not only did they propose to incorporate the *Convention* and *Protocol* directly into Canadian law, but Bill C-24 also permitted the minister the discretion to admit non-*Convention* refugees on humanitarian grounds should the need ever arise.[23] Recognizing that a deluge of claims would place considerable strain on both the immigration system and the Canadian economy, most MPs were satisfied with the proposed reforms.[24] Facing little sustained opposition, Bill C-24 was passed overwhelmingly on 25 July 1977 by a vote of 115 to 8. At the time, few believed that there was anything inherently unfair or unbalanced with the new law.[25] Refugee advocates, including the CCC, disagreed.

The new refugee determination system outlined in the *Immigration Act, 1976*, was both complex and cumbersome. Section 45 of the new act established the procedures for handling a claim once it was made. Individuals were permitted to make a claim but only during their initial immigration inquiries. In the event of a claim, the inquiry would be adjourned, and a removal order or departure notice would be issued to the individual. The claimant would then be examined under oath by a senior immigration officer (SIO) and permitted to obtain legal counsel should he or she desire it.[26] A transcript of the examination, along with the claim, would then be referred to the minister. The individual making the claim would also receive a copy of the transcript and be allowed to make corrections if necessary. Following this, the minister would then refer the case to the newly established Refugee Status Advisory Committee (RSAC), which would advise the minister as to whether the claimant fit the definition of a *Convention* refugee. The minister would then inform the claimant and the SIO who conducted the initial inquiry of his or her decision.

Depending on the claimant's place within the process, the system allowed for a number of appeals. If the minister's decision was positive, an adjudicator would determine whether the claimant should be allowed to remain in Canada. Under sections 4(2) and 55, *Convention* refugees could be expelled if they were considered to be a potential threat to public order or national security, but they could appeal the negative decision before the IAB.[27] If the minister's decision was negative, the claimant could launch an appeal for redetermination to the IAB under sections 70 and 71.[28] The appeal would then be allowed to continue if – and only if – the IAB determined that there were "reasonable grounds to believe" that the claim was legitimate and had a chance of being successful. At this point, the claimant would be entitled to a full oral hearing before an adjudicator, with a representative from the minister's office present if the minister deemed it necessary. If successful, the claimant would then resume the initial immigration inquiry to determine whether he or she should be allowed to remain in Canada. However, if the claimant still did not qualify as a *Convention* refugee, an adjudicator would resume the initial inquiry and issue a removal order or departure notice as if the claim had never been made in the first place.[29]

The claimant could launch a second appeal under section 84, this time to the Federal Court of Appeal, but only on matters of law, not the decision itself, and have his or her case referred to the Special Review Committee for "consideration on humanitarian and compassionate grounds."[30] If still unsuccessful, the claimant had fifteen days to file for "redetermination" before the IAB, at which point the board would decide whether an oral hearing before a three-member panel was warranted. If the decision was still negative, the last option available to the claimant would be, once again, to seek judicial review on matters of law before the Federal Court of Appeal.

The new law came into effect on 10 April 1978, and almost immediately the federal government started to have reservations about the efficacy of the new system. Given the number of stages and appeals, it found that the determination process was ill suited to handle more than 4,000 or 5,000 claims per year.[31] Consequently, it was susceptible to backlogs, which in turn encouraged fraudulent claims from individuals who wished to sidestep the traditional immigration process and prolong their stay in the country. This option was not lost on a great number of immigration consultants who saw the refugee determination system as a backdoor means to secure residence in Canada for their clients.[32]

Meanwhile, the CCC's relationship with Ottawa had become increasingly strained over the Trudeau government's handling of various refugee crises, which it believed were full of contradictions and driven not by a sense of humanitarian obligation but by domestic politics and Cold War alliances. Its opposition to government policy stemmed, in part, from the larger theological changes taking place within the CCC. The 1960s and early 1970s were a time of considerable transformation for many of its members. For some, such as the United and Presbyterian churches, gone were the social conservatism and overt piety of the past, only to be replaced by what they referred to as the "radical seventies," a renewed sense of Christian activism that coincided with Canadians' growing acceptance of pluralism and more liberal social norms.[33] The CCC's work with refugees was influenced a great deal by this transition, which had evolved alongside emerging norms and ideas concerning refugees, both domestically and internationally. Still rooted firmly in a commitment to ecumenism, pacifism, and Christian compassion, the CCC no longer focused solely on Europe and the Middle East but on crises in Africa, Asia, and Latin America.[34]

At no time was the stress on the relationship more pronounced than during Ottawa's response to the refugee crisis in Chile following the 1973 military coup d'état. Prompted by accounts of widespread human rights abuses by the Chilean military, and calls for solidarity from churches in Chile, both the Protestant and the Catholic churches of Canada responded by establishing the Inter-Church Committee on Chile (later renamed the Inter-Church Committee on Human Rights in Latin America [ICCHRLA]), which had a mission to "promote human rights and social justice" throughout the Americas.[35] Led by the Reverend Dr. Floyd Honey, general secretary of the CCC, and George Cram of the Anglican Church of Canada, the Inter-Church Committee on Chile and the CCC together called on the Canadian government to denounce the human rights abuses and grant asylum to Chilean refugees located both inside Chile and in neighbouring Argentina.

Andras and Minister of External Affairs Mitchell Sharp remained reluctant to do so. At the urging of Canadian Ambassador to Chile Andrew Ross, the Canadian government had recognized the Pinochet junta on 29 September 1973 on the grounds that it was the only authority in the country.[36] This decision was not well received by refugee advocates. Many, including the churches, questioned whether the Canadian government was displeased to see the Allende government fall. For their part, Andras and Sharp feared that terrorists, communists, and other subversives were among the refugees.[37] Only after considerable outcry from various civil society groups did they go back on this position and begin the process by which Canada would take in more than 4,500 Chilean refugees by the end of 1976.[38]

Neither the Inter-Church Committee on Chile nor the CCC was content with Ottawa's handling of the crisis. The slow response led many to become increasingly suspicious of Ottawa's commitment to refugees. As several scholars of Canadian immigration and refugee policy have noted, the response to the crisis helped to foster the perception that the federal government was far more willing to accommodate refugees fleeing communist regimes on the left than those escaping fascist regimes on the right.[39] It was this growing concern with the treatment of refugees fleeing oppressive regimes in South and Central America throughout the 1970s that eventually prompted the CCC to establish an additional inter-church committee, the Refugee Concerns Project, in late 1979 (later renamed the Inter-Church

Committee for Refugees [ICCR]). Its purpose was to "monitor the world refugee situation and Canadian responses, keeping the participant churches informed and concerned."[40]

According to Kathleen Ptolemy, the churches' advocacy on behalf of Latin American refugees provided them with firsthand exposure to the new immigration system.[41] What they saw was a set of policies and procedures that contravened established norms relating to openness and due process. In 1977, church delegates lobbied the government to allow claimants "the right to appear in person before the RSAC," a recommendation that was rejected because of fears that such a move would place undue strain on the system.[42] A year later, Cram and a number of other church officials teamed up with a series of human rights groups and concerned immigration lawyers from the Toronto area to discuss the problems of Canada's new refugee determination system. Among those present were delegates from the CCC, the ICCHRLA, the Canadian Conference of Catholic Bishops, the Ontario Federation of Labour, and Amnesty International Canada, as well as a number of independent legal and medical organizations. Appropriately, they referred to themselves as the Delegation of Concerned Church, Legal, Medical, Labour, and Humanitarian Organizations. Their hope was that a united front from a large segment of Canada's refugee advocacy community might prompt the federal government to enact reforms.[43]

The consensus within the delegation was that the new system was not designed with the best interests of the claimant in mind. First, they found that neither the minister's office nor the RSAC was present at the SIO's examination and instead relied only on the written transcript of the initial interview. These transcripts often contained errors, sometimes serious ones. Second, there were few checks on either ministerial discretion or the procedures for guiding the minister's decision, both of which added a degree of arbitrariness to the process. Third, many immigration officials, because of inadequate resources and training, were unfamiliar with the ever-changing political events from which the individual was seeking refuge. Fourth, hearings were adversarial, the burden of proof resting with the claimant, not the state. This was particularly problematic given that many claimants did not receive adequate legal counsel, and refugee advocates found that the quality of the interpretations was not high for those who spoke neither French nor English. Taken together, these shortcomings often placed undue stress on claimants, compounding the trauma that had accompanied their flight from persecution. Equally troubling was that these deficiencies increased the risk that mistakes would be made.[44]

In March 1979, the delegation submitted a brief to Cullen, the minister of employment and immigration, which contained a series of recommendations that, if acted on, would theoretically lead to a friendlier and more accessible system. Many of the suggestions involved relatively simple yet significant administrative improvements: hiring competent translators, providing more adequate training for immigration officers, allowing immediate family members to be included in a claim, and holding the hearing at the closest immigration centre to the claimant's desired destination to relieve many of the financial costs to the individual.[45]

Other recommendations were less straightforward. The delegation was particularly concerned that the system was prone to errors that were easily preventable. It suggested that claimants be provided with immediate legal counsel and that claims be admissible at any point in the immigration process, not simply during the initial inquiry. Moreover, the delegation recommended that claimants and their legal counsel be given an opportunity to correct any mistakes in the transcript before it was forwarded to the RSAC. Both the claimant and counsel should also be given access to the information used by the RSAC and minister in their cases and be given the reasons for a negative decision, which the government was not obliged to disclose under section 45 of the *Immigration Act, 1976*.[46]

Much of the delegation's criticisms were aimed directly at the IAB. According to the delegation, IAB personnel often showed a disturbing lack of understanding of either refugee issues or world events. This had been all too apparent during the inadequate handling of the second wave of Chilean refugees to Canada, who were once again uprooted following the Argentine military coup d'état of 24 March 1976, an event that marked the beginning of Argentina's now infamous "Dirty Wars" of 1976 to 1983 and led to the torture, execution, and disappearance of thousands of opponents of the junta. The IAB had also shown that it was inconsistent in its determinations and, in the minds of the delegation, unduly adversarial, too eager to jump on any discrepancies in a claimant's story.[47] Given that a claimant could only appeal a negative decision to the Federal Court of Appeal on the grounds that there had been an error in law, there was little room within the appeal process to correct any mistakes. The delegation thus saw little value in the current IAB. It advocated replacing the body with a new, independent Refugee Review Board that would deal exclusively with refugee claims by fulfilling the dual function of hearing and determining claims referred to it by the Refugee Status Advisory Committee.

The delegation also pressed the Canadian government to provide an oral hearing before the body responsible for the final hearing for all but the "manifestly unfounded claims," the term used to describe the most frivolous cases that are clearly fraudulent. Any system, it contended, that did not allow a claimant the opportunity to respond to the case against him or her at either the determination or the appeal stage was fundamentally unjust, especially when decisions were based solely on written transcripts and not intangible yet crucial factors such as body language and tone of voice of the claimant.

The Canadian government's initial reaction to the delegation's recommendations was lukewarm at best. Cullen disapproved of many of the suggestions, particularly the addition of an oral hearing. His fear, shared by the Department of Immigration, was that any dramatic changes would add layers of bureaucracy and substantial costs to an already complicated and overtaxed system.[48]

Cullen's successor, Lloyd Axworthy, was more receptive to the delegation's concerns.[49] Despite overseeing cuts to immigration levels that were prompted by the economic recession of the early 1980s, Axworthy was sympathetic to the plight of refugees and genuinely committed to the task of designing a more compassionate and accurate process of determination. Shortly into his tenure, he appointed W.G. Robinson, a lawyer from Vancouver and the former executive director of the Liberal Party of Canada, to head up a Task Force on Immigration Practices and Procedures on the Refugee Status Determination Process. Robinson consulted widely with a number of refugee advocacy groups, including the delegation.

Not coincidentally, many of his conclusions mirrored those that had initially been raised with Cullen. He found that the system was unnecessarily inefficient, often unfriendly, and under-resourced. He concluded that the refugee determination system was in need of being streamlined, recommended that the law be amended so that all claimants receive an oral hearing (which the UN high commissioner for refugees also recommended), and advised that the current three-stage process be replaced by "a single body [preferably the RSAC] to hear and decide all [but the 'manifestly unfounded'] refugee claims."[50]

To Axworthy's credit, the report did spark a number of changes, some significant. More liberal guidelines for applying the definition of a refugee and assessing his or her credibility were drafted, and additional resources were invested into the system. Particularly noteworthy was Axworthy's announcement on 2 May 1983 that the federal government was prepared to launch experimental pilot projects in Toronto and Montreal, Canada's two largest destinations for claimants, granting oral hearings before the RSAC.[51]

Still, there remained a number of problems with the way in which the system was administered. According to Howard Adelman, the pilot projects were "cumbersome and subject to many levels and a myriad of delays."[52] Many claimants at ports of entry continued to be denied adequate counsel, the system still relied on poorly qualified translators, and decisions did not always reflect the realities of political situations abroad.[53] And still the backlog continued to grow. By the spring of 1983, it had risen to approximately 3,500 cases.[54]

On 12 September 1983, John Roberts replaced Lloyd Axworthy as minister of employment and immigration. A cautious minister, Roberts commissioned two new studies on the failings of the system.[55] The first was conducted by University of Ottawa law professor Ed Ratushny, who submitted his report, *A New Refugee Status Determination Process for Canada*, to Roberts in May 1984.[56] Then, in a move that many interpreted as little more than a stalling tactic, he turned to Rabbi W. Gunther Plaut and asked him to gauge the response of Canada's refugee advocacy community to Ratushny's report.

Plaut was an exceptional, though not obvious, choice. A former refugee who had fled Nazi Germany in 1935, he was, at the time of his appointment, serving as the vice-chair of the Ontario Human Rights Commission, a position he had held since 1977. Since his arrival in Canada from St. Paul, Minnesota, in 1961 to take up the position of rabbi of Holy Blossom synagogue in Toronto, he had been a leading voice for Canada's Jewish community and one of Canada's foremost human rights thinkers and activists. He saw refugee protection as a "moral dilemma," as much an issue of religion and faith as it was of law.

Plaut understood that at the heart of the dilemma was a tension between seemingly competing norms of individual rights and state sovereignty. He did not dispute that the federal government had a duty to control entry into the country. But Plaut also believed that federal authorities had an ethical duty to protect individuals from harm, a duty rooted in the country's Judeo-Christian traditions.[57] His challenge was to devise a system that accommodated both duties.

Thanks to the federal election of 1984, Roberts would never get the chance to act on Plaut's recommendations. On 4 September, Brian Mulroney and the Progressive Conservatives won an overwhelming 211 of the 282 seats in the House of Commons. With the exception of Axworthy, the Trudeau Liberals had shown little enthusiasm for adopting more than cosmetic changes to Canada's refugee determination program. The various reports that they had commissioned had, by and large, gone ignored. Consequently, the Tories inherited a refugee backlog estimated to have grown to approximately 15,000 cases.[58]

Much to the dismay of refugee advocates, the new government had little appetite for altering the system. And once it did act, the reforms that it instituted were no friendlier to refugees. Rather, the Progressive Conservatives would come to favour tighter restrictions, in part because of events at the Supreme Court of Canada involving the CCC that directly contested its right to control how it determined who was a legitimate refugee and who could be turned away.

On 16 February 1984, the Supreme Court of Canada agreed to grant leave to appeal in seven cases involving refugee claimants who had been denied refugee status under the terms of the *Immigration Act, 1976*. Six of the claimants – Harbhajan Singh, Sandu Singh Tandhi, Paramjit Singh Mann, Kuwal Singh, Charanjit Singh Gill, and Satnam Singh – were Indian Sikhs who claimed that they would be persecuted if returned to India because of their ties to the Akali Dal party. The seventh claimant, Ms. Indrani, a woman from Guyana of Indian extraction, also feared for her life if deported but on "racial and religious," not political, grounds. In each case, the minister of employment and immigration, acting on the advice of the RSAC and the transcripts of the initial hearings, had ruled that there was no reasonable evidence to suggest that any of them qualified as *Convention* refugees. All seven had appealed the decision to the IAB and the Federal Court of Appeal to no avail as both bodies had dismissed the appeals. The claimants had applied for leave to appeal to the Supreme Court on the grounds that the transcripts of their hearings did not reflect the extent of their respective fears of persecution. This would have been clearer, their counsels contended, had they received oral hearings with officials from the Department of Employment and Immigration who could have considered factors such as their tone of voice and body language.

On 30 April 1984, the Supreme Court consolidated the seven cases into one hearing, *Singh et al. v. Minister of Employment and Immigration*,[59] thereby putting the fairness of Canada's refugee determination system on trial. Specifically, the Supreme Court considered whether sections 45, 70, and 71 of the *Immigration Act, 1976,* were in contravention of section 2(e) of the *Canadian Bill of Rights* and section 7 of the nascent *Charter of Rights and Freedoms*. The legal issue in question was whether claimants should be guaranteed the right to an oral hearing before those who were responsible for deciding their fate. Politically, however, the case pitted refugee advocates, through the CCC, against a federal government that was leery of extending greater protections to claimants than those already in place with the Supreme Court as the arbiter between the two.

At the urging of the ICCR, the CCC sought intervener status for the trial.[60] Justice Bertha Wilson, responsible for reviewing applications, was sympathetic to its concerns. In a decision that would have significant ramifications for the outcome of the trial, she agreed on 27 April 1984 to the CCC's request but on the condition that it submit a joint factum with the Counsel for the Federation of Canadian Sikh Societies (FCSS), which had also applied for intervener status.[61]

Both groups sought the counsel of some of Toronto's most prominent immigration lawyers. The FCSS turned to Mendel Green, a long-time advocate on behalf of refugees. The CCC recruited Barbara Jackman, a bright young lawyer and leading expert on Canadian immigration and refugee law, and Michael Schelew, Amnesty International Canada's chief spokesperson on refugee issues. Schelew's presence was both personal and strategic. A long-time critic of the *Immigration Act, 1976,* Schelew had been one of the original members of the delegation and knew the CCC leaders well, having accompanied them, beginning in the late 1970s, on a number of high-profile advocacy meetings with government officials. AI Canada's mandate at the time did not permit the organization to intervene directly in cases before the courts (this amendment was still a few years away); however, Schelew's participation was intended to send a signal to the Supreme Court that the CCC's intervention had the implicit, if not explicit, approval of Canada's largest and most recognized human rights organization. Green, Jackman, and Schelew understood that *Singh* was not simply about the seven individuals whose cases were in question. They knew that the case represented a golden opportunity to realize – through the courts – the reforms that they had been unable to secure through more traditional forms of lobbying. All offered their services pro bono.

Singh contained three pivotal questions. The first was whether section 7 of the *Charter,* which protected the "life, liberty and security of the person," applied to non-citizens physically present in Canada. Building on this question, the second asked whether a claimant's expulsion from Canada based on the terms of the *Immigration Act, 1976,* constituted "a deprivation of liberty otherwise than in accordance with the principles of fundamental justice." If the answers to questions one and two were yes and no, respectively, the third contemplated whether such a deprivation could be justified under section 1 of the *Charter,* which permitted reasonable limits on the rights and freedoms set out in sections 2 through 7 and 15 should they be "demonstrably justified in a free and democratic society."[62]

Predictably, counsel for the federal government, Eric Bowie, offered the Supreme Court a narrow interpretation of the applicability of section 7 of the *Charter* to Canada's refugee determination process, suggesting that the answers to the questions facing the court were no, yes, and yes, respectively. He began by arguing that section 45 of the *Immigration Act, 1976,* which established the procedures for handling a claim once it was made, was irrelevant to the trial since that was the "administrative," not the "judicial," stage of the process. Therefore, only sections 70 and 71, which dealt with appeals to the IAB, could come under the ambit of section 7 of the *Charter.*

But even this, Bowie argued, was debatable. Under common law, Canadian courts had established that entry into Canada was a "privilege" and not a "right," a precedent that Ottawa hoped the Supreme Court would uphold. Moreover, section 6(1) of the *Charter,* which dealt with mobility rights, stated explicitly that only Canadian citizens, not foreigners, had the right to enter and remain in Canada.[63] Still, perhaps unconvinced by his own line of reasoning, he conceded that the term "everyone" found in section 7 of the *Charter* could be interpreted to include refugee claimants as well as Canadian citizens.

Bowie tried to convince the Supreme Court that the federal government should be absolved of any wrongdoing that might result from an inaccurate assessment. He suggested that a claimant's removal from the country did not automatically result in a violation of his or her right to life, liberty, and security of person, even though the chance of this occurring remained possible. But he made it clear that Canadian officials were not the ones who committed the human rights abuses. Therefore, any potential complicity of the Canadian government resulting from the administration of Canada's refugee laws should be considered insufficient grounds to invoke a *Charter* challenge.[64]

Bowie also argued that an oral hearing before the body responsible for the final decision was not a necessary prerequisite to meeting the principles of fundamental justice. These, he submitted, were intended to apply only to the establishment of "impartial and unbiased" tribunals, not refugee hearings.[65] Because sections 70 and 71 of the *Immigration Act, 1976*, allowed claimants ample opportunity to make their cases in writing, the absence of an oral hearing did not automatically mean that the process was any less just.

The combination of ballooning costs and the growing backlog within the IAB did, however, impinge on the system's overall effectiveness. Indeed, this was Bowie's trump card. In the event that the Supreme Court found that sections 70 and 71 contravened section 7 of the *Charter*, Ottawa's position was that the current appeal system should nonetheless be saved under section 1. Ironically, Bowie suggested that prescribing automatic oral hearings would actually be detrimental to the well-being of refugees because the added task would hamper the appeals process and compromise the IAB's ability to carry out its functions in a timely manner. This, he argued, would needlessly exacerbate the ever-increasing strains on the system, the result of which "would be to diminish the capacity of the Board to exercise jurisdiction in other cases."[66]

Predictably, counsel for the appellants as well as the interveners disagreed with all three of the federal government's claims. Ian Scott, the court-appointed counsel for six of the appellants, C. David Coveney, Satnam Singh's attorney, and the FCSS-CCC lawyers all advocated a broad interpretation of section 7 of the *Charter*. All agreed that Canadian law should make special allowances for refugee claimants that were otherwise unavailable to those aliens who had applied for residency via the traditional immigration process. Together they stressed the inherent shortcomings of Canada's refugee determination system and dwelt on the absence of procedural safeguards to protect claimants against inaccurate assessments. Most of all, they challenged the assumptions that, in this new *Charter* era, the Canadian government had absolute control over the nation's borders and that the state's interests automatically took precedence over those of the individual who had a well-founded fear of persecution.

Despite their general consensus, each answered the questions before the court differently. With respect to the first question, all believed that the term "everyone" should apply alike to Canadian citizens and refugee claimants physically present in Canada. Scott's main contention was that the very act of arbitrarily detaining claimants, either to examine or to remove them from the country, violated their right to "life and liberty," the very things that section 7 was intended to prevent. However, Jackman, who assumed the role of lead counsel for the interveners, offered a slightly alternative, if more creative, line of reasoning. First, she contended that there were precedents for extending greater procedural rights to foreigners. The 1951 UN *Convention* and the 1967 *Protocol,* despite their narrow definitions, clearly recognized refugees as a distinct group in need of unique protections; so too did sections 3(g), 45, 55, and 72 of the *Immigration Act, 1976*. Consequently, it was not unreasonable for the Canadian government to treat them differently than it did other aliens attempting to gain entrance into Canada.

Whether recognition meant protection under the *Charter,* however, was less clear. Canadian courts had largely been reluctant to challenge the view that the state was the lone arbiter responsible for determining which non-citizens could enter and stay in Canada.[67] Nonetheless, Jackman argued that granting greater procedural rights to foreigners was not without precedent. The courts had previously ruled that refugee claimants in Canada had the right to seek *habeas corpus* to contest unlawful detention and had upheld the right of a past claimant to refuse deportation under the terms of the 1952 *Immigration Act*.[68]

Responding in part to concerns about cost overruns, Jackman took aim at the practical deficiencies of the system. Affording all claimants protection under section 7, she contended, would alleviate some of the inconsistencies within the application of the law. At the time, only refugee claimants who had already been admitted to Canada or who had established residency in Canada were considered to be protected by the *Charter,* whereas those who made their claims at a port of entry fell outside the purview of the Constitution. This, Jackman argued, had the dual effect of not only limiting access to the system but also rewarding those who were prepared to "mislead a port of entry officer in order to gain admission to Canada."[69] She submitted that extending the scope of section 7 to include all claimants – regardless of where they made their claims – not only had some precedent in Canadian law but also was a sensible measure that would help stem the abuse currently taking place within the system.

Counsel for the appellants and interveners were also in general agreement on the second question, though again for different reasons. Scott submitted that the absence of an oral hearing either before the RSAC or the IAB contravened the principles of fundamental justice found in section 7. Without an oral hearing before a "visibly impartial" and "open" tribunal, the current system operated in such a manner that claimants were not permitted to learn, let alone respond to, either the case against them or the reasons for the minister's negative decision. This deficiency with the law prompted the charge that "the substantive rights conferred by [sections 45, 70, and 71 of] the *Immigration Act* are more illusory than real."[70] But for Jackman, Schelew, and Green, the central rationale for invoking section 7 of the *Charter* to force the Canadian government to grant oral hearings to all claimants was not so much impartiality of the system (though this had been a long-standing complaint of the delegation) as protection of legitimate *Convention* refugees against refoulement, something, they reminded the court, that the Canadian government was obliged to do under Articles 32 and 33 of the 1951 *Convention* and section 55 of the *Immigration Act, 1976*.[71]

Still, the principal issue was whether a well-founded fear of persecution was sufficient to warrant the application of section 7. Predictably, the interveners believed that it did, arguing that a fear of persecution, grounds for being granted refugee status, was tantamount to a fear of deprivation of life, liberty, and security of person.[72] Thus, if the Supreme Court accepted both the earlier contention that *Convention* refugees constituted a "distinct class of aliens" that fell under the ambit of the term "everyone" in section 7, and that those individuals whose life, liberty, and security of person were at risk of persecution, then failure to provide adequate safeguards against refoulement – specifically through an oral hearing before the body responsible for the decision – did indeed constitute a violation of the principles of fundamental justice.[73]

On the third question – whether the absence of any reference to an automatic oral hearing in sections 45, 70, and 71 of the *Immigration Act, 1976*, could be justified under section 1 of the *Charter* – both counsel for the appellants and counsel for the interveners agreed that the answer should be no. All conceded that the federal government had reasonable grounds to be concerned about the cost of the system, yet none believed that such fears were compelling enough to allow the legislation to stand in its current form.

They made two requests of the court. The first was to ask the justices to reverse the Federal Court of Appeal's ruling in each case. The second was far more sweeping. In light of the absence of an oral hearing, they called on the Supreme Court to strike down the current provisions that dealt with appeals of negative decisions. The implications of this request were tremendous. They were, in essence, calling for a complete overhaul of the system. It was a direct assault on Parliament's authority to determine the terms of entry into the country.

The justices on the bench were divided on the question of whether the *Charter* was the most appropriate instrument for reviewing Canada's refugee determination system. Conscious of the magnitude of the decision before them, they asked each party on 7 December 1984 to resubmit its arguments based on the rights found in the 1960 *Canadian Bill of Rights*. Specifically, they wanted to know whether the sections of the *Immigration Act, 1976*, that outlined the refugee determination process violated section 2(e), which protected the right to a "fair hearing in accordance with the principles of fundamental justice for the determination of his rights and obligations."[74]

It was, in many respects, a peculiar request. Prior to *Singh*, the *Bill of Rights* had exerted a relatively minor influence on Canadian law. With the exception of the 1970 *Drybones* case, in which the *Bill of Rights* had been used to strike down portions of the *Indian Act*, the Supreme Court had treated it as a statutory document with virtually no constitutional authority.

Counsel for the appellants used the request to highlight once again the failings of Canada's refugee determination system. Scott (with Coveney concurring) maintained that his clients had not been given a fair hearing and argued that sections 45 and 71 of the *Immigration Act, 1976*, were in compliance with section 2(e) of the *Bill of Rights* only if claimants were granted an oral hearing before the body responsible for the decision in which they could hear the case against them and contest it accordingly. Section 45(4), Scott wrote, should either be revised to allow claimants an oral hearing before the minister or, along with 45(5), be discarded altogether, thereby giving the RSAC the authority to make the final decision. Similarly, he argued that section 71 should be revised so as to permit an oral hearing before the IAB for all claimants who apply for redetermination.[75]

Jackman, Schelew, and Green agreed, asserting once again that, given the potential for inaccurate assessments and refoulement, the state had an obligation to grant refugee claimants more than simply a "paper hearing."[76] On the question of the relevance of the *Bill of Rights*, they conceded that Canadian courts had not traditionally extended the protections found in the document to non-citizens. However, they submitted that the document was nonetheless relevant if the "rights" referred to in section 2(e), which prohibited the federal government from depriving "a person of the right to a fair hearing in accordance with the principles of fundamental justice for the determination of his rights and obligations," were those identified in section 7 of the *Charter*.[77]

Bowie's interpretation of the relevance of the *Bill of Rights* differed considerably from those offered by Scott and the CCC-FCSS. Once again, Bowie maintained that the current process was sufficiently fair. The real problem, he suggested, lay not with the law itself but with the "threshold" by which the IAB determined whether a case exhibited a likely chance of success and thus warranted an oral hearing. Thus, if the *Bill of Rights* had any relevance at all, it was at the administrative level. Any alteration to the law that either required an oral hearing for all claimants before the IAB or gave quasi-judicial status to the RSAC was, he concluded, unreasonable.[78]

The Supreme Court disagreed. On 4 April 1985, it sided with the appellants, issuing a six to zero decision in their favour. All six justices agreed that the original judgments should be overruled and ordered that each of the seven appellants be given an oral hearing before the IAB. This, however, was where the unanimity ended. The justices were split on the reasons behind their ruling. Half believed that *Singh* was predominantly a case for the *Charter*, and half thought it a matter to be decided solely by the *Bill of Rights*. The difference between the two was not inconsequential. Each reflected a distinct view of not only how the law should be interpreted but also the rightful place of the Supreme Court within the Canadian democracy.

Chief Justice Brian Dickson and Justices Antonio Lamer and Bertha Wilson believed that *Singh* was a *Charter* case. Writing on behalf of the group, Wilson drew on many of the arguments that had been put forth by the interveners and to a lesser extent Scott. On the first question, she agreed that the term "everyone" in section 7 included those who claimed to be *Convention* refugees. She also rejected Bowie's contention that the Canadian government lacked any culpability for the fate of those individuals whom it removed from the country, and she ruled that, even if the court accepted Bowie's call for a narrow interpretation of section 7, any reading of the phrase "security of the person" must nonetheless "encompass freedom from the threat of physical punishment or suffering as well as freedom from such punishment itself." Hence, removing a *Convention* refugee to face such a potential fate was, according to her logic, tantamount to a violation of the *Charter*.[79]

With respect to the two remaining questions, Wilson was even less charitable to Bowie. Unconvinced that the provisions found in sections 70 and 71 of the *Immigration Act, 1976*, allowed claimants an adequate opportunity to challenge the cases against them, she ruled that they were incompatible with the principles of fundamental justice as stipulated in section 7. Nor was she persuaded by Bowie's assertion that the added costs of administering oral hearings would place undue strain on an already taxed system. Citing the 1981 report of the Task Force on Immigration Practices and Procedures that Axworthy had commissioned (which had recommended oral hearings for all claimants), Wilson insinuated that the main obstacle impeding the creation of a system consistent with principles of fundamental justice and due process was not cost but government indifference, concluding that "the guarantees of the *Charter* would be illusory if they could be ignored because it was administratively convenient to do so."[80]

Justices Beetz, Estey, and McIntyre concurred, though they would not go as far as their colleagues. Relying on section 2(e) of the *Bill of Rights*, Beetz, who wrote on behalf of the three justices, agreed with Scott that the RSAC and IAB had failed to assess the potential dangers facing the seven appellants should they be deported. Their reason for focusing on section 2(e) of the *Bill of Rights* rather than section 7 of the *Charter* was that the latter applied only to breaches committed by the Government of Canada. The *Bill of Rights*, however, was less stringent. The appellants had to prove not that their rights had been violated but that "their 'rights' fail to be 'determined' by federal law." This meant that all they had to do was successfully make the case that the refugee determination system's inability to identify potential threats to life and liberty by a foreign state was inconsistent with liberal conceptions of a fair hearing and thus in violation of section 2(e). Alarmed that the appellants were not permitted either to learn of or to respond to the case against them, Beetz wrote, "in my opinion, nothing will pass muster short of at least one full oral hearing before adjudication on the merits [of the cases]."[81]

Despite taking different routes to get there, both rulings established that section 71(1) of the *Immigration Act, 1976*, was unsatisfactory. But Beetz, Estey, and McIntyre were far more guarded than their colleagues. The two approaches reflected a profound philosophical split on the bench: one side comfortable using the courts to challenge the Westminster tradition of parliamentary supremacy, the other side far more deferential. Aware of the stakes involved, Beetz cautioned that, though it was not unreasonable for the courts to carry out "relatively crude surgery on deficient legislative provisions," they should not be in the business of performing "plastic or reconstructive surgery."[82] He was willing to accept that section 71(1) was inoperative – but only for the seven cases in question. Nonetheless, despite the misgivings of half of the court, Wilson and those who sided with her carried the day. The result was a constitutional requirement to provide oral hearings to all claimants. Thanks in part to the CCC, a "facelift" was now mandatory. Unfortunately for it and other refugee advocates, the operation that followed was no more appealing.

The responsibility for reforming the refugee determination system initially fell to two members of the Mulroney cabinet, Minister of Employment and

Immigration Flora MacDonald and Minister of State for Immigration Walter McLean. Both "Red Tories," the two seemed to be well suited to the task. As minister of external affairs in the short-lived Joe Clark government, MacDonald had been one of the co-architects of the federal government's decision in 1979 to accept more than 50,000 Vietnamese boat people fleeing communist Vietnam, which marked the largest response to a refugee crisis in Canadian history and led the United Nations to award Canada the Nansen Medal for service to refugees in 1986. Similarly, McLean, whose first cabinet portfolio was secretary of state and minister responsible for the status of women, was a long-time social activist, both domestically and internationally, having specialized in development issues facing Africa. While at the University of Toronto in the early 1960s, McLean co-founded the Canadian University Students Overseas (CUSO), heading up its work in Nigeria. In 1971, he was the minister for Knox Presbyterian Church in Waterloo, Ontario, a position that he held until his election to office in 1979. McLean was also the former chair of the CCC's Commission on World Concerns. Yet from the perspective of refugee advocates, including many with the CCC, MacDonald and McLean would eventually come to be seen as disappointments, as neither seemed to be able or willing to devise a more equitable and efficient determination system in keeping with the spirit of the Supreme Court's ruling.

On 17 April 1985, Rabbi Plaut presented MacDonald with his revised report, which he had updated following the *Singh* decision, titled *Refugee Determination in Canada: Proposal for a New System*.[83] By most accounts, it was an excellent report. Plaut proposed three alternative models for the refugee determination system, all of which were designed to satisfy the obligations laid out by the Supreme Court while still allowing for cost effectiveness and efficiency. In his first model, claimants would receive an initial interview with a refugee officer, followed by an oral hearing by a three-member panel of the Refugee Board. Either the claimant or the minister of employment and immigration would, depending on the outcome, have the option to appeal the decision to the Federal Court of Appeal.[84] In theory, the entire process would take approximately three months to complete. Although it was economical, Plaut conceded that its major shortcoming was that it did not provide for a review within the determination stage. The second model was slightly more comprehensive. As with the first model, there would be an initial meeting with a refugee officer. It would be followed by a one-person oral hearing with the Refugee Board. If the claim was rejected, a review panel in Ottawa consisting of three members would then rule on the case, followed by a subsequent appeal to the Federal Court of Appeal. The advantage of this proposal was that it offered a consistent review process even though only one official would be present for the oral hearing to assess the claimant's credibility.[85] The estimated total time for a claim to be processed would be about five and a half months. Finally, the third model differed from the second model in that the claimant would receive two oral hearings. One would be with the new Refugee Board, the other with a three-member regional panel of the IAB. Of the three, this last model was the most expensive yet offered the greatest protection to the claimant.

Plaut's models represented clear breaks from past practices. All three reduced the decision-making role of the minister of employment and immigration – except in cases involving national security concerns – and gave more authority to immigration officials who would be present at the oral hearings.[86] Hearings were also to be co-operative, not adversarial, and more resources would be invested in the system. Finally, Plaut called for the creation of a new Immigration Refugee Board (IRB) that would be responsible for handling the administrative functions of the IAB and the Refugee Board. Although Plaut was mindful of the needs of the state, his models were tremendously favourable to the rights of claimants.

Meanwhile, the backlog of claims continued to mount, reaching approximately 21,500 cases by late 1985. Many of the claimants were economic, not political, refugees. To stem the flow, McLean introduced legislation that, if passed, would drastically increase the number of IAB members from eighteen to fifty. Still, part of the problem was of the Canadian government's own making. Throughout 1986, more than 3,600 Portuguese claimed to be Jehovah's Witnesses fleeing religious persecution in Portugal (neither aspect of the claim was true). Fearful of alienating Canada's Portuguese community, the Mulroney government refused to issue a travel visa against visitors from Portugal, preferring instead to wait the problem out.[87] Much to the government's displeasure, these were not the only offenders, as hundreds of false claims were made by visitors arriving from Turkey and Brazil as well.[88] The result was widespread consensus that Canada's refugee determination system was rife with abuse and that the world was taking advantage of Canada's generosity. Many critics blamed the *Singh* decision for the problem.

In the spring of 1986, McLean conceded that the situation was beyond repair. Responding to the growing backlog, he announced with great reluctance on 21 May that the federal government was prepared to grant a "case-by-case administrative review," a move that many interpreted to be a blanket amnesty designed to eliminate the backlog.[89] McLean also introduced a series of reforms to the refugee determination process. According to the proposed legislation, claimants would be given an oral hearing before a two-member panel of a newly established Refugee Determination Board. A claim would be successful if one of the two members believed that the person's fear of persecution was well founded. Still, the proposed changes were not entirely sympathetic to claimants. Also contained in the reforms were criteria that placed restrictions on who was eligible to make a claim in the first place. Moreover, claimants would be permitted only one appeal to the Federal Court of Appeal and only on matters of law.

Refugee advocates were quick to denounce the reforms and McLean. Many interpreted the new measures as little more than a thinly veiled attempt to nullify the *Singh* decision. On 23 May, two days after the announcement, McLean addressed the Standing Conference of Canadian Organizations Concerned for Refugees (the precursor to the Canadian Council for Refugees [CCR]), a conference consisting of roughly 100 refugee advocacy groups. It was a hostile crowd. Those in attendance, including George Cram and Tom Clark, who had become the ICCR's co-ordinator in 1983, condemned the new measures. McLean pleaded for their assistance in making the new system work. Most would have none of it. Several participants even called for the secretary of state for immigration's resignation.[90]

On 29 June 1986, they got their wish. Following a cabinet shuffle, McLean was named special representative on South Africa and Commonwealth affairs and Canadian delegate to the UN General Assembly. MacDonald was also moved, becoming the new minister of communication. However, their replacements, Gerry Weiner (secretary of state for immigration) and Benoît Bouchard (minister of employment and immigration), were no less controversial. Neither was overly sympathetic to the concerns of refugee advocates. Nor did Canadians necessarily want them to be. As Victor Malarek revealed in his 1987 book *Haven's Gate: Canada's Immigration Fiasco*, the mood of the nation, prompted by the unhealthy combination of a shaky economy and a growing sense of disillusionment with a refugee determination system that seemed to be rife with abuse, had become increasingly hostile toward immigrants and refugees.[91]

It was the arrival off the coast of Newfoundland of a boat containing 155 Tamils from Sri Lanka on 11 August 1986 that spurred the Mulroney government into introducing reforms to the *Immigration Act, 1976*. There was a great deal of hysteria surrounding their arrival, as large segments of

Canadian society believed that they were queue-jumpers, even terrorists. To his credit, Mulroney announced that "Canada would not turn its back on the Tamil castaways." Many in Canada's refugee advocacy community, including Jackman and Clark, found the prime minister's stance to be reassuring amid the anti-immigrant backlash that had emerged throughout much of the country.[92]

But it was later revealed that the Tamils had misled the public about their journey. Contrary to their initial claims, they were not *Convention* refugees fleeing persecution, nor had they ever been. Rather, they were all migrants who had secured passage to Canada via West Germany through a human smuggling ring. Their arrival, coupled with the system's inability to reduce the backlog (in March 1987, cabinet would deem it necessary to grant a second amnesty to all claimants), prompted nervous speculation within the CCC and a number of other groups that the federal government was exploring new ways of limiting claimants' access to the system.[93]

Their fears were soon realized. On 5 May, Weiner introduced Bill C-55, *An Act to Establish a New Refugee-Determination Process*, in Parliament. Although technically in keeping with the *Singh* decision, the proposed new system was no "friendlier" to refugee claimants than was the old system.[94] In Bill C-55 was a proposal to establish a new body, the Immigration Refugee Board, which included a new Convention Refugee Determination Division responsible for conducting oral hearings and determining the merits of any claim. But also contained in the bill were a number of amendments to the *Immigration Act, 1976*, designed to limit access to the system. One was a proposed screening process that would bar any claimant who was already a recognized *Convention* refugee in another country from making a claim in Canada. A second granted the Refugee Determination Division the authority to dismiss any claim that it believed lacked a "credible basis." A third was the addition of a "safe third country" clause that would permit the federal government to return any claimant to the country through which he or she had travelled en route to Canada, provided that doing so would not lead directly to a case of refoulement.[95] Claims would be permitted only at the onset of an immigration inquiry, and appeals would be limited to the Federal Court of Appeal and restricted to matters of law.[96] Opposition MPs accused the federal government of being unnecessarily hostile toward refugees, and Plaut dubbed it the "deportation" bill.[97] But Weiner remained unapologetic. Those who attacked the bill, he countered, were naive, unwilling to consider "realistic solutions."[98]

Events in the summer of 1987 seemed to confirm that "realistic solutions" were indeed necessary. On 12 July, 174 East Indian Sikhs landed off the coast of Nova Scotia after having secured passage on a vessel headed to Canada from the Netherlands. All claimed to be *Convention* refugees. The federal government's reaction was swift and forceful. Upon arrival of the vessel, Canadian authorities seized it and arrested its crew. The government then sought permission from an immigration adjudicator to detain the ship's passengers for an initial period of seven days. Bouchard defended the move on the grounds that his department was acting responsibly and needed to send a "signal [to the rest of the world] that Canada will not tolerate illegal actions such as [human smuggling]." He continued, "if another boat arrives on our shores, the government will act as promptly and effectively as we did this time."[99] The federal government then recalled Parliament from its summer recess for an emergency session. In the hope of preventing a flood of claims, it introduced companion legislation to Bill C-55 (which had not yet made it to second reading), Bill C-84, *An Act to Amend the Immigration Act, 1976, and the Criminal Code in Consequence Thereof*, on 11 August 1987. The purpose of the reforms was simple: to deter large-scale human smuggling into Canada.[100]

With Bill C-84, Ottawa proposed to expand its ability to deal expeditiously with any claimant suspected of violating the *Immigration Act, 1976*. Like Bill C-55, the bill contained a number of new and controversial powers. Among them, the federal minister of justice and the solicitor general would be granted the authority to issue security certificates signifying inadmissibility into Canada to those persons believed to be threats to national security or public safety. Any individual who received a certificate would subsequently be ineligible to make a refugee claim and would face detention followed by deportation. Only the Federal Court of Appeal would have the jurisdiction to reverse the decision. If the minister thought it necessary, reviews by the court, which would not be subject to appeal if negative, could be conducted in secret without the presence of either the individual in question or his or her legal counsel.[101]

Under the new *Immigration Act*, federal authorities would have the power to order ships suspected of being involved in human smuggling within twenty-four nautical miles of Canada's coast to remain beyond twelve nautical miles of the shore. Although the minister would be obliged to consider both the safety and the well-being of the passengers and Canada's international obligations to *Convention* refugees, the reforms would allow the federal government to enforce any order prohibiting entry into Canadian waters through "such force as is reasonable in the circumstances."[102] Moreover, the new law would permit authorities to detain any persons unable to satisfy an immigration officer of their identity or deemed to be security threats for a period of up to seven days, up from the forty-eight hours that had previously been required by the law, before they would have to be brought before an immigration adjudicator.[103]

Bill C-84 also targeted those who brought inadmissible persons into the country. If the bill passed, airlines and other transportation companies would be obliged to ensure that all their passengers held valid travel documents, such as passports and visas, or risk facing a fine of $5,000. The penalties for individuals or organizations caught aiding those persons who lacked proper documentation were even stricter. Depending on the number of people being assisted, punishments ranged from thousands of dollars in fines, to imprisonment, to the "seizure and forfeiture" of any vehicles used in committing the act. Although the aim of the legislation was to deter human smuggling, no distinction was made between those whose intentions were criminal and those whose intentions were humanitarian.

Once again critics were quick to denounce the proposed reforms. In a letter to the minister sent on 12 August, UN High Commissioner for Refugees Jean-Pierre Hocké criticized the proposed new legislation for its lack of adequate safeguards against refoulement (a charge that the Canadian government refuted),[104] while in the House of Commons opposition members accused the minister of a xenophobic and heavy-handed response that was comparable to trying to "kill a gnat with a cannon."[105] Undeterred, the federal government pressed on, sending Bill C-84 to committee on 14 August 1987, only days after it had first been introduced into the House of Commons.

Among the civil society groups that appeared before the committee was the ICCR.[106] Although it supported the federal government's desire to institute a more efficient system and deter future abuse, its position was that the aims of Bill C-84 were misguided, that the Mulroney government had devised callous responses to a very human problem. Keeping security risks and criminal elements out of Canada was a legitimate objective, but it should not come at the expense of due process. For this reason, the ICCR opposed the proposed new role of the Federal Court of Appeal and argued that the new measures aimed at deterring human smuggling unfairly punished claimants for the predicament in which they found themselves.

The ICCR called for the legislation to be reformed so that any criminal sanctions were directed solely at the "shippers," not at the "shipped."[107] It proposed that the government amend the sections of Bill C-84 that penalized individuals who lacked proper travel documents on the grounds that proper identification documentation was a luxury often not available to those fleeing persecution. Penalizing those individuals, it contended, would not only make worse an already harrowing experience, it would also be ineffective, since criminals who had access to forged or stolen documents would have little trouble circumventing the system. Finally, fearing that the churches were being lumped together with smugglers, it urged parliamentarians to ensure that the law distinguished between the two.

Meanwhile, committee hearings for Bill C-55 continued. Soured by the hastiness of hearings for Bill C-84, which had lasted for only one week, church officials were reluctant to appear before the committee. Nevertheless, the ICCR agreed, albeit reluctantly, to participate in the proceedings. Of particular concern were the clauses that dealt with the return to third safe countries and the pre-screening of claimants based on the "credible basis" tests. Both, it found, were ambiguous and open to a broad range of interpretations. Like many of the groups that appeared before the committee, the ICCR feared that the result would be a highly unfair determination process.[108] And like others, it too cautioned that, if substantial improvements were not made, another court challenge would be imminent.[109]

This was not a hollow threat. Despite overwhelming concern from refugee advocacy groups that the reforms would hurt genuine refugees, few meaningful changes had been made to either bill. Both bills were reintroduced in the House of Commons in the autumn of that year, and Parliament passed Bill C-84 on 14 September by a vote of 92 to 52 and Bill C-55 on 21 October by a convincing vote of 115 to 48.[110] Disheartened, refugee advocates appealed to the Liberal-dominated Senate in the hope that it would defeat both bills. Its efforts were to no avail. After a drawn-out exchange over the merits of the bills with the new minister of employment and immigration, Barbara McDougall, the Senate dropped its opposition to Bills C-55 and C-84, conceding that, amid the public's growing irritation with the regular reports of fraud and a widespread fear that the backlog of claims was spiralling out of control, tougher measures were necessary. Dismayed, a coalition consisting of the churches, immigration lawyers, and human rights organizations appealed to Canada's judiciary to intervene, their hope being that the courts would find the new laws to be unconstitutional. But unlike in

Singh, this time around the courts were far less willing to become the instrument through which the rights of refugees were advanced at the expense of the will of Parliament.

Canadian Council of Churches v. The Queen and the MEI was less about the legality of the new law and more about whether third parties should be permitted to seek standing with the courts. On 28 December 1988, three days before the new provisions in Bills C-55 and C-84 were to come into effect, McDougall announced a $100 million clearance program, the intent of which was to deal once and for all with the estimated 85,000 claims that had accumulated within the system since the two earlier amnesties. Despite the news, the CCC, with Jackman once again as its counsel, filed a statement of claim in the Trial Division of the Federal Court on 3 January challenging the constitutionality of Canada's new refugee determination system on the grounds that it was acting pre-emptively on behalf of all refugees, lawyers, and church workers who could be adversely affected by it. Their hope was that the courts would be sympathetic to their arguments that many of the provisions found in Bills C-55 and C-84 contravened sections 7 and 15 of the *Charter* and sections 1(a), (b), and 2(e) of the *Bill of Rights*.[111] But the decision to secure reforms through the courts was made only reluctantly and after great deliberation. Refugee advocates within the churches had become increasingly frustrated with Ottawa; many thought that their commitment to social justice compelled them to take legal action against the government.[112] There were, however, considerable risks with this strategy. The costs of litigation were high, and, in the post-*Singh* political environment, the odds of success were low.

For its case even to be heard, the CCC first had to obtain "public interest standing" from the courts, which meant that it had to pass three tests. First, the issue being contested had to be of "fundamental public importance." Second, the group had to be either directly affected by or have "a genuine interest in the validity of the legislation." Third, there could be "no other reasonable, effective or practical manner in which the issue may be brought before the Court."[113] That the CCC's claim satisfied the first two requirements was never really in doubt. The courts had already recognized the protection of refugees as an important matter, and the CCC had proven long ago that it had "genuine" interest in their well-being. But whether the CCC met the third condition was not so clear.

The courts were divided on the question of whether to accept the CCC's constitutional challenge. During the initial hearing at the Federal Court,

Jackman argued that the CCC had an obligation to challenge the determination system in its entirety because refugee claimants were unlikely to do so because of the difficulties associated with litigation. Conceding that there were a number of serious flaws that could render the law unconstitutional if challenged in a higher court, the Federal Court judge accepted her arguments and granted the CCC "public interest standing" to proceed with its challenge. But the judge was not prepared to go any further. Given the infancy of the new system, he was unwilling to strike down the new *Immigration Act* on the grounds that many of the system's perceived shortcomings had yet to play out.[114]

Displeased with the outcome, the Mulroney government appealed the decision to the Federal Court of Appeal. On 12 March 1990, that court overturned the initial ruling, at least partially. It ruled that the lower court had erred in accepting Jackman's claim in its entirety and not as a series of related but distinct complaints. Reviewing her submission point by point, the Court of Appeal found that there was little in it to warrant granting the CCC the opportunity to challenge the constitutionality of the revamped *Immigration Act, 1976*, and dismissed all but four of her complaints.[115]

Neither the CCC nor the federal government was pleased with the compromise ruling, and both turned to the Supreme Court of Canada to settle the matter. Predictably, the CCC maintained that the new system was inherently unfair to legitimate refugees and should thus be deemed inoperative. In contrast, the government wanted the remaining four points dismissed and the CCC's public interest standing revoked.[116]

On 10 January 1991, Justices Antonio Lamer, John Sopinka, and Beverley McLachlin granted both parties leave to appeal and leave to cross-appeal, respectively.[117] For all intents and purposes, the battle lines between the CCC and Ottawa had been drawn, and the responsibility for determining the "winner" rested in the hands of Canada's top court. At stake was much more than simply the fate of Canada's refugee determination system. *Canadian Council of Churches v. Canada* was ultimately about the larger question of whether the judiciary could, on principle, use its constitutional authority to advance rights claims stemming from Canadian civil society, even noble ones such as the rights of refugees.

The CCC's efforts were ultimately all for naught. On 23 January 1992, the Supreme Court of Canada sided unanimously with the federal government. Justice Peter Cory, who wrote the decision on behalf of the court, concurred that the CCC had met the first two criteria needed to gain public interest standing before the courts by showing, first, that the issue of refugee determination was a serious matter and, second, that as one of the principal organizations that offered aid to refugees it had a genuine interest in how the system functioned. What Cory could not accept, however, was the CCC's claim to the third criteria. He ruled that the CCC had failed to prove that refugees lacked adequate recourse to the nation's courts to challenge the particular failings of the determination system.[118] Consequently, he dismissed the CCC's appeal, accepted the federal government's cross-appeal, and refused to consider the second question, whether there was any merit to the CCC's original critiques of the new laws. The stated rationale for the decision was a concern that offering public interest standing to concerned interest groups, except in the most exceptional cases, would have a "detrimental, if not devastating[,] effect" on Canada's judicial system.[119] Suggesting a degree of frivolousness to the CCC's challenge, he wrote, "the courts must not be allowed to become hopelessly overburdened as a result of the unnecessary proliferation of marginal or redundant suits brought by well-meaning organizations pursuing their own particular cases."[120]

The CCC's case against the federal government had raised awkward questions about the appropriate role of the Supreme Court within the larger Canadian democracy. To grant interest groups standing to challenge the constitutionality of a law would open the court up to accusations that its real intent was not to fulfill its role as an adjudicative institution but to make law. Understandably, the CCC was disappointed with the ruling. But it was not surprised. It had become increasingly disheartened with the Mulroney government's handling of the refugee determination process. Now it extended this disillusionment to the Supreme Court of Canada.

Following the decision, the federal government placed further restrictions on the legal protections available to refugee claimants who arrived at Canada's doorstep. Responding to growing criticisms that the Immigration Refugee Board was neither effective nor efficient, the Mulroney government amended the *Immigration Act* for a third time, passing Bill C-86 in June 1992. As Dirks notes, the main purposes of Bill C-86 were to reduce the potential for backlogs and long delays by streamlining the determination process and to make entry into Canada more difficult for those claimants who lacked proper documentation.[121] The bill codified what James Hathaway and Alex Neve describe as a policy of "deflection," whereby individuals who arrived in Canada via a "designated country," as determined by the federal cabinet, were prohibited from making a claim for refugee status. Not unlike the safe third country proposal found in Bill C-55, the purpose of the policy was to grant the federal government the means to limit access to inland and port-of-entry claims and still avoid the issue of refoulement, since the responsibility of identifying *Convention* refugees would fall to the country from which the individuals had arrived.[122] In addition, Bill C-86 made membership and participation in a terrorist organization grounds for exclusion from the refugee determination process. Under sections 53(1)(b) and 19(1) of the *Immigration Act*, the minister of citizenship and immigration now had the authority to deport refugee claimants who the federal government had reason to believe "had" engaged or "would" engage in terrorism or were members of organizations believed to be engaged in terrorist activities, even if the deportation might lead to the individual's refoulement.[123] Predictably, Canada's refugee advocacy community, including the churches, once again reacted negatively to the changes, believing them to be overly stringent and unfriendly to refugee claimants. Whereas before they had tried to convince the courts that Canada's refugee laws violated the *Charter* and *Bill of Rights*, this time they appealed, with limited success, to both international and domestic bodies, their hope being that Canada's refugee laws would be found to be in contravention of international human rights law and that Ottawa would be shamed into making reforms.

In the mid-1990s, the United Church of Canada sponsored a delegation to appear before the Organization of American States (OAS) Inter-American Commission on Human Rights (IACHR), the purpose of which was to convince the commission that Canada's refugee laws contravened the *American Declaration of the Rights and Duties of Man*. The strategy seemed to work. Although Canada was not a signatory to the *Declaration*, the IACHR nevertheless announced on 17 October 1997 that it would be conducting a three-day fact-finding mission in Toronto, Ottawa, and Montreal "for the purpose of observing and gathering information concerning Canada's refugee determination process and the domestic remedies available to refugee claimants."[124]

After extensive consultations, the IACHR issued its report in February 2000. Although generally complimentary toward Canada's policies, the report's conclusions and recommendations vindicated many of the delegates' concerns about the refugee determination system. Among its findings, the IACHR questioned the fairness and impartiality of the screening processes within the IRB, particularly for claimants who lacked proper travel documents or who were deemed to be a threat to public order or national security. Moreover, it criticized the Canadian government for initiating a system that did not permit a case to be reopened should new evidence become available, a shortcoming that could result in cases of refoulement.[125]

Shortly after the release of the OAS report, the Chrétien Liberals, who had taken office in 1993, introduced Bill C-31, the *Immigration and Refugee Protection Act* (*IRPA*), in April 2000. The bill received mixed reviews. Among the more positive additions was the creation of a Refugee Appeal Division, which would permit a claimant who had received a negative decision to launch an appeal on matters of both law and fact.[126] But in many respects the new law was more restrictive than the one that preceded it. Michael Bossin notes that, among other shortcomings, Bill C-31 expanded the grounds for ineligibility, did nothing to distinguish between criminal and non-criminal offences committed by claimants, and established strict guidelines for the overseas interdiction of individuals who lacked proper documentation.[127]

Bill C-31 eventually died on the order paper; however, *IRPA* was reintroduced in early 2001, this time as Bill C-11. In a letter to members of the Senate Human Rights Committee dated 30 March 2001, Jack Costello and Jan Drews, co-chairs of the ICCR's board, lamented that Bill C-11 was not in keeping with international human rights treaty obligations and drafted "before the recommendations of the Inter-American Commission on Human Rights could be properly considered."[128] Appearing before the Standing Committee on Citizenship and Immigration hearings five days later, ICCR delegates urged members to enact greater safeguards to ensure that all claimants who fit the *Convention* definition received a fair hearing and had the right to a "meaningful appeal" that included access to the courts for those who risked facing ill treatment or torture if returned to the country from which they had fled.[129] Their efforts were to no avail. The House of Commons passed the new law on 13 June 2001.

The terrorist attacks on New York and Washington, DC, on 11 September 2001 brought renewed attention and scrutiny to the refugee determination system. Although curbing inefficiency and preventing the potential for abuse remained key priorities for the federal government, protecting national security and checking the threat of terrorism took on new urgency. The prevailing concern was that terrorists could secure entry into Canada via a refugee system prone to long delays, backlogs, and drawn-out proceedings. Amid the heightened anxieties that followed the attacks, Minister of Citizenship and Immigration Denis Coderre announced in April 2002 that, because of increased demands on the refugee system, the federal government had decided to hold off on its promise to establish the Refugee

Appeal Division, preferring instead to permit claimants who had received a negative decision to apply for judicial review to the Federal Court, Trial Division.[130] Then, on 5 December, Ottawa signed a Safe Third Country Agreement with the United States, the purpose of which was to regulate movement across the Canada-US border and prevent claimants from engaging in "asylum shopping." It came into effect on 29 December 2004.[131] Both Coderre's announcement and the agreement represented more than just an attempt to co-ordinate policies with Washington. For all intents and purposes, they were the culmination of two decades of measures designed to limit the protections that had been granted to refugee claimants as a result of that fateful decision at the Supreme Court in 1985.

Indeed, *Singh* remains a seminal event in a larger debate about which branch of government has been most responsible for the failings of the refugee determination system. For scholars and writers critical of the restrictiveness of the system, such as Adelman, fault lay primarily with the Mulroney government and the senior bureaucrats at the Department of Immigration for purposely allowing the backlog to grow so as to justify reforms that "moved the process back in the direction of ministerial discretion and mandarin control."[132] Along the same lines, in their book *Closing the Doors: The Failure of Refugee Protection,* David Matas and Ilana Simon describe the new system devised under Bill C-55 as an "abysmal failure" in which "fairness and common sense have given way to the insistence on speed."[133] But others – including those on both the left and the right – have stressed the role of the Supreme Court in mandating an oral hearing for all claimants. Michael Mandel has argued that, despite the noble intentions of the Supreme Court, the decision "dictated the form" of the government's response but did little to relieve the plight of refugees, at least not in the long run.[134] Jeffrey Simpson of the *Globe and Mail* has pointed on several occasions to the *Singh* decision as the chief obstacle preventing a fair and efficient system, as a poorly conceived by-product of an over-zealous Supreme Court that had little appreciation for or understanding of the burden that it was placing on the federal government.[135] Simpson is by no means alone. F.L. Morton and Rainer Knopff, two leading conservative critics of judicial activism in the *Charter* era, have described *Singh* as a "classic example of the unintended consequences of judicial policy reform."[136] Daniel Stoffman, in his 2002 book *Who Gets In: What's Wrong with Canada's Immigration Program – and How to Fix It,* takes this idea a step further, suggesting that, in the wake of the terrorist attacks of 11 September 2001, the time has come for "a government that is attentive to the national interest" to "invoke the notwithstanding clause of the *Charter of Rights* to nullify [*Singh*]."[137]

Despite its experiences in both *Singh* and later *Canadian Council of Churches v. Canada*, the CCC has continued to view the Supreme Court of Canada as a venue for securing more claimant-friendly reforms to the refugee determination system.[138] On 11 January 2001, the court heard the case *Suresh v. Minister (Citizenship and Immigration)*.[139] Manickavasagam Suresh was a *Convention* refugee from Sri Lanka who had been granted refugee status in Canada in 1991. In the mid-1990s, the Canadian Security Intelligence Service (CSIS) found evidence that he was an alleged fundraiser for the Liberation Tigers of Tamil Eelam (LTTE), a group believed to have engaged in acts of terrorism against the Sri Lankan government during that country's protracted civil war. Suresh was detained in October 1995 on the grounds that he was suspected of being a member of an organization alleged to have committed terrorist acts, and he was issued a security certificate stating that he was "inadmissible to Canada" under the terms of section 19(1) of the *Immigration Act*. On 29 August 1997, the Federal Court found that the security certificate was warranted. The minister of citizenship and immigration at the time, Lucienne Robillard, then informed him that he was to be deported back to Sri Lanka on the grounds that he represented a "danger to the security of Canada."[140]

In response, Suresh presented the minister with written reports about the human rights situation in Sri Lanka. His hope was that he might convince her, *prima facie*, that he would face torture if returned. An immigration officer was assigned to review his case. After reviewing the file, the officer informed the minister that, "on balance, there are insufficient humanitarian and compassionate considerations present to warrant extraordinary consideration."[141] Robillard thus saw little reason not to proceed with the deportation, scheduled for 19 January 1998. Receiving no reply, Suresh appealed his case to the Federal Court of Appeal. His counsel was none other than Barbara Jackman.

Jackman challenged the minister's decision on three grounds. The first was that the minister had acted unreasonably. The second was that sections 53(1)(b) and 19(1) of the *Immigration Act* violated the principles of fundamental justice since Suresh had neither been provided with a copy of the immigration officer's report nor allowed to respond to the evidence against him. The third was that the same sections, which allowed for the possibility of refoulement, violated sections 7, 2(b), and 2(d) of the *Charter*, which covered the rights to "life, liberty and security of the person," "freedom of expression," and "freedom of association," respectively. However, the Federal Court of Appeal was unconvinced, ruling against Suresh on all three counts. Predictably, Suresh appealed the decision.

In *Suresh*, the Supreme Court was asked to determine whether sections 53(1)(b) and 19(1) of the *Immigration Act* were constitutional. Specifically, it was asked to determine whether the ministerial discretion to return someone to face possible torture, as permitted in section 53(1)(b), violated section 7; whether membership in an organization believed to be engaged in terrorist activities violated sections 2(b) and 2(d), which protected freedom of expression and freedom of association; and whether the terms "danger to the security of Canada" and "terrorism" found in sections 53(1)(b) and 19(1), respectively, were so vague that they contravened the principles of fundamental justice found in section 7. *Suresh* attracted considerable attention from a number of interest groups. In total, eight, including the CCC (represented this time by two of Canada's most well-known defence lawyers, Clayton Ruby and Marlys Edwardh), were granted intervener status.[142] All supported Suresh's bid not to be deported.

The court issued its judgment on 11 January 2002. Not surprisingly, the events of the previous three months had a considerable influence on its interpretation of the two provisions of the *Immigration Act* in question. In a unanimous decision, it sided with the federal government on all three counts. Although the decision was not necessarily unexpected, it was the court's answer to the first question that was most troubling to the refugee advocates. The court ruled that, though refoulement was a violation of section 7, the law, which permitted ministerial discretion, was not in and of itself unconstitutional provided that it was applied in such a manner that the individual in question not be deported to face torture. The court ruled that Suresh, who had made a *prima facie* case that he would be tortured if deported, was entitled to a new hearing with the minister. But the court then went a step further. Ever conscious of the need to balance individual liberties with collective security, it ruled that refoulement might be justifiable under section 1 of the *Charter* in an "exceptional" case.[143] The court's ruling might well have been different had it occurred prior to 9/11. Indeed, it might have opted to do away with ministerial discretion altogether. But in the climate of early 2002, in a case involving national security, it reaffirmed that refoulement was legal, if only in the most extenuating circumstances.[144]

The CCC's battles with Ottawa were not over. In 2004, Minister of Citizenship and Immigration Judy Sgro brought renewed attention to the churches' role in the refugee system after she threatened to do away with the *de facto* right of the churches to provide sanctuary to claimants who had been denied refugee status and were scheduled to be deported. Understandably, the news did not sit well with the churches. They chastised Sgro for attempting to violate a centuries-old tradition in which state officials had recognized and respected the churches' moral duty to protect those facing persecution. Eventually, Sgro backed down, albeit reluctantly.[145]

Shortly thereafter, in December 2005, the CCC, along with Amnesty International Canada and the Canadian Council for Refugees, filed a court challenge with the Federal Court, contending that the Canada-US Safe Third Country Agreement violated refugees' rights. Two years later the Federal Court upheld the challenge on the grounds that, in addition to a number of procedural shortcomings, US refugee policy did not comply with the UN *Convention against Torture* and the UN *Refugee Convention*. Following the ruling, all three parties called on the federal government to suspend operation of the agreement.[146] However, Ottawa successfully appealed the decision; the Federal Court of Appeal overturned the ruling on 27 June 2008. Much to the dismay of refugee advocates, including the Canadian Council of Churches, the Supreme Court of Canada denied leave to appeal on 5 February 2009, proving once again that, of the many human rights norms that challenge state sovereignty, those relating to the rights of refugees remain the hardest to secure.

Howard Adelman once wrote that "refugee policy is the litmus test of the concept of justice of a society."[147] Since the end of the Second World War, there have been moments when Canada has passed this test admirably, showing great compassion toward those in need of refuge. At other times, however, its generosity has been in short supply. On these occasions, the aim of the state has been to reinforce the notion that entrance into the country remains a privilege and not an automatic right.

Although refugees obtained legal recognition as a distinct category of individuals, first internationally with the 1951 *Convention* and subsequently in Canadian law through the *Immigration Act, 1976*, norms relating to the rights of refugees have had a tenuous hold and have been prone to backsliding. As Dirks has aptly noted, "neither formal legislation nor authoritative administrative structures guarantee humanitarian and compassionate refugee admissions programmes or a fair and just set of procedures for the determination of refugee status."[148] The reason is that, at their core, refugee rights involve a contest between two competing and seemingly incompatible norms that pit the protection of the individual against the interests of the state.

The Canadian Council of Churches has played an important role in advancing refugee rights in Canada. Since its founding in the mid-1940s, the CCC has lobbied Ottawa to respond with compassion to refugee crises around the world and to enact a determination process that is fair and, above all, not susceptible to incidents of refoulement. In the post-*Charter* era, the organization has appealed to the courts to secure these aims, as it first did in *Singh*. But more than any other case that the CCC has been involved with, *Singh* revealed the limits of judicial activism for the defence of non-citizens most in need of protection. The case and the events that followed suggest that, in states with a Westminster parliamentary system, reforms through the courts can often be temporary. Parliament, if it chooses to, can always respond with new measures designed to reclaim authority that was lost and tilt the scales back in favour of the state. Indeed, until notions of sovereignty change, borders are made more permeable, and global migration flows dissipate, there is little chance that this dialectical struggle between refugee advocates, such as the CCC, and the state – with the judicial branch as arbiter – will ever be fully resolved.

2

The "Misuse" of Freedom?
The Canadian Jewish Congress, the Canadian Civil Liberties Association, and the Limits of Expression

Human rights are often held to be indivisible and inalienable. Although this claim operates well at the rhetorical level, and arguably is even necessary for the advancement of rights generally, it offers little guidance to politicians and policy makers who must weigh individual liberties against the collective well-being of citizens. For Canadians, nowhere has this tension been more acute than in controversies surrounding the 1970 hate propaganda law, which criminalized certain expressions of hate. Drafted in the mid-1960s as a response to the perceived rise in hate literature and the emergence of neo-Nazis and white supremacist groups in Canada, the law operated on the principle that individual freedom of expression is earned and can legitimately be restricted by the state when used to further harmful ideas directed at vulnerable minorities.

The story of the hate propaganda law and the subsequent constitutional challenges against it at the Supreme Court of Canada beginning in the 1980s is also the story of a series of contests of ideas between two organizations, the Canadian Jewish Congress (CJC) and the Canadian Civil Liberties Association (CCLA). Rooted in the collective historical experiences of the Jewish community in Canada and abroad, the CJC advanced the position that freedom of speech is not absolute and can be misused for the purpose of undermining the well-being of Canadian society. Therefore, it can legitimately be curbed. In turn, the CCLA challenged the merits of this assertion, contending that there can be no legitimate grounds for prohibiting non-violent ideas, no matter how unpopular or abhorrent they might be, and that it is far more advantageous to confront messages of hate through open public debate than through criminal sanction. In their own ways, both organizations provided much of the intellectual capital for a fundamental yet unresolved debate that all liberal democracies, including Canada, must grapple with: namely, whether free expression – the very foundation of a democratic society – can justifiably be limited when the ideas promoted are deemed to be so offensive that they are inimical to the core of the free society.

Founded initially in 1919 as an umbrella group for Canada's Jewish community, the Canadian Jewish Congress had an inauspicious beginning. Unable to co-ordinate a divided and fractious community, it was "on the rocks of internal disharmony" in the 1920s, only to be reconstituted in 1933 and 1934 in response to growing antisemitism in Canada and abroad.[1] As historians Irving Abella and Harold Troper recount in their book *None Is Too Many: Canada and the Jews of Europe, 1933-1948*, much of the organization's early history is the story of failed efforts to persuade the Mackenzie King government to provide sanctuary to large numbers of Jewish refugees fleeing the horrors of Nazism.[2] But combatting homegrown incidents of hate directed at Jewish Canadians – whether the virulent writings of fascist Adrian Arcand, the overtly antisemitism teachings of the Catholic Church in Quebec, the anti-Jewish conspiracies of the Social Credit Party in Alberta, or the discriminatory practices of so many of Canada's institutions, particularly those of higher learning – was a core part of its mandate from its early days.[3]

Although antisemitism in Canada long predated the Second World War,[4] it was Hitler's rise to power, culminating with the Holocaust, that brought a new sense of urgency to confronting antisemitism specifically and racism generally. For many within the CJC, the war revealed the irrationality of entire populations during times of duress. For them, the terrible events of the 1930s and 1940s cemented the view that all societies, democratic or otherwise, were inherently fragile, susceptible to hateful ideas that, if left unchecked, could undermine social harmony and public order. After the war, several of the CJC's executive became convinced that the solution was for the state to play an active role in inhibiting the promotion of open hostilities between different groups within society.[5]

Yet the CJC executive struggled with the implications of what they were calling for. They recognized that freedom of expression is the cornerstone of a democratic system, not its Achilles heel. They also understood that ill-conceived limits on speech and other forms of communication could be detrimental to free societies, leading them down the path toward totalitarianism. Consequently, the executive adopted the argument that freedom of expression is a function of the individual's greater responsibility to contribute to the overall well-being of society. Hate-mongers, they contended, offered nothing positive to society, their principal aim being to deprive certain classes of people of their right to personal fulfillment. Any costs of censoring these individuals would be small, particularly compared to the costs that might result from allowing them free rein.

This, in essence, is what the CJC told the House of Commons Special Committee on the *Criminal Code of Canada* in March 1953 during a briefing on the provisions of the law that dealt with sedition, public mischief, and spreading false news. The CJC delegation was led by Professor Bora Laskin of the University of Toronto's Department of Law. Laskin had not fought in the war, nor had he witnessed the concentration camps of Europe firsthand. But his brother Saul had. As Philip Girard explains in his biography of Laskin, Saul's experience had a profound effect on the future chief justice of the Supreme Court of Canada, focusing his energies on combatting racial and religious discrimination in Canadian society.[6] Laskin warned the committee that "preservation and maintenance of our essential freedoms" should not be confused with a "licence to those who would arouse hostility among different classes of our people or publish malicious falsehoods to drive a wedge between such classes. Conduct of this character undermines our democratic rights, sabotages the national welfare and destroys national unity. It exploits our democracy for evil ends."[7]

The CJC had been concerned that existing Canadian law offered no meaningful protection to racial, ethnic, and religious minorities that might be vulnerable to messages of hate. Sections 62 and 166 of the *Criminal Code* prohibited, respectively, sedition and "spreading false news" with the intention of causing "injury or mischief to a public interest." But neither had been designed to criminalize expressions intended to provoke violence against a particular group within society.[8] In light of these "deficiencies," Laskin and his colleagues recommended that the committee insert explicit references to group defamation in both sections and suggested a sentence of two years' imprisonment for anyone found guilty of either offence.[9] The committee passed on the advice. Unconvinced of the harm that could result from promotions of hate, the members opted against placing any new limits on Canadians' right to freedom of expression.[10]

The early 1960s brought a renewed sense of urgency to the matter for the CJC. As historian Franklin Bialystok has argued, in the early years of the decade the Holocaust came to be seen as an integral part of Canadian Jewish identity, prompted, in part, by the attention surrounding the 1962 trial of Adolf Eichmann, the Nazi SS officer and architect of Hitler's "final solution," whom Israeli forces abducted from his home in Argentina in 1960, tried, and eventually executed for crimes against the Jewish people, crimes against humanity, and war crimes.[11] This period also saw a marked, though indeterminable, rise in the proliferation of antisemitism and racist materials throughout the country. Most of it arrived via the southern United States, from states such as Virginia, Alabama, and California. A smaller percentage was homegrown, originating in parts of southwestern Ontario.[12] Overwhelmingly, the materials espoused the doctrines of white superiority, endorsed the Holocaust, and advanced the view that both communism and the United Nations were part of a larger Jewish conspiracy to control the world.[13] To many in Canada's Jewish community – especially survivors of the Holocaust – the spread of these materials was proof that "the disease of antisemitism" was very much alive and that something needed to be done about it.[14]

In a letter dated 12 March 1964, three members of the CJC executive – Michael Garber, Sydney Harris, and Saul Hayes – raised the issue of drafting hate propaganda legislation with the Pearson government, cautioning that, though still relatively small, the problem had grown to such a point that it could no longer be left alone.[15] The three focused their efforts on obstructing the distribution of hateful materials. At the time, section 153 of the *Criminal Code* granted the postmaster general the authority to block the distribution of mail on the grounds that its content was considered "indecent" or "immoral, "seditious" or "disloyal," "scurrilous" or "libellous," or "fraudulent" or "illegal."[16] The fear was that the courts would refrain from including materials that defame identifiable groups in their interpretation of "scurrilous," opting for a narrow reading in which the term's application would be restricted to materials deemed to be slanderous only to individuals. Consequently, the executive members called on the federal government formally to expand the list of grounds on which an individual's postal privileges could be revoked to include materials that promoted violence or hatred against religious, racial, or ethnic groups. Just as Laskin had argued in the

1950s, they maintained that certain ideas deprived vulnerable groups of their right to live a dignified existence and that censoring these ideas was not only reasonable for the sake of shielding these groups but also in the best interests of society.

> It is no exaggeration to say that, however confident we are of the strength of our democracy, this hate movement, if it is not met, and met squarely, bears within itself a potent threat to our society. In the early 1930's few were prepared to say that the highly civilized society of Germany could succumb through inaction and inertia on the part of those who had nothing in common with Nazism to the extent of permitting that destructive doctrine to gain the upper hand. Yet history has shown what can happen in the face of passivity or inaction.[17]

In October 1964, Garber, Hayes, and Maxwell Cohen, dean of law at McGill University in Montreal and long-time CJC supporter, met with Guy Favreau, the minister of justice, to discuss the possibility of striking a committee to study the matter.[18] The meeting was a success. Three months later Favreau announced that the federal government was establishing the Special Committee on Hate Propaganda in Canada, which would have a mandate to reexamine "the parameters of permissible argument" for Canadian society.[19] Cohen was named its chair.[20] Its seven members were picked for their particular expertise and understanding of both the law and the larger philosophical questions involved in restricting expression. Joining Cohen were J.A. Corry, professor of political science and law at Queen's University; L'abbé Gérard Dion, a sociologist at Laval University; Shane MacKay, executive editor of the *Manitoba Free Press;* Pierre Elliott Trudeau, professor of law at the University of Montreal at the time;[21] Saul Hayes of the CJC; and Mark MacGuigan, professor of law and chair of the CCLA Board of Directors.

Originally influenced by the success of the American Civil Liberties Union (ACLU), civil liberties organizations first emerged in Canada in the 1930s and 1940s as ad hoc and temporary responses to specific (and flagrant) encroachments on individual liberties.[22] Dormant throughout the 1950s, the CCLA was formally revived in 1964 following the Robarts government's decision to increase the powers available to Ontario's police forces.[23] Committed to protecting and extending Canadians' civil liberties and fundamental freedoms against undue encroachments by the state, the CCLA took a hallowed view of freedom of expression. Although its stance was by no means absolutist, its position was that free speech was the single greatest safeguard shielding democracies from the perilous road toward authoritarianism. In the minds of its members, many of whom were prominent lawyers, journalists, and academics, it was the "marketplace of ideas" – free and uncensored public debate – that protected Canadians against "unjust governments and unjust policies."[24]

Also taking exception to the announcement was the editorial board of the *Globe and Mail*. Given the motto on the paper's masthead – "the subject who is truly loyal to the Chief Magistrate will neither advise nor submit to arbitrary measures" – its opposition was not out of character.[25] In an editorial on 12 January 1965, the paper questioned the wisdom behind the government's decision, in essence damning the committee before it even began its work. Its view was that a hate propaganda law would invariably interfere with the freedom of expression of all individuals, not just hate-mongers, and have the unintended effect of driving hate-mongers underground, thus "leaving the spirit of anti-Semitism to fester in hidden recesses of the community."[26]

Cohen remained unconvinced that ignoring the problem was the most appropriate course of action. Like Hayes, he shared many of the CJC's fears about the fragility of democracies and held a particularly pessimistic view of human nature. All individuals, he believed, no matter how well educated, were capable of moments of irrationality, sometimes even cruel and violent irrationality. So too were whole societies, especially during times of social duress when the temptation to malign or scapegoat a particular group within society could be great. For Cohen, passing laws that prohibited the promotion of hate was, in effect, an "insurance policy" that society took out against its own potential for acts of brutality.[27] Although he understood that this approach was neither perfect nor comprehensive, he subscribed to the belief that legislation could deter sentiments of hate from manifesting themselves in overt acts of violence and give targeted groups legal recourse to confront those who vilified them or, worse still, called for their destruction.[28]

The Allan Gardens Riot of late May 1965 in Toronto marked a low point in the larger debate over the appropriate response to the proliferation of hate propaganda in a democratic society. The incident began after a number of news outlets announced that William John Beattie, leader of the National Socialist Party of Canada, and his supporters were planning to hold a public rally for the end of the month at the Allan Gardens.[29] At the time, Toronto City Council could do nothing to stop the rally as none of its bylaws granted it the authority to bar public gatherings in the city's parks.[30] Events turned violent. On 30 May, a mob of roughly 5,000, many of them Holocaust survivors who had immigrated to Canada from Eastern Europe after the Second World War, descended on Beattie and his supporters. Whether the violence was premeditated was not entirely clear, but given that many of them were armed it was apparent that their intention was to intimidate the neo-Nazis into silence. After much commotion, police eventually separated the two groups, rescuing Beattie and members of a motorcycle club who happened to be in the vicinity of the rally before anyone was seriously injured. Nine of the rioters were arrested, including Beattie and eight Jews. All were charged with causing a disturbance to the peace, though only Beattie and one other rioter were ever convicted.[31]

Many were quick to denounce the riot, with the harshest condemnations coming from the CJC executive.[32] Both Sydney Harris, the organization's vice-president, and Benjamin Kayfetz, the executive director of the Joint Community Relations Committee (JCRC), which was made up of delegates from the congress and B'nai Brith, criticized the rioters for acting "irresponsibly." Two days after the incident, Harris told reporters that he had "no sympathy with any group that has pre-determined it is going to act in a militant manner." Kayfetz added that the CJC did not condone violence, nor did it support individuals or groups in the Jewish community that did.[33] Both accused the organizers of the riot of acting "with little regard for the consequences to the community."[34]

Whether the CJC liked it or not, the riot had tremendous implications for both the congress as an organization and its campaign for a hate propaganda law. According to Bialystok, the clash exposed the deep cleavages within Canada's Jewish community and marked the "arrival of the survivors as a force" that had been excluded from the "corridors of power" of the CJC. But perhaps more importantly, it revealed a wider dissatisfaction with the CJC's seemingly passive response to neo-Nazism and prompted calls for a more aggressive, systematic, and inclusive strategy for combatting antisemitism in Canada.[35]

The Cohen committee submitted its report to the federal government on 9 November 1965, only eleven months after it had begun its work. Cohen and his colleagues all agreed that freedom of expression, albeit fundamental to the overall health of any democracy, was not absolute. They concluded that ideas that vilified whole groups of people could exact a tremendous toll – psychologically, socially, and physically – on those targeted, all the while jeopardizing the well-being of society. Although the evidence suggested that the dissemination of hate literature was restricted to a small percentage of the Canadian populace, Cohen and his colleagues believed that, in the wake of the Allan Gardens Riot, the problem was too pressing to ignore.[36] Moreover, in an era in which Canadians owned radios and televisions en masse, the capacity for messages of hate to reach new and larger audiences was, at the time, unprecedented. Believing that the worst-case scenario was not out of the realm of possibility, the committee assumed that Canadians were no less vulnerable to the "triumphs" of fascism or Nazism than either Italy or Germany had been during the first half of the twentieth century.[37] For them, the harms that might arise from allowing such ideas to go unchallenged, though ostensibly minimal given the relative size of the problem and the general economic prosperity of the mid-1960s, nonetheless seemed pressing. They recommended that the state enact measures to deal with the problem pre-emptively, before it "mushroom[ed] into a real and monstrous threat to our way of life."[38]

The consensus among the group was that the various provisions in the *Criminal Code* that limited certain types of expression offered inadequate recourse for confronting the dissemination of hate propaganda. Section 166, which dealt with acts of sedition, applied only to "facts" that the individual in question knew were "false" yet published anyway, and it was never intended as a remedy against the spread of hate against identifiable minorities.[39] Section 153, which granted the postmaster general the authority to suspend the delivery of certain types of "scurrilous" materials, had only been applied to materials deemed to be "immoral" and of a "sexual character."[40] Section 5(1)(b) of the *Broadcasting Act* for radio and television prohibited the broadcasting of "abusive comments" or pictures toward any "race or religion," but the law allowed charges to be laid only against the station or network involved, not the person who committed the offence on air.[41] To address these shortcomings, the committee recommended that new legislation be drafted that criminalized three types of speech. The first would prohibit either the advocacy or the promotion of genocide. The second would forbid statements that incited "hatred or contempt against any identifiable group" – which it defined as "any section of the public distinguished by religion, colour, race, language, ethnic or national origin" – in a public place that is "likely to lead to a breach of the peace." The third would prohibit group defamation, regardless of the outcome. The penalties for anyone found guilty of violating any of the three types of speech, the committee suggested, should be imprisonment for five, two, and two years, respectively.[42]

Although neither the first nor the second recommendation was inordinate, the third was more problematic. No one, in good conscience, could argue that advocating genocide or inciting violence against a vulnerable minority had any place in a democratic society. However, the dilemma was to find a way to prohibit speech that did not cause any immediate physical harm to the targeted group without placing undue restrictions on freedom of expression. To solve this problem, the committee added four qualifiers to its recommendation relating to non-violent group defamation. First, promotion of hate needed to be "wilful." Second, individuals could not be found guilty if they could prove that what they had said was true. Third, they could not be convicted if they could prove that the subject matter was in the "public interest," that discussion of the subject was "for the public benefit," or that they had "reasonable grounds" to believe that their statements were indeed "true," though the onus was on them, not the state, to show this.[43] Fourth, to prevent "frivolous or unwarranted prosecutions," the committee recommended that only the federal and provincial attorneys general be allowed to bring charges against individuals believed to be in violation of the law.[44] With these safeguards in place, the committee surmised that the bar had been set high for any limitations on speech and that the courts would have little trouble differentiating hate-mongering from legitimate speech.

Released on 4 April 1966, the Cohen committee's report drew mixed reactions. Not surprisingly, the CJC was highly supportive of the report, content that Cohen and his colleagues had crafted a sensible and well-reasoned solution to the problem of hate propaganda. Others, including the prime minister, were less convinced that the committee had succeeded in accomplishing what it had set out to do. Pearson, who in the 1950s had been accused by Joseph McCarthy of being a communist, was uncomfortable with the ambiguity of the recommendations. He feared that such a law could be used "against those of us who believe in civil rights."[45] The *Globe and Mail*, which had been leery of the committee's work from the beginning, was equally disturbed, for the report seemed to confirm many of the fears that its editorial board had raised the year before. The paper maintained that the proposed limits on expression were dangerous for Canada. Although the recommendations were intended for neo-Nazis and hate-mongers, the *Globe and Mail* believed that the net could be cast much farther, perhaps even used to silence those who were critical of social and economic inequities within society.[46]

The CCLA also had reservations about the report. Despite MacGuigan's involvement, the organization had serious concerns about the proposal to criminalize speech deemed hateful but not violent.[47] Steadfast in its suspicion that any infringement on freedom of expression was tantamount to allowing the state to be the "arbiter of truth," it dismissed much of the reasoning behind the proposed new law on the grounds that neither the absence of criminal sanction nor the potential threat to society posed by the promotion of hate was sufficient to warrant censoring discussion that, though offensive to a particular group or groups, could be of some social value.[48] The CCLA remained firm in its conviction that open debate offered a far more appropriate response to the problem of hate propaganda than did the threat of litigation.[49]

The question of "appropriate" media exposure for neo-Nazis and hate-mongers posed a considerable dilemma for the CJC. On the one hand, the CJC favoured efforts to reveal the activities of those who publicly promoted hate, believing awareness to be an important step toward insulating society against destructive ideas. On the other hand, it saw a great danger in giving "currency and notoriety" to these ideas, particularly if the news organization was attempting to display a semblance of "balance" in its coverage.[50] Nowhere was this more apparent than during the CJC's public feuds with the Canadian Broadcasting Corporation (CBC) over its engagement with various neo-Nazis in the late 1960s.

In January 1967, the JCRC learned that Adolf von Thadden, the deputy chairman of the German ultranationalist National Democratic Party (NPD), was planning a tour of Canada to win international support for his party and that the CBC hoped to interview him. Angered, the JCRC mobilized the Jewish community, as well as churches, labour unions, and veterans' groups, to attend a public rally at Nathan Phillips Square in Toronto to protest both von Thadden's arrival and the resurgence of Nazism in Germany.[51] Just as troubling for the organizers was the CBC's seemingly cavalier attitude toward a man whose platforms included the eradication of Jews.[52]

The network initially proposed having von Thadden on as a "mystery guest" on *Front Page Challenge*, an entertainment-news show in which a panel of reporters were first given four minutes to identify the guest through a series of yes and no questions and then allowed to question the individual. Livid, the JCRC accused the CBC of "glorifying and idealizing" Nazism rather than exposing the dangers that such ideas posed to Canadian society. Amid the pressure, the CBC conceded that this was an inappropriate forum for von Thadden. Instead, it chose to interview him on the public affairs show *Sunday*.

The leaders of Canada's Jewish community remained angry and warned the CBC that any program on von Thadden would undoubtedly be accompanied by protests outside the studio. Secretary of State Judy LaMarsh, the minister responsible for the public network, even weighed in on the controversy and chastised the network for adopting a reckless attitude toward public safety.[53] Again the CBC retreated. But it did not acquiesce, at least not entirely. In lieu of interviewing von Thadden in Toronto, it sent its production crew to Germany to interview him there. As had been forewarned, roughly 3,000 demonstrators protested outside the CBC studio in Toronto while the show aired on 22 January.

The quarrel between the CBC and Canada's Jewish community did not end there. In December 1968, the CJC accused the CBC of once again showcasing a hate-monger to the Canadian public. Once again the controversy involved *Front Page Challenge,* only this time the individual in question was British fascist and outspoken antisemite Sir Oswald Mosley. Unlike von Thadden, he did appear as the "mystery challenger." This time the CJC's attack drew the ire of author and journalist Pierre Berton. A civil libertarian and vocal proponent of freedom of the press (and a regular panellist on the show), Berton defended the CBC's right to allow individuals such as Mosley onto its programs, accusing the CJC of trying to confine the airwaves to "right-o's" who were uncontroversial and "dull."[54]

The disputes did little to dispel fears that the CBC was granting these individuals platforms to present an "apologia for Nazism" that would otherwise have been unavailable to them.[55] But more than this, they revealed just how little recourse was available to targeted minorities that wished to halt such public displays of racism from reaching thousands of viewers. It confirmed in the minds of many within Canada's Jewish community that the need for a hate propaganda law remained pressing.[56]

In January 1966, a delegation from the Canadian Jewish Congress met with the secretary of state for external affairs and acting prime minister Paul Martin to discuss the federal government's plans to adopt the recommendations of the Cohen Report. Martin was noncommittal. He told the delegation that the federal government planned to hold off on introducing any new legislation to Parliament until after it had a chance to translate the Cohen Report into French, at which point it would make a decision on any future course of action.[57] Only in November did Solicitor General Lawrence Pennell introduce Bill S-49, *An Act to Amend the Criminal Code (Hate Propaganda),* not in the House of Commons but in the Senate.

Bill S-49 was, for all intents and purposes, identical to the Cohen committee's recommendations, the only notable exception being that the bill omitted the terms "religion," "language," and "national origin" from its definition of "identifiable groups."[58] Like the report, the bill was highly divisive. Few senators – Liberal or Conservative – supported it without reservation. Most were sympathetic to its aims but uncomfortable with its potential applications. A vocal few remained convinced that it posed a perilous affront to civil liberties.[59] Although the bill was allowed to die on the order paper in March 1967, the Senate resumed its work the following year, this time reintroducing the legislation as Bill S-5. In February 1968, a special Senate committee began hearings on the bill. Predictably, it called on the expertise of the organizations and individuals that had had a hand in drafting the proposed legislation.

The CJC was among the first group of witnesses to appear before the committee. Its delegation consisted of nine representatives from various Jewish organizations, one of whom was Saul Hayes.[60] Little had changed in its position since the 1950s. The CJC's support for Bill S-5 remained rooted in the belief that open societies are not invulnerable to the destructive power of hateful ideas. Conspiracies about Jewish plots to dominate the world, its representatives argued, had been around for centuries. They were not new. But Joseph Goebbels, the mastermind behind the Nazi propaganda machine, had taken "Jew-baiting" to new heights by devising the "big lie technique," which operated on the premise that people will believe any lie if it is repeated frequently enough.[61] Convinced that hatred toward Jews never really disappeared but came in waves that ebbed and flowed, the delegates warned that the worst-case scenario – another Holocaust – remained a possibility, if a remote one. On this point, Sydney Harris, now the vice-chairman of the Central Region of the CJC, was adamant:

> Now, the climate of Canada is different and there is not the slightest reason to think that the climate of Canada will ever resemble that of Germany. Nevertheless, we live in a generation where it happened, and we have with us today at least one person who survived the European holocaust. So that he knows that you can grow up in an atmosphere where you do not think it is possible for that to happen but then you see it happen.[62]

Ever conscious of the concerns raised by civil libertarians, the CJC maintained that Bill S-5 did not stifle "legitimate" speech. Expressions of hate, its delegates reiterated, offered no redeeming value to society. Nothing sacred was lost by censoring speech that could cause great physical and psychological harm to whole communities. Again Harris was particularly adamant on this point:

> It is my concern that too much stress has been laid upon the privileges of the individual, as an isolated person, an island unto himself, and not enough upon the duties and obligations which are his as a member of that society. In my view, it is the "rights" of society that are experiencing a subtle but continual erosion, and individual liberty, far from diminishing, is expanding to the detriment of the collective safety and welfare.[63]

For the CJC, the safeguards in the law protecting freedom of expression – the defence of "truth," "public interest," and "public benefit" – were sufficient and not that different from the provisions found in Canada's libel laws.[64] Nor did the delegates take issue with the "reverse onus" aspects of the legislation, suggesting that there was little wrong with placing the responsibility on the accused to prove the validity of his or her statements, as it was unreasonable for the courts to require members of the aggrieved group to prove the falsity of the attack against them. Finally, the CJC did not place any stock in the criticism that Bill S-5 would, in effect, operate as a sort of "gag law" that could be used to silence individuals pre-emptively, since it was a reactionary measure that allowed the state to respond only to promotions of hate already in the public domain.[65]

Not all members of the special Senate committee were convinced. Some senators remained unsure of the need for the legislation on the grounds that many potential vulnerable minorities did not share the same sense of urgency. CJC delegates responded by suggesting that Bill S-5 would also protect French Canadians from hate propaganda originating in English Canada. To this claim, a skeptical Lionel Henri Choquette responded, "you do not find French Canadians who will try to shove this type of legislation down people's throats. You see the difference."[66]

The hate propaganda legislation was once again put on hold, this time by the federal election of 1968, which saw Trudeau win a majority government. Unlike his predecessor, Trudeau was far more comfortable with the idea of a law prohibiting hate speech. In September 1968, members of his government told delegates from the CJC that the prime minister planned to adopt the legislation as a government measure. Undoubtedly, his involvement in the Cohen committee influenced his thinking.[67] But more than this, Trudeau believed that the purpose of the state was to create a society in which Canadians were allowed both freedom and equality of opportunity. Despite his libertarian leanings, he was not opposed to direct government intervention in the lives of Canadians, as long as the justification for doing so was to allow greater freedom and opportunity for the disadvantaged.[68] True to his word, the legislation was reintroduced as Bill S-21. Hearings in the Senate began anew in February 1969, and this time the Senate turned to the CCLA for guidance.

The CCLA sent four representatives: Eamon Park, one of the organization's vice-presidents; Wilson Head, a sociologist in race relations from Atlanta who had been a member of the National Association for the Advancement of Colored People prior to moving to Canada in 1965; Graham Parker, special counsel to the CCLA and an expert in criminal law at York University's Osgoode Hall; and Jill Armstrong, the organization's executive assistant. Also appearing before the committee, though as an independent witness, was Osgoode Hall dean of law Harry Arthurs, one of the CCLA's founders in 1964.[69] Absent from the CCLA's delegation was MacGuigan, who had left academe for politics, winning the seat for the riding of Windsor-Walkerville. For MacGuigan and the CCLA, the Cohen Report and subsequent hate propaganda bills had marked a philosophical parting of ways. Although MacGuigan remained a strong supporter of and a good friend to the organization and its executive, he had been persuaded of the need for legislation to deal with hate-mongers. This was something his former colleagues simply could not accept.[70]

The CCLA delegates saw little need for the law, save the prohibitions against the promotion of genocide and the advocacy of violence. Although sympathetic to the intent of the legislation, they were uneasy about its potential application. They questioned the assumption that tension among groups in society had no redeeming value, contending that it often acted as the spark that ignited positive social change. "History," Park explained, "has taught us that so often tomorrow's social reform grows out of today's verbal attack." Although the CCLA did not condone hate-mongering, the dilemma facing any democratic society, he argued, was to draw the "line between creative tension and destructive hate."[71]

To those representing the CCLA, Bill S-21 simply did not define this equilibrium. Were the times different, were inter-group tensions boiling over into systematic outbreaks of violence, the group conceded, the case for such legislation might be stronger. But they held to the view that the social climate of the late 1960s was such that, even with the von Thaddens,

Mosleys, and Beatties of the world, the "breeding ground for extremism" was "not very fertile." They questioned the virtues of legislation that used "truth" as the barometer of innocence while simultaneously granting the courts the power to "set the framework of democratic political polemics" by giving them the authority to decide which subjects of debate were of "public interest."[72] The danger, they warned, was that the law could affect people who bore "no resemblance to the Nazis or hatemongers who sparked the bill." The real solution was not to prohibit certain forms of speech but to strengthen the human rights legislation across the country while simultaneously eliminating the social and economic inequities within society that fuelled feelings of hate, which, at least in theory, would force the hatemonger to operate in a "virtual vacuum."[73]

The CCLA's arguments resonated with Bill S-21's detractors. On 24 April 1969, two days after Park and his colleagues had appeared before the Senate Committee, the *Globe and Mail* printed excerpts of its testimony and lauded the organization in that day's editorial column for advocating non-legal remedies to the problem of hate-mongering.[74] Much of the appeal of the CCLA's position was that it offered, in effect, an intellectual counterweight to the arguments put forth by the CJC without minimizing concerns about the need to oppose ideas of hate.

But the CCLA's arguments were not persuasive enough to change the Trudeau government's mind. On 17 June 1969, after two and a half years, the Liberal-dominated Senate passed Bill S-21 by a convincing vote of thirty-seven to twenty-one. Two days later the legislation was introduced in the House of Commons but died on the order paper when Parliament broke for the summer. In October 1969, the federal government reintroduced it as Bill C-3, *An Act to Amend the Criminal Code (Hate Propaganda)*. On 13 April 1970, after much heated debate, Parliament passed the law by a count of eighty-nine for and forty-five against. One hundred and twenty-seven members – nearly half the House of Commons – were absent for the vote. Why so many members were not present for the vote that day is not clear. Although poor attendance for a bill's third reading is not necessarily out of the ordinary, Stefan Braun has speculated that their absence can be attributed to "a fear of being perceived to be on the wrong side of hate, a yielding to growing political pressure, public indifference, political weariness, or some combination of all four."[75]

True to form, the editorial board of the *Globe and Mail* disapproved of the outcome: "This is a dangerous bill. We have only begun to see the dark waves circling out from it to thunder at the foundations of our most precious institutions."[76] And in the Upper Chamber, an equally disturbed Liberal senator, Daniel Lang, called on his fellow senators, albeit unsuccessfully, to suspend their review of the legislation until the Supreme Court of Canada could determine whether it was constitutional under the 1960 *Bill of Rights*.[77]

The 1970s saw a marked drop in the number of known incidents involving the distribution of hateful materials in Canada. With this decline, the fears of a widespread neo-Nazi resurgence of the late 1960s seemed to fade.[78] But the unease about the potential application of the hate propaganda law did not. It remained on the minds of those who had had so much input into the construction of the law.

Some members of the JCRC believed that they should lobby various provincial governments to invoke the law broadly, even for relatively minor incidents of public antisemitism.[79] That they would take such a position, particularly after 1973, is understandable. As Bialystok has suggested, for many within Canada's Jewish community, the Six Day War of 1967, the War of Attrition from 1967 to 1973, and the 1973 Yom Kippur War "brought home in some measure the reality of the Holocaust – that Jews had to be vigilant, that antisemitism was a palpable threat, and that Jews must never allow themselves to become captive to totalitarian regimes based on racial or religious exclusion."[80] But others were not as convinced that this was a wise idea. Following the 1970 *Drybones* decision at the Supreme Court, some members feared that the hate propaganda law would not survive a constitutional challenge.[81] Hence, the predominant view within the CJC was that pressure to have the law invoked should be restricted only to cases in which the outcome would be "clearcut," as a hasty and ill-conceived trial risked undoing what had taken decades to achieve.[82]

Alan Borovoy, the general counsel for the CCLA, was equally unconvinced of the constitutionality of the law. He had joined the organization in 1968, quickly becoming its principal public spokesperson as well as the intellectual force behind many of its positions. Like many civil libertarians, Borovoy was uncomfortable with far-reaching state intrusions into the lives of individuals, especially in times of peace. For him, a healthy democracy hinged on the right of disaffected groups to influence the social consensus through non-violent forms of pressure. Freedom of expression lay at the heart of this ability to effect social change.[83] In an article that appeared in *Canadian Forum* in 1971, Borovoy wrote that Canada's hate propaganda law leaned "too heavily and unnecessarily toward the protection of peace at the expense of speech" by restricting "the right to speak where the threat to the peace is non-existent, minimal, or capable of adequate protection in other ways."[84]

A long-standing member of the JCRC, Borovoy was deeply disturbed by both the faith that the CJC placed in the safeguards of the law and its silence on the question of whether such a law might "catch the wrong people."[85] A pragmatist, he suspected that any application of the hate propaganda law would be inherently counterproductive. He feared that it would have the undesired effect of transforming little-known soapbox orators into national figures by allowing them an undeserved moment in the sun and, perhaps more troubling, creating unwelcome martyrs for free speech.

A former protégé of Adrian Arcand, Ernst Zündel was a Holocaust denier from Germany who first came to the attention of Canada's Jewish community in the mid-1960s following the release of his book *The Hitler We Loved and Why*, which he wrote under the pseudonym Christof Friedrich.[86] By the early 1980s, his Toronto publishing company, Samisdat Publishers, had become the largest distributor of antisemitic literature in the world, mailing hate propaganda to destinations throughout North America and Europe. On 13 November 1981, Postmaster General André Ouellet issued an interim prohibition against Samisdat under the terms of section 41 of the *Canada Post Corporation Act*, which permitted him to revoke the company's ability to send and receive mail until the case could be examined by a Postal Review Board.[87] Ouellet justified the decision on the grounds that the company's mailings violated section 281.2(2) (now 319(2)) of the *Criminal Code*, the portion of the hate propaganda law that prohibited the distribution of non-violent messages of hate.[88] A self-proclaimed champion of freedom of expression and a defender of the German ethnicity, Zündel believed that he was the "victim of Zionist persecution."[89]

But he was not the only individual with an antisemitic agenda and an appetite for the spotlight. Beginning in the early 1970s, James Keegstra taught his high school students in Eckville, Alberta, that Jews were responsible for much of the evil in the world.[90] Like Zündel, Keegstra believed that the Holocaust had been a fabrication, a ploy to create favour for Jews with the rest of the world.[91] Students in his grades 9 and 12 social sciences classes who supported his views on exams and in essays were rewarded with high marks; those who did not did poorly in his classes.[92] Following complaints from some parents and a protracted battle with the Alberta Teachers' Association, Keegstra was dismissed and stripped of his teaching licence on

8 December 1982. Although the former teacher was no longer in a position to influence young minds, the matter did not end there. On 11 January 1984, after some initial reluctance, the Lougheed government in Alberta charged Keegstra with violating the hate propaganda law.[93]

Representing both men was Doug Christie, a lawyer based in Victoria, British Columbia. A devout Roman Catholic, Christie was a controversial figure in his own right. In the 1970s, he had founded a political party known as the Western Canada Concept, its mandate being to secure separation of the four western provinces from the rest of Canada.[94] Avowedly anti-"big government," he considered it his duty to defend unpopular individuals whom no one else would take on as clients, including Zündel, whom he first met at Keegstra's preliminary hearing in June 1984. Many observers were not so sure that his motives were so principled. There was a strong suspicion that his attraction to Keegstra and Zündel involved more than just the defence of freedom of expression. In preparing for Zündel's defence, Christie was reported to have read all that he could about revisionist "interpretations" of the Holocaust, spending considerable time at Zündel's home in Toronto. Many observers suspected that little separated client from counsel.[95]

In 1983, Parliament initiated a study on the *Participation of Visible Minorities in Canadian Society*, which included a review of the hate propaganda law. Responding to pressure from a number of minority groups, the committee responsible for the study recommended a series of alterations to the law, all of which would, if passed, remove or diminish the provisions safeguarding freedom of expression found in the hate propaganda law.[96] Among other things, the committee concluded that the law required too much of the prosecution, thus making convictions difficult to secure. It recommended that the law be amended so that the state no longer had to prove that the accused "wilfully" promoted hate and that consent of the attorneys general would no longer be required to initiate proceedings against an individual.[97] The report was indicative of growing support among many minority groups that the state required greater authority to censor the Zundels and Keegstras of Canadian society, individuals whose ideas were not only deeply hurtful but also posed a threat to their members' well-being and safety.[98]

Borovoy was deeply troubled by the proposed changes. In a speech delivered at the 1984 Conference of the Canadian Institute for the Administration of Justice, he maintained that, though inadequate, these provisions did offer minimal safeguards against undue encroachments of freedom of expression.[99] Moreover, he argued that Canadian society was not only strong enough to withstand the ideas of hate that came from a relatively small group of extremists but also had demonstrated this fortitude in recent months. Keegstra, Borovoy noted, had already been removed from the public realm. Not only had he been dismissed from his teaching position, but he had subsequently lost his bid for re-election as mayor of Eckville. Keegstra had later tried his hand at national politics, winning the candidacy for the Social Credit, which had a history of antisemitic platforms, in the riding of Red Deer in the federal election of September 1984. But here too he had been rebuffed. Both he and his party had floundered, winning roughly 0.6 percent of the popular vote, only slightly more than the Rhinoceros Party's 0.4 percent.[100] For Borovoy, this was proof that the solution to individuals such as Keegstra was not litigation but raising "political hell whenever racist utterances emanate from people of authority or social standing," with the objective being either to remove the person in question from his or her position or to garner a meaningful public apology. As for "peripheral racists," those who might be tempted to find scapegoats for their relative standing in society, Borovoy once again suggested that the solution was to remove discriminatory barriers within society, his rationale being that confronting racist "deeds" would likely diminish the effect of racist "words."[101]

Not everyone was satisfied with Borovoy's assessment. Many Canadians, including many members of the Jewish community, believed that the exercise of attempting to rectify the long-term ills of society that allowed racist ideas to take hold was an inadequate and inappropriate response to an immediate problem. Increasingly, they began to look to the courts for a solution.

In late 1984, the Canadian Holocaust Remembrance Association, which had broken off from the CJC in the late 1970s because of what it believed was a passive response toward hate-mongers, took Zündel to court, not for violating the hate propaganda law, but for violating section 177 (now 181), which prohibited the "spreading of false news" and did not require the consent of the attorney general.[102] Zündel seemed pleased with the turn of events. In a fundraising letter to his supporters, he wrote that this was the "Great Holocaust Trial" in which history itself was being judged.[103] Drawing on George Orwell's famous novel *Nineteen Eighty-Four*, he wrote that the Zionists were "enemies of truth, freedom and justice" and warned that, if he lost, not only would he go to prison and Samisdat be shut down but also "all those who question Zionist behaviour and interests will be liable to similar legal actions."[104]

Christie's antics in the courtroom added further fuel to the debate over the usefulness of the trial. During the proceedings, the Crown, which had been unsuccessful in its bid to convince the court to grant judicial notice that the Holocaust was an indisputable event in history, called on survivors to take the stand in the hopes of proving that Zündel was not only wrong but also knew that he was wrong yet promoted his theories anyway.[105] Christie was unforgiving in his cross-examinations. He challenged the authenticity of the survivors' memories, accusing many of the witnesses of lying about what they had lived through. He even called on witnesses of his own, "revisionist experts," one of whom was Keegstra.[106]

Zündel was eventually found guilty on the first count of spreading falsehoods about the Holocaust and was sentenced to fifteen months in prison. Throughout the trial, Christie had done his best to convince the jury that a conviction would be tantamount to undermining freedom of speech in Canada; however, his case had fallen apart after the Crown was able to dispel Zündel's claim that he was a revisionist historian.[107] Outside the courtroom, a dejected Christie told journalists, "we would be wise not to question anything in this country for a while."[108]

Many within the CJC applauded the ruling and hoped that the conviction would act as a deterrent against others like Zündel. They contended that a passive response had thus far accomplished little, that the Holocaust denier had gone unchallenged for almost two decades, with the result being that Samisdat had become one of the most prolific distributors of hate propaganda in the world.[109]

Still, many remained skeptical of the wisdom of the trial. Rabbi W. Gunther Plaut of Toronto's Holy Blossom Temple called it an "error." His concern was that Zündel had been handed both a platform of unprecedented scale and an undeserved credibility that only came with treating his ideas seriously. In a rather blunt assessment of the situation, he commented, "if someone calls your mother a whore, that is not a fit subject for a debate."[110] Predictably, the CCLA remained convinced that litigation was a mistake.[111] In an opinion-editorial in the *Toronto Star*, Borovoy wrote:

> What, then, was the point of the exercise? Was Zundel prosecuted because he was a man of such standing and stature? Was his presence so commanding that he simply had to be cut to size? The fact is that Zundel hovered on our periphery. His constituency was virtually non-existent. His influence approached zero. What made the prosecution so foolish, therefore, is the fact that it was so gratuitous.[112]

Keegstra's appeal had the potential to be just as jarring. The initial trial had been gruelling, lasting seventy days, concluding with the judge ruling that the hate propaganda law was indeed constitutional and the jury finding Keegstra guilty of wilfully promoting hate, fining him $5,000.[113] For the initial hearing, the CJC had sent a team of observers and had helped the Alberta Crown to build its case. But ever conscious of the optics of the proceedings, it had decided against seeking intervener status for fear that the trial would be perceived exclusively as a "Jewish" issue.[114] The caution was warranted. The former mayor of Eckville's appeal to the Alberta Court of Appeal was set for the spring of 1985. Already he had become a symbol of freedom of expression for the extreme political right of western Canada.[115]

As Borovoy had believed with Zündel, he believed that pursuing Keegstra through the courts had unnecessarily given a "fringe" extremist a platform to broadcast his ideas.[116] Hoping to avoid a reoccurrence, the CCLA approached the CJC and proposed that the two organizations together call on the federal government to submit a judicial reference to the Supreme Court of Canada to determine whether the section of the hate propaganda law that criminalized non-violent hate speech was constitutional.[117] Borovoy reasoned that, if the federal government agreed, Keegstra's trial would undoubtedly be adjourned until a decision had been rendered. Conversely, if, in the context of the reference, the Supreme Court ruled that the law was unconstitutional, any trial for Keegstra would be moot. However, if found that the law did not contravene the *Charter*, the issue would be settled, and Keegstra would be unable to challenge its legality on the grounds that it violated his freedom of expression.[118]

The CJC was not keen on the idea. There was a feeling among its executive that support for such a reference could be easily misunderstood and even exploited. The fear was that the public would not recognize that the CJC and CCLA were engaging in a pre-emptive move to disrupt Keegstra's defence. Rather, they were nervous that any questioning of the validity of the law, even if the request was ignored, could ultimately undermine any future defence of its constitutionality.[119]

For the CJC and Canada's Jewish community at large, the first Zündel and Keegstra trials had been Pyrrhic victories. In both cases, the decisions had been favourable to the Jewish community. Yet they had had to relive the events of the Holocaust and combat centuries-old theories about the existence of an international Zionist conspiracy. Whether the costs had been worth it was debatable. Following his sentencing, an unrepentant Zündel had confirmed the fears of those who had opposed the trial in the first place, boasting to journalists outside the courthouse, "it cost me $40,000 in lost work, but I got a million dollars worth of publicity for my cause," and "I wouldn't have missed a second. I enjoyed myself thoroughly."[120] It is little wonder that historian Irving Abella began his address to the plenary session of the CJC's 1986 annual general meeting with the words "only slowly have Canadian Jews emerged from the trauma of 1985."[121]

But the trauma was not over.

Pressure began to mount on the CCLA to intervene in Zündel's and Keegstra's appeals, which once again placed the organization in a difficult position.[122] Luckily for Borovoy, a public feud with Christie in 1986 erased any doubts regarding the CCLA's interest in the two cases. At the time of the initial trials, Christie made a number of public statements that echoed those of his clients, expressing doubts about the Holocaust and suggesting that Jews were responsible for his clients' respective convictions.[123] Infuriated, Borovoy wrote to Christie, informing him that the CCLA's "counsel had been instructed not to cooperate with you in any way in connection with the presentation of argument or otherwise, except as may be stricltly required" until he clarified his views on the Holocaust and the "theory" of an international Zionist conspiracy.[124] Christie responded by accusing Borovoy of committing a "serious impropriety" and referred the letter to his own lawyer.

The letter, however, turned out to be a mixed blessing for the CCLA. At the initial hearing for Zündel's appeal at the Ontario Court of Appeal, Zündel's supporters distributed copies to those in attendance, including the media. However, Zündel had made a few additions to it. He had included a note on the first page: "Alan Borovoy is a lawyer who styles himself 'a defender' of our civil liberties. Yet, he has written the following vicious, arrogant and prejudiced diatribe against a true defender of civil liberties, Mr. Douglas Christie." It continued:

> Borovoy's letter drips with the hatred of one whose tribal prejudices have superseded any real love for civil and human rights and it must be read in its entirety so that real defenders of civil liberties may be warned as to Borovoy's real intentions. When Borovoy describes "anti-democratic extremists" who attempt "to don the mantle of civil liberties in order to clothe their ideologies in an aura of respectability," isn't he really describing himself?[125]

Still, the Ontario Court of Appeal rejected the CCLA's application on the ground, that Borovoy's letter to Christie contained "intimidating overtones."[126] Whether this was a large factor in the court's decision is debatable, given that the court had also rejected earlier applications for intervener status from the CJC and B'nai Brith. Nonetheless, Borovoy was angered by the court's narrow resolve. Given the potential for the case to set a powerful legal precedent, he rebuked the court publicly for allowing rights to free speech to be defended by a lawyer who took "instruction from a known Nazi."[127] Adding insult to injury, the Ontario Court of Appeal reaffirmed the original decision and ruled that the "conscious spreading of falsehoods" is not covered by the freedom of expression protections found in the *Charter*.[128]

The Alberta Court of Appeal, however, was far more receptive to the concerns of the CCLA, granting it intervener status in Keegstra's appeal.[129] In the original trial, the trial judge had ruled that section 281.2(2) was not a *prima facie* infringement of section 2(b) of the *Charter* and that, even if it were, the limiting effect on expression was minimal and thus justifiable through section 1. Unlike the Ontario Court of Appeal, the Alberta Court of Appeal overruled the original decision. In a three to zero ruling issued on 6 June 1988, it struck down section 281.2, ruling that the hate propaganda law violated both sections 2(b) and 11(d), which guaranteed a constitutional right to be presumed innocent until proven guilty, and could not be "demonstrably justified" under section 1.[130]

Civil libertarians applauded the decision. The following day Borovoy told Canadian Press, "I believe the hatemongers in this country can be effectively counteracted without relying on such dangerous language ... [Keegstra] should have been allowed to wallow in the obscurity he so richly deserves."[131] Similarly pleased, the *Globe and Mail*'s editorial board lamented that the only shortcoming of the ruling was that it applied only to Alberta. The paper called on the Government of Alberta to appeal the decision to the Supreme Court of Canada in the hope that the appeal court's decision would be extended across the country.[132]

Subsequent events suggested that the chances of the *Globe and Mail* getting its wish were good. Nearly two months after the *Keegstra* decision, the Ontario Court of Appeal upheld the same section of the hate propaganda law in a similar case involving Donald Clarke Andrews and Robert Wayne Smith, members of the Canadian Nationalist Socialist Party. In 1985, both men had been convicted and sentenced to twelve months and seven months in prison, respectively, for wilfully publishing and distributing their neo-Nazi newsletter, the *Nationalist Reporter* (both also happened to be friends of Keegstra and had supported him in his failed bid for leadership of the Social Credit Party the year before).[133] The Ontario Court of Appeal's decision was almost completely at odds with that of its counterpart in Alberta. Two of the three justices ruled that the law was not an unreasonable infringement of section 2(b), and all three believed that it was not so sweeping that it could not be justified under section 1 if need be. Unlike the Alberta court, the Ontario court based its decision on the aims found in sections 15 and 27 of the *Charter*, which covered equality rights and enhancement of Canada's multicultural heritage, respectively. In what was perhaps the most eloquent defence of the law, Justice Cory wrote, "what a strange and perverse contradiction it would be if the *Charter* was to be used and interpreted so as to strike down a law aimed at preserving our multicultural heritage by limiting in a minimal and reasonable way freedom of expression."[134]

The result, however, was two different laws for different parts of the country. Given the inconsistency in the law, the Supreme Court of Canada agreed to hear the *Keegstra* and *Andrews and Smith* appeals concurrently on 8 June 1989. Keegstra was not pleased with the prospect of seeing his appeal overturned. When asked by journalists about his feelings toward the trial, he responded defiantly, "I was just persecuted because they said that's not what you can believe – in other words, we have thought control in Canada."[135]

Like the two provincial appeal courts, the Supreme Court was charged with determining whether section 281.2 of the *Criminal Code* was constitutional. Specifically, it was asked to answer four questions. Did section 281.2(2) infringe on section 2(b) of the *Charter?* If so, could it be saved through section 1? Also, did section 281.2(3)(a) violate section 11(d) of the *Charter?* And if so, could it be justified under section 1? On questions two and four, the court employed the Oakes test, which it had devised to provide some consistency to section 1 analyses. The test operated on the premise that a law deemed to be unconstitutional could be salvaged if it was "rationally connected to the objectives," if it "impaired" the right in question as little as possible, and if its effects were "proportional" to its objectives.[136] It was – and remains – the Supreme Court's tool for rationalizing limits on the rights of individuals for the purpose of protecting the collective good.

R. v. Keegstra was not about the teachings of James Keegstra as much as it was about whether the Cohen committee had, back in the 1960s, been successful in striking an appropriate balance between two seemingly incompatible rights. Not surprisingly, the case caught the attention of a wide array of third parties, both governmental and non-governmental. The federal and provincial attorneys general for Ontario, Manitoba, Quebec, and New Brunswick all sought and were granted leave to intervene. The Supreme Court also awarded intervener status to five interest groups: four that defended the law, one that did not.[137] The four in support of the Government of Alberta were the CJC, the League for Human Rights of B'nai Brith Canada, InterAmicus, and the Women's Legal Education and Action Fund (LEAF). That they would choose to intervene was not at all surprising. Given both Keegstra's vilification of Canada's Jewish community and their respective connections to the hate propaganda law, both the CJC and B'nai Brith had a great deal at stake in the trial. Similarly, InterAmicus was a human rights centre based in the Department of Law at McGill University and was chaired by Irwin Cotler, former president of the CJC, and LEAF was an organization whose mandate was to "realize the *Charter*'s promise of equality rights for women" and develop "equality jurisprudence" through litigation in precedent-setting cases. They were included for their respective expertise in human rights law.[138] The lone intervener for the respondent was the CCLA.

During the trial, the arguments raised by the CJC, B'nai Brith, InterAmicus, and LEAF were variations on old CJC ideas of the 1950s and 1960s now couched in the language of the *Charter*. All took the position that the hate propaganda law neither represented an unreasonable limit on the freedom of expression provision found in section 2(b) of the *Charter* nor violated a defendant's right under section 11(d) of the *Charter* to be innocent until proven guilty. All suggested that the law was consistent with both the *Charter*'s equality and multicultural protections found in sections 15 and 27, respectively, and various statutes found in international law and could easily be upheld under section 1 if need be.

For the first two questions, all four contended that section 2(b) of the *Charter* did not protect absolute freedom of expression. They told the Supreme Court that pronouncements of hate were not about the pursuit of truth but about depriving the targeted minority of its rights and freedoms. Such pronouncements carried no merit for society and thus warranted no constitutional protection. Section 15, which protected minorities against formal discrimination in law, offered a constitutional safeguard against those whose ultimate aim was to deny vulnerable minorities an equal standing in society. Similarly, section 27 embodied a vision of what the hatemonger hoped to destroy, namely, a pluralistic, multicultural Canada.[139] All but LEAF buttressed their arguments by claiming that Canada's hate propaganda law was consistent with Article 4(a) of the *International Convention on the Elimination of All Forms of Racial Discrimination (ICEFRD)*, which explicitly prohibited the dissemination of hateful ideas and, thus, was in keeping with Canada's international obligations.[140]

Collectively, they rejected the position that limits on non-violent forms of freedom of expression were justified only when faced by a "clear and present danger." Citing the experience of the Holocaust and the emotional and mental anguish that came with being the target of hateful ideas, all three suggested that requiring a tangible danger minimized the cumulative effects of hate propaganda. Like the Cohen committee, all maintained that it was better to nip hate in the bud before it blossomed into full-fledged acts of violence and that any impairment of freedom of expression was minimal and proportional to the larger goal of censoring hate.[141]

For questions three and four, none believed that the law violated the presumption of innocence found in section 11(d) of the *Charter*. All agreed that the defence of truth found in section 281.3(a) was intended to protect the accused and to allow truthful speech that might have some redeemable value to society. The CJC contended that there was still a heavy burden on the Crown to prove that the individual's intentions had been "wilful" and that he or she had actually "promoted hate."[142] Given the potential for harm and disruption as a result of ideas of hate left unchallenged, any infringement of section 11(d) was, in their thinking, entirely justified. All four submitted that placing the burden on the Crown to prove the truthfulness of a statement would render the law "toothless."[143]

Bruce Fraser, counsel for the Government of Alberta, also submitted that the answers to the questions before the court were no, yes, no, and yes, and he suggested that it was the Ontario Court of Appeal that had reached the correct decision in *R. v. Andrews and Smith*. And like the majority of the interveners, Fraser contended that the promotion of hate was beyond the parameters of section 2(b) of the *Charter*, on the grounds that such speech was antithetical to the aims of a multicultural society. Indeed, there was little that separated the arguments of the interveners who supported the law and those of the Government of Alberta.[144] Fraser's section 1 defence similarly relied heavily on a combination of the Cohen Report and norms in international law, including Article 4(a) of the *ICEFRD*, and Fraser supported the notion that "individual freedom of expression must give way to the broader interests of social cohesion and racial and religious freedom."[145] Given the combination of the objectives, and the various defences found within section 281.2 that protected freedom of expression, he too submitted that the hate propaganda law met the criteria of the Oakes test.

As for questions three and four, the same logic applied. Fraser submitted that the "defence of truth" requirement of section 281.2(3) was not an unreasonable burden on the defendant, particularly since the Ontario Court of Appeal had ruled in the *Zundel* case that the promotion of falsehoods was not protected under section 2(b) of the *Charter*. Rather, section 281.2(3) should be seen as an added safeguard against infringements on freedom of expression. Nor did Fraser contend that it was unfair to require the accused to prove the truthfulness of his or her statements, since, given the subjectivity of theories about history, to place that responsibility on the state would render the law "inoperable" and "unenforceable." Citing the Cohen Report once again, he suggested that, if it did violate section 11(d) of the *Charter*, it was a justifiable violation that interfered minimally with the defendant's right to be presumed innocent.[146]

The CCLA took a different view of the constitutionality of the law. Representing the organization was Marc Rosenberg. Little had changed in the CCLA's position toward the law since the late 1960s and early 1970s. Section 281.2, he maintained, was poorly designed and had been based on noble but misguided intentions; it was simply too vague and thus in contravention of section 2(b) of the *Charter*. To establish this point, he raised many of the same misgivings that the CCLA had presented to the Senate back in 1968. He did not discount the premise that certain non-violent speech should be limited simply because it appeared to be "devoid of redeeming merit." Rather, he warned how the murkiness of terms such as "wilful," "hatred," and "truth" made it impossible to distinguish speech that was "worthy of protection and that which should be proscribed" and impeded the right to dissent in a free society.[147]

On this point, he took particular issue with the findings of the Cohen committee. In the mid-1960s, Cohen and his colleagues had suggested that the law was necessary, not because of *what* was happening, but because of what *could* happen should hate be allowed to go unchallenged. Like Borovoy, Rosenberg contended that there had not been a "clear and present danger" from hate-mongers in 1965 when the Cohen Report was issued, nor was there one almost twenty-five years later. Consequently, there was "no basis to conclude that the fabric of Canadian society and its democratic institutions are so fragile as to be unable to withstand the rantings of a limited number of players on the fringe of society."[148]

The law, he suggested, failed all three criteria of the Oakes test. Section 281.2(2) had not been "rationally" devised on account of its vagueness, and its capacity to impair free expression was strong. Here, he suggested that the law could have a "chilling effect" on speech, which would do little to serve the interests of a multicultural society. On the question of proportionality, he reasoned that maintaining the law on the basis that ideas of hate *might* take hold in mainstream society in the future was an insufficient justification. And just as Borovoy had done on so many occasions before, he told the court that the law was counterproductive, that censorship through litigation gave individuals such as Keegstra and Zündel an undeserved air of "legitimacy." "Placing such racist propaganda on the front pages of our national newspapers as if it were worthy of debate," he concluded, "in no way serves the purpose of the legislation and is a gratuitous affront to racial dignity."[149]

Predictably, Christie's answers to the questions before the court were also yes, no, yes, and no. On the first two questions, the rationales behind his arguments were not that different from those of the CCLA. Like the CCLA, he too contended that section 281.2(2) was in clear violation of section 2(b) of the *Charter*, as it was vague and subjective, open to broad interpretation and unequal application. Moreover, Christie found that the defence of truth was highly speculative, and he questioned the assumption that unpopular speech could not be an important instrument of social change. And like the CCLA, he suggested that the law gave too much power to the attorneys general and the courts to determine the parameters of legitimate speech and that the appropriate recourse to hate-mongering was not the courts but public condemnation. Furthermore, Christie argued that section 281.2(2) did not pass the Oakes test and thus could not be saved under section 1 of the *Charter*, particularly since there was no tangible evidence that Keegstra's teachings had caused any physical harm to Canada's Jewish community.[150]

Whereas Rosenberg offered a measured critique of the law, Christie was inflammatory, wildly doctrinaire. According to him, section 281.2(2) of the *Criminal Code* and the charges against Keegstra were part of a larger state-sanctioned movement to "criminalize immoral speech" orchestrated by "advocates of silence," the provincial attorneys general, the CJC, B'nai Brith, InterAmicus, and LEAF.[151] Their collective goal, he contended, was not to foster a climate of equality but to create a "multicultural despotism" in which "freedom of expression" was restricted to "freedom of good faith, multicultural, egalitarian, rational and unemotional, tolerant, legitimate speech."[152]

For Christie, this was tantamount to state-sponsored hate-mongering.[153] He belittled the Cohen Report, suggesting that its "sweeping generalizations such as 'Freedom of speech does not mean freedom to vilify'" offered little guidance and that its assumption that Canada could become the next Weimer Republic if pronouncements of hate were allowed to go uncontested was misguided.[154] Furthermore, he rejected arguments based on international law, suggesting that they had little bearing on the Canadian experience, particularly because the interveners had been quick to dismiss American jurisprudence, which favoured a high threshold for any limits on speech.

As for the Oakes test, Christie contended that it failed the proportionality aspect, that the threat of criminal sanction when there was no evidence of any substantial effect was a harsh penalty for expressing an opinion, no matter how objectionable it might be. On this point, he contended that the "highest objective of a society is the pursuit of true knowledge." Hence, "a person who perceives a religious conspiracy to be evil must be free to say so even if it promoted hatred of that sect or group because it may be the truth."[155]

Brazenly, Christie suggested that the law was an exclusive tool belonging to Canada's Jewish community. His contention was that the hate propaganda law was not "an instrument of justice, but of selective oppression," used only to censor instances of antisemitism, not the defamation of other groups – "Austrians or Palestinians or Arabs" – that had a history of friction and hostility toward Jews and the state of Israel.[156] In his oral presentation to the court, he cited Elie Wiesel's 1968 book *Legends of Our Time*, in which Wiesel recommends that, because of the Holocaust, all Jews should reserve a "zone of hate" for Germans. Smugly, Christie defended Wiesel's words on the grounds that they could serve a "social purpose."[157]

On the third and fourth questions, Christie charged that the defence of truth found in section 281.3(a) was an unreasonable burden to place on the accused. Truth, when dealing with theories about the past, simply could not be proven. Ironically, given that Zündel was also his client, Christie argued that the defence of truth might make sense only if the individual in question knowingly spread falsehoods. But even then he contended that it was insufficient to censor all hate simply because it might include some lies.[158] Nor did he believe that the law could be saved under section 1 since it began with a "presumption of guilt," which he suggested was "neither necessary for the protection of society nor beneficial to the fundamental interest of a free and democratic society."[159] In dramatic fashion, Christie warned that convicting Keegstra would be equivalent to sanctioning an "official state history," the effects of which would be to remove the need for "individual judgment, conscience, or intelligence" and to set a precedent for future limitations on expression.[160]

The Supreme Court disagreed. In a four to three decision delivered on 13 December 1990, it ruled that sections 281.2(2) and 281.3(a) of the *Criminal Code*, despite infringing on sections 2(b) and 11(d) of the *Charter*, respectively, were constitutional according to the parameters of section 1. Chief Justice Brian Dickson wrote for the majority, Justice Beverley McLachlin for the minority.[161] Despite the uncertainties and tensions inherent in the law, the ruling affirmed the view not only that free expression comes with responsibility but also that state intervention was permissible in cases where this responsibility has been ignored.

Although Dickson rejected the arguments that the promotion of hate was congruous with violence and that section 281.2(2) did not infringe on section 2(b), he believed that the law could be saved through section 1. Adopting the arguments put forward by the appellant and the four civil society interveners that defended the law, his judgment revealed remarkably little faith in the "marketplace of ideas" to deal with messages of hate yet tremendous confidence in the courts to convict only the tried and true hate-monger. Given that the respondents appearing before the court were Keegstra, Smith, and Andrews, this was not necessarily an unreasonable assumption. But Dickson also subscribed to the view that hate had no redeemable value to society and was inconsistent with the pursuit of truth. Rather, its purposes were to "deny respect and dignity to vulnerable minorities, and were antithetical to the aims of a democratic society," aims articulated in the *Charter* as well as international law.[162] Dickson also rejected the argument that the law had been poorly designed. Instead, he found that, given the various defences first offered by the Cohen committee, it was a rationally constructed law, the ultimate aim of which was to combat racism within Canadian society. Any infringement that might occur to freedom of expression was minimal and easily outweighed by the gains accrued from a harmonious, pluralistic Canada. He found that the same was true of the question about section 281.3(a): although it contravened section 11(d), the benefits that came from such an infringement far outweighed the potential harms.[163]

McLachlin's judgment was, in turn, far more in line with the ideas put forth by the CCLA and to a lesser extent those of Christie. McLachlin supported the aims of the hate propaganda law but not the means by which it set out to criminalize certain speech. Unlike Dickson, she had considerably more confidence in Canadian society's ability to withstand ideas of hate and considerably less in the courts' ability to separate legitimate speech from that deemed to be illegitimate.[164] Thus, she found that section 281.2(2) was unconstitutional. She rejected the arguments that other sections of the

Charter and international law could inform the court's understanding of section 2(b), as all were too ambiguous to provide much guidance. Moreover, she disagreed that Keegstra had violated section 15 and ruled that that section of the Constitution should have no bearing on the decision. She came to a similar conclusion with regard to section 27. The term "multiculturalism," she wrote, was an "abstract value." There was no tangible evidence to suggest that section 281.2(2) enhanced it.[165] And like the CCLA, McLachlin found that the hate propaganda law did not pass the Oakes test and thus could not be saved under section 1. She wrote that the law placed an unreasonable burden on the judiciary to determine speech that was in the "public interest."[166] Moreover, the reverse onus on the accused could create a "chilling effect," such that any impairment on freedom of expression was far from minimal. And like Rosenberg, she concluded that the hate propaganda law was ultimately counterproductive. Trials such as this gave the Keegstras and Zundels of Canadian society "a million dollars worth of publicity."[167]

Reaction to the decision was mixed. At the time of the ruling, the CJC's Manuel Prutschi speculated that had "the decision gone the other way, the noxious level of hate propaganda would have risen." Borovoy countered that the true "casualties are likely to include very legitimate dissenters."[168]

To no surprise given the split decision, the controversy surrounding the hate propaganda law did not end there. Following the ruling, Keegstra's initial conviction was set aside and a new trial ordered. As in 1984, Keegstra was once again found guilty of wilfully promoting hate and this time was charged a $3,000 fine. Christie appealed the decision on the grounds that the trial judge had misled the jury. The Alberta Court of Appeal agreed, quashing the conviction and ordering that Keegstra be granted a new trial. But it was only a partial victory for the defendant and his lawyer. Ever the martyrs, they appealed the decision to the Supreme Court of Canada on 31 October 1994, once again on the grounds that Canada's hate propaganda legislation contravened sections 2(b), 7, 11(d), and 15 of the *Charter*. The federal government, in turn, responded by filing a motion to have the appeal quashed, arguing that the Supreme Court lacked the jurisdiction to hear the case since Keegstra had already raised the *Charter* arguments in the Alberta Court of Appeal. The Supreme Court sided with neither. On 18 May 1995, it dismissed the motions, quashing both in a nine to zero ruling.[169]

Following the ruling, the federal government contested the Alberta Court of Appeal's decision to quash Keegstra's conviction. In response, Christie filed a cross-appeal, contesting that, in addition to a number of procedural errors by the Alberta trial judge, the reverse onus provisions of section 281.3

(now 319(3)(a)) of the *Criminal Code* infringed on his client's right to be innocent until proven guilty under section 11(d) of the *Charter*. Again the Supreme Court was unanimous. In an oral ruling delivered by Justice Frank Iacobucci on 28 February 1996, the court determined that the issue of section 319(3)(a)'s constitutionality had already been decided in the original *Keegstra* trial and was not in need of being revisited. Again the Supreme Court overruled the decision of the Alberta Court of Appeal, dismissed Christie's cross-appeal, and restored Keegstra's earlier conviction of a fine of $3,000.[170] As far as the court was concerned, the issue of the hate propaganda law's constitutionality was closed.

The Supreme Court of Canada has revisited, however, the law prohibiting the "spreading of false news," prompted once again by the publishing activities of Ernst Zündel. In the early 1990s, Zündel was again charged with spreading falsehoods after publishing an updated version of his pamphlet *Did Six Million Really Die?*[171] Once again the CJC, B'nai Brith, and the CCLA intervened in his trial. But this time the Supreme Court struck down the law, again in a split four to three decision. McLachlin, this time writing for the majority, ruled that section 177 of the *Criminal Code* contravened section 2(b) of the *Charter* and could not be saved under section 1. As she had before, she found the law to be overly "broad," "invasive," and "draconian" and believed it could create a "chilling effect" on speech.[172]

In striking down the falsehoods law but not the hate propaganda law, there was a certain inconsistency to the Supreme Court's decision making and a clear division among the justices on the bench. Through the latter law, certain expressions remained criminalized; however, in striking down the former law, the bar had been raised. Gone was the public's ability to instigate criminal proceedings against individuals who promoted hate. Such decisions now rested exclusively in the hands of the state.[173]

The legacies of the hate propaganda law and the first *Keegstra* trial on both expression and racial tolerance in Canada have been hotly contested by both scholars and activists. A proponent of the law, Joel Bakan has criticized the Supreme Court for accepting the argument that antisemitic hate speech is "*prima facie* protected" by section 2(b) of the *Charter*, suggesting that, had the court truly been interested in protecting vulnerable minorities from racist remarks, it would not have resorted to a section 1 defence.[174] Similarly, Warren Kinsella, a lawyer and former special assistant to Prime Minister Jean Chrétien, has criticized the dissenters on the bench – and unfairly so – for ruling that "the law should be thrown out and that Jim Keegstra should be free to preach hatred to children."[175] In contrast, civil libertarians have argued that there has been a gradual slide toward greater censorship of expression, a slide that they believe has upset the balance between freedom of speech and protection of minorities that had first been sought by the Cohen committee.[176] Both Alan Borovoy and Stefan Braun have suggested that the political left, together with the judiciary, has become increasingly adept at recategorizing dissenting views concerning progressive social agendas as a form of hate worthy of censorship, making litigation (or at least the threat of litigation) the tool of choice for limiting socially offensive forms of expression.[177] Similarly, Joseph Magnet has argued that "Canada's hate propaganda controls have had little or no real effect on Canada's hate literature predicament or the underlying causes of racism and intolerance which motivated it."[178] Philosopher L.W. Sumner has criticized the Supreme Court for taking an "instrumentalist view of rights," in which "rights themselves and their limitation are justified by reference to the appropriate underlying values or interests [equality and multicultural heritage] which they enhance or protect," regardless of whether the hate propaganda law actually produces this desired effect.[179]

Although antisemitism has become "socially unacceptable" within mainstream Canadian society,[180] there is evidence that, globally, the opposite trend is occurring. "Revisionist scholars" as well as their supporters continue to deny that the Holocaust ever took place.[181] The Internet has become their medium of choice to broadcast their ideas, taking advantage of both its lack of regulation and its international reach.

Several observers, including members of the CJC, have also suggested that the tensions arising from the political turmoil of the Middle East have given rise to a "new" antisemitism, in which Islamists and Arabists have come together with elements of the political left and right to discredit the state of Israel and Zionism by equating the inequities of capitalism and economic globalization with the age-old myth that international Jewish financiers have conspired to control the world economy.[182] Although it is difficult to gauge the cumulative impact of this anti-Zionism on the attitudes of Canadians, the fear is that this singular attention on Israeli policies and practices provides both "cover and respectability" for acts of physical violence against Jews, both in Canada and elsewhere.[183]

Predictably, the Canadian Jewish Congress and the Canadian Civil Liberties Association continue to disagree on the question of how best to confront the threat posed by old and new antisemitism specifically and racial intolerance more broadly. In the words of Borovoy, the central question is whether to "muzzle or marginalize" individuals who wilfully engage in the promotion of hate.[184] Indeed, the fundamental issue facing every liberal parliamentary democracy, including Canada, is how to respond to expressions deemed to be threatening to the security of the collective.

Through their respective engagements with the hate propaganda law, including at the Supreme Court of Canada, the CJC and the CCLA defined the parameters of the debate. For the CJC, the bar rests with dehumanizing speech intended to sow the seeds for future violence against those who are targeted. For the CCLA, the test is whether the speech represents a "clear and present danger to society"; for all other hateful speech, responsibility rests with the public, not the state, to provide an appropriate and measured rebuke.

That both organizations remain dissatisfied with the current state of Canadian law is telling, a reflection of how difficult the governance challenges facing the democratic state are when freedom is "misused." Too weak a response by the state can lead to the disintegration of social cohesion, the undermining of minority equality rights, and acts of violence (physical and psychological) against the targeted population. Too strong a response can result in infringements on all speech, not just that deemed to be hateful. That neither organization has been completely successful in its efforts suggests that the respective norms that they are advancing and defending may never be fully internalized. Nor should they be because of the stakes involved. But through their quarrels, both organizations have shaped Canadians' understanding of the threats posed by hate propaganda and the pitfalls of criminalizing speech. Canadians are better off for it.

3

Shocking the Conscience? Amnesty International Canada and Abolition of the Death Penalty

The belief that rights belong to everyone is one of the cornerstones of the modern human rights regime. In theory, little is controversial about this idea: rights operate on the principle that, by virtue of being human, all individuals are guaranteed certain inalienable and immutable entitlements. Of course, in practice this ideal has rarely, if ever, been realized, particularly in cases in which the state must respond to acts of violence. In Canada, as in much of the democratic world, norms relating to abolition of the death penalty are relatively recent, products of the emerging rights consciousness of the 1960s and 1970s. And as in much of the democratic world, these norms have had a tenuous hold, at odds with competing norms relating to retributive justice, collective security, and state sovereignty.

Amnesty International (AI) Canada has played an instrumental role in advancing and defending the abolitionist norm in Canada. Since 1973, it has opposed the use of capital punishment on the principle that an individual's right to life or to be free from cruel and unusual treatment cannot be forfeited, regardless of the heinousness of the crimes that he or she has committed. In a high-profile case at the Supreme Court of Canada involving two violent fugitives from the United States, AI Canada contested the legality of Canada's extradition treaty with the United States, which permitted an individual's fate to be determined by the federal government's desire to place conditions on his or her surrender to a foreign state. AI Canada challenged the Canadian government's sovereign authority to conduct external relations free of constitutional considerations. In doing so, it established that, in matters involving extradition and the death penalty, international norms matter when interpreting the Constitution and cannot be disregarded even in difficult cases involving individuals whose real or alleged crimes are indefensible and who pose a direct threat to public safety.

Founded in 1961 by an idealistic English lawyer named Peter Benenson, Amnesty International began as an organization in defence of non-violent freedom of expression. First launched as a one-year letter-writing campaign called the Appeal for Amnesty, 1961, its purpose was to mobilize grassroots support for the release of all "prisoners of conscience" (POC), those "forgotten" individuals who had been imprisoned for their political or religious beliefs but who had neither advocated nor used violence.[1]

Chief among its aims were the defence of freedom of opinion, the establishment of fair trials for all political prisoners, and the expansion of mechanisms for seeking asylum (including helping political refugees to find work in the host country). [2] The campaign sought to accomplish these goals by calling on concerned individuals from around the world to write letters on behalf of the POCs in solidarity with those in prison and to let governments know that their abuses were not going unnoticed. As Tom Buchanan reveals in his history of the origins of the organization, the Appeal for Amnesty emerged out of a combination of Benenson's desire after the Second World War to confront the "increasing prominence of political imprisonment" by the fascist regimes in Greece, Portugal, and Spain and his frustration with similar "amnesty" campaigns led by communist organizations going on at the time, whose underlying purpose was to discredit their ideological opponents.[3]

Described by Stephen Hopgood as a "quasi-religious response to globalization" and secular "free church" rooted in the Christian ecumenical spirit,[4] the Appeal for Amnesty quickly grew in popularity, particularly in western Europe.[5] Indeed, Benenson and his colleagues were able to tap into a collective sense of frustration among those who shared their sense of injustice but longed for an apolitical outlet for their activism. Encouraged by their initial success, they decided to establish a permanent, membership-based, international movement with national sections around the world. Thus, Amnesty International was born.

Much of the attraction of AI stemmed from its relatively limited and cautious mandate. The purpose of the organization was, as Hopgood notes, to "bear witness," to bring international attention to individuals whose "crimes" were not really crimes at all.[6] The majority of the prisoners that AI adopted were often themselves defenders of freedom of expression, arrested for voicing ideas and opinions that challenged the injustices of an austere democracy, a vicious dictatorship, or a repressive communist regime.

There was an easy legitimacy associated with coming to their aid. They were neither armed insurgents nor violent criminals. Their pacifism was what made their detention worthy of public outcry. Although AI did call for the establishment of fair trials for political prisoners who had resorted to or advocated violence, its initial allure rested on its ability to distance itself from individuals whose actions, though potentially political in motivation, were criminal and deserved a punitive response from the state.[7]

In 1973 came a watershed moment for AI and the international abolitionist movement. That year the organization revisited its position on capital punishment. There were several reasons for this decision. One was that, by the early 1970s, it had become increasingly difficult for the organization to determine whether the individual being detained fit the definition of a POC. Often there simply was not sufficient information available to determine whether a prisoner had used or advocated violence. Moreover, policy prevented AI from adopting prisoners who had been falsely accused of violent acts since this too was difficult to verify. But there was also a philosophical shift taking place within the organization.

Certain senior members were beginning to question the morality behind opposing the death penalty only for certain individuals and not others. Still, this view was by no means unanimous within the organization. Many were uncomfortable with any move that could be seen as an endorsement of violent behaviour. They saw a blurred line between political and criminal violence and were nervous that taking up the cause of such prisoners would "radicalize" the organization's image, undermine its work on POCs, compromise its impartiality, and "erode the moral strength of [its] non-violent pressure on governments."[8] They feared that any loosening of the policy toward violence would create an expectation that AI would be obligated to come to the defence of criminals, a shift that risked creating deep divisions within the organization's grassroots membership.[9]

Conscious of the potential costs to the organization, AI's International Council Meeting, the highest and only decision-making body within the organization with the authority to alter the mandate, nevertheless accepted that the time had come for AI to incorporate into its mandate unconditional opposition to the death penalty. In doing so, it committed the organization not only to becoming a leading international voice for the abolitionist cause but also to adopting the difficult cases involving individuals accused of committing the most serious acts of violence, cases from which, prior to 1973, it had deliberately made a point of distancing itself.[10]

Canada's road toward abolition of capital punishment began in the early 1960s, when many Canadians were beginning to question the virtues of a justice system that allowed the state to take an individual's life. The 1950s and early 1960s constituted a period of sporadic reliance on the death penalty in Canada, the last two executions taking place in December 1962.[11] By the middle of the decade, attitudes were changing, albeit slowly. Although the majority of Canadians continued to favour use of the death penalty for certain violent crimes, many came to see it as an outdated sentence that belonged to a passing era in Canadian history.

Beginning in 1963, the Canadian government slowly began to move away from capital punishment as a punitive measure. Even though it was still permitted under the *Criminal Code of Canada*, once in office the government of Lester B. Pearson effectively removed it as an option for the courts. By virtue of its executive authority, it intervened in all of the capital cases before the courts, commuting each death sentence to one of life imprisonment. In essence, it turned Canada into an unofficial abolitionist state.

Nonetheless, a *de facto* law lacked the certainty and consistency of one that was *de jure*. By the end of the decade, Parliament's enthusiasm for the death penalty, at least in its contemporary form, continued to wane. In 1967, a series of bills on capital punishment was introduced in the House of Commons. At the centre of these reforms was a larger philosophical debate that questioned the meaning of punitive justice in a modern and pluralistic society. Legislators struggled to find the appropriate balance between an individual's right to self-fulfillment and the state's duty to protect society's well-being. Some parliamentarians saw it as a retributive punishment that had no place in the judicial system. Still others believed that it was a legitimate response to certain acts of violence that constituted an affront to the decency and tolerance of an ordered and peaceful nation.[12]

Predictably, the various reforms tabled in the House of Commons favoured only modest changes to the law and were intended to make Canada's sentencing laws more "humane." One private member's bill advocated replacing the hangman's noose with lethal gas, the rationale being that the latter was more compassionate and merciful.[13] A second suggested that, instead of an automatic execution, judges be given the discretion to decide whether to sentence to death individuals found guilty of committing capital crimes. A third called for a "trial" abolition period of three years, with each death sentence to be replaced by a sentence of life imprisonment and parole to be determined by the National Parole Board and the governor-in-council.[14]

In late 1967, the Pearson government introduced Bill C-168, which proposed an experimental five-year moratorium on imposition of the death penalty in all cases except those involving the murder of police officers, prison staff, or any other individuals "employed for the maintenance of the public peace."[15] The stated intent of the legislation was to study whether the death penalty was indeed a deterrent to violent crime. But Bill C-168 was about much more: it was about revisiting norms around which the state could, in good conscience, take a life. Were the legislation to pass, first-degree murder, treason, and piracy would no longer be crimes punishable by death. But it did not favour total abolition in order to allay fears that the safety of law enforcement officials would be put at risk by criminals undeterred by the prospect of a life in prison without parole.

Bill C-168 represented an incremental step toward abolition, a cautious reform made by a minority government that recognized that capital punishment was still considered to be a legitimate sentence by much of the country. Given the divisions in the House of Commons, Pearson wisely opted for a free vote on the bill. Unwilling to risk an election on the issue, he permitted parliamentarians to break from party discipline and vote according to conscience while simultaneously ensuring that the bill's defeat would not mean the end of his government. The House of Commons passed Bill C-168 by a comfortable, but not overwhelming, tally of 105 in favour and 70 against.

The opportunity for a more permanent solution did not present itself until 1976.[16] When Bill C-168 had expired in 1973, Prime Minister Pierre Trudeau, who also had the misfortune of presiding over a minority government, had decided to renew the moratorium for a second five-year period. But his government had won a majority in the election of 1974. In 1976, Solicitor General Warren Allmand introduced Bill C-84, *An Act to Amend the Criminal Code in Relation to the Punishment for Murder and Certain Other Serious Offences*.[17] Unlike Bill C-168, which favoured incremental change, the intent of Bill C-84 was simple and straightforward: to remove the death penalty completely from the *Criminal Code*. Allmand was a staunch abolitionist. He believed that to grant the courts and the federal cabinet the right to determine an individual's fate was to give the state authority beyond its legitimate jurisdiction. For him, the death penalty was not in "keeping with the end or values which [Canadians] as a society embrace."[18]

The prime minister shared Allmand's distaste for capital punishment. A month prior to the vote on Bill C-84, he delivered an impassioned appeal to Parliament in support of the legislation. At stake, he contended, was a question whose answer was "as awesome as that of life or death." For Trudeau, capital punishment was the emotive response of a "socially bankrupt" society, not one that was rational and modern. To retain it, he warned Parliament, would be to "abandon reason in favour of vengeance; to abandon hope and confidence in favour of a despairing acceptance of our inability to cope with violent crime except with violence."[19]

In total, 119 parliamentarians spoke to the bill over a period of several months. Reactions – and rhetoric – were highly charged. There were deep divisions not only within the House of Commons but also within the Liberal and Conservative parties.[20] Knowing full well that the fate of Bill C-84 was anything but certain, Trudeau and Allmand, like Pearson before them, opted for a free vote on the bill, wisely removing the chance that its defeat would result in a loss of confidence in the government.

Those who opposed Bill C-84 attacked it from a variety of angles. Several MPs questioned the popularity of the bill, citing recent polls indicating that over 70 percent of the population still favoured capital punishment; some went a step further and called for a referendum on the issue. Others challenged an earlier claim by Allmand that there was no causal link between the death penalty and crime rates, substantiating their charge with a Statistics Canada report indicating that the number of incidents of violent crime had actually risen during the two moratorium periods. Still others accused the government of weakening an already lenient justice system and denounced it for minimizing victims' suffering while proposing to leave police officers exposed to acts of violence. Several MPs questioned, albeit rhetorically, the point of these reforms since the federal government had no intention of refraining from using its executive authority to intervene in capital cases. A number of detractors even challenged the timing of the bill, accusing the government of pushing the legislation midway through the second moratorium so that its expiration would not coincide with the next federal election, still a few years away.[21]

Uniting opponents was a common belief that Bill C-84 was an inadequate response to some of the uglier realities of Canadian society. They played upon fears of terrorism, insurrection against the state, and a general sense of insecurity. One MP dredged up memories of the October Crisis of 1970, when members of the Front de libération du Québec kidnapped and murdered Quebec minister of labour Pierre Laporte, and suggested that capital punishment would be an appropriate response to any future acts of terror.[22] Several others, including former prime minister John Diefenbaker, even raised the spectre of the tragic assassination of the Israeli athletes at the 1972 Olympic Games in Munich by suggesting that passing such a law so close to the Montreal Olympic Games would send the wrong message to international terrorists. Finally, some claimed that Canada was experiencing a rise in organized crime and therefore needed the death penalty to confront it.

Predictably, many attempted to water down Bill C-84 with amendments that, if accepted, would permit exceptions within the law for various violent crimes. For some, maintaining the status quo by reserving capital punishment for individuals convicted of murdering officers of the peace was sufficient. Others wanted to go further. One proposal called for the death penalty as an option for any offender convicted a second time for first-degree murder. Another would have made it available for "crimes of mass killing," such as placing a bomb aboard an airplane.[23] A third, which came from Diefenbaker, advocated execution for certain crimes of treason. During the debate, Diefenbaker remained adamant that the death penalty be available for individuals who attempted either to assassinate the queen or overthrow the government. Trudeau was unmoved. Flippantly, he accused the former prime minister of being an abolitionist "in general" but a retentionist "in particular."[24]

Even on the last day of debate, as the bill moved through its third reading, those in favour of retention continued their efforts to take the teeth out of the legislation. There was a last-ditch attempt to delay the vote until Parliament's resumption in the fall, the rationale being that MPs would use the summer to consult their constituents on how to vote on the issue. The government refused to balk, calling the matter to vote. A reluctant and emotionally drained Parliament passed Bill C-84 by a narrow margin of 130 to 124 on 14 July and then broke for the summer recess.

Removing the death penalty from the *Criminal Code* marked an important victory, though by no means a definitive one, for the Trudeau government. Still, the impact of the reform was immediate: since the death penalty was no longer part of the *Criminal Code* (though it was still an option for a number of military crimes under the *National Defence Act*), the three individuals scheduled to be hanged that day all had their sentences commuted immediately to life in prison, as did the other eight individuals on death row at the time.[25] Nonetheless, the closeness of the vote, combined with majority support for capital punishment among the Canadian population, meant that few politicians believed that the issue was settled.[26] Given that five of the seven members absent during the vote supported retention and that party discipline had been invoked for all members of cabinet, the bill's passing appeared to be tenuous, even a little lucky.[27] This was not lost on those who had contested Bill C-84. Sparing little time, opponents vowed to make reinstatement an election issue, believing – with good reason – that much of Canada did not support Trudeau's and Allmand's conception of justice.

The year 1976 proved to be significant in the effort to advance abolition for another less pronounced but no less significant reason. On 22 March of that year, the Canadian government ratified a new extradition treaty with the United States. Prior to 1976, Canadian extradition law dated back to the Ashburton-Webster Treaty of 1842 between Britain and the United States. In the early 1970s, both nations agreed that a new extradition treaty reflective of the realities of the latter half of the twentieth century, not the first half of the nineteenth century, was long overdue.

One question to settle was what to do about foreign fugitives charged with capital crimes. In 1971, when the treaty was being negotiated, the United States was in the midst of a moratorium of its own on use of the death penalty. Washington had insisted that an abolitionist state be allowed the discretion to seek assurances that the death penalty not be carried out should the individual extradited be found guilty of a capital offence. If assurances were not granted, the state holding the person in question had the right to refuse extradition.[28]

But much had changed in both countries during the five years between the treaty's drafting and its ratification. Whereas Canada removed capital punishment from the *Criminal Code* in 1976, the United States reinstated it. Thus, what had originally been a clause granting the United States recourse to intervene in the Canadian justice system became an avenue through which the Canadian government could bring its foreign policy in line with its domestic law.

"Discretion" was the key term in the agreement. Depending on the nature of the crime and the current state of bilateral relations between the two countries, the Canadian government had the option of extraditing individuals without placing any demands on the types of sentences that would be available to US courts. In practice, this meant that, even with Bill C-84's passing, the Trudeau government's commitment to abolition was far from absolute, its new conception of "Canadian justice" not necessarily in line with the longer-standing principle of non-interference in the domestic affairs of a sovereign neighbour.

Bill Domm, the MP for Peterborough, was first elected to office in 1979 as a member of Joe Clark's Progressive Conservative government. The son of a Presbyterian minister, Domm believed that capital punishment brought a measure of security to an insecure world. This belief was consistent with the teachings of his faith.[29] A populist, Domm was a firm believer in government that acceded to the will of the majority, particularly on issues of conscience and morality. At the time of the election, a Gallup poll revealed that 82 percent of Canadians favoured a referendum on capital punishment, as did a number of non-governmental organizations, many of which included police associations and various evangelical Christian groups.[30] The combination of his own convictions and public opinion proved to be too tempting for him not to act. Armed with what he believed was a clear mandate, he made reinstatement of the death penalty for crimes of high treason and first-degree murder his top priority.

Domm's opening came in 1984 following his party's election victory under new leader Brian Mulroney. During the campaign, Mulroney had pledged to reopen the debate if elected. Domm made sure that, once in office, Mulroney held true to his promise. In the autumn of 1986, he submitted a private member's motion to the Standing Committee on Justice and the Solicitor General that, if passed, would require the committee to examine arguments both for and against reinstatement of the death penalty. This, he hoped, would then set the stage for a vote in the House of Commons.

Although Domm's motion was not adopted formally, it was accepted in principle. On 13 February 1987, Deputy Prime Minister and President of the Privy Council Don Mazankowski tabled a similar motion in which Parliament would be asked to decide, again in a free vote, whether capital punishment was a legitimate sentence within Canada's criminal justice system. Mazankowski instructed the House that, if the motion failed, the matter would be settled. However, if it passed, the government would establish a fifteen-member parliamentary committee to draft appropriate legislation for reinstatement.

Domm was elated. The general feeling on Parliament Hill at the time was that the motion would pass by a margin of about two to one. To many observers, the 1976 changes to the *Criminal Code* seemed to be in danger of becoming undone. Moreover, the majority of Canadians were supportive of reinstatement. Two Gallup polls conducted in May 1987 revealed that, though support for capital punishment was waning, more than 60 percent of the country still favoured the practice, believing that it was an important deterrent against violent crime.[31]

Founded in 1973,[32] Amnesty International Canada had not played a large role in the 1976 decision to remove capital punishment from the *Criminal Code;* however, it was determined to be a player in the debate on reinstatement. It had hoped that the Progressive Conservatives would "forget" about their campaign promise. When it became apparent that Mulroney planned to hold true to his word, the organization launched a multifaceted campaign to persuade the federal government that there was significant opposition to the motion, not only within Canada but also throughout the international community. In a strongly worded letter to Prime Minister Mulroney, Bob Goodfellow, then president of the section's executive board, warned that such a move would be in keeping with neither the *Charter of Rights and Freedoms* nor international norms and that "Amnesty International will actively oppose any attempt to bring back civilian executions."[33]

It was not an idle threat. Shortly after the Canadian government announced its intention to revisit the issue, Amnesty International launched a two-tracked campaign to have the motion defeated. At the international level, the International Secretariat, along with a number of sections around the world, wrote to the prime minister and other key MPs, warning them that such a motion was not in keeping with the values of the global community. In Canada, volunteers and staff at the national office in Ottawa kept records on each parliamentarian's position and then encouraged AI community groups to write letters to, and even meet with, MPs who they believed could be won over to the abolitionist side.[34] They also joined forces with like-minded NGOs, such as the Church Council on Justice and Corrections and the Canadian Labour Congress, to form an umbrella group known as Coalition against the Return of the Death Penalty (CARDP).[35]

Luckily for AI Canada and CARDP, they had an ally in the prime minister.[36] Mulroney was ardently opposed to the motion to reintroduce capital punishment into the *Criminal Code.* Like Trudeau, he saw the death penalty not as an effective deterrent but as a "repugnant" and "profoundly unacceptable" practice that favoured passion and vengeance over reason and justice.[37] And like Trudeau, he did not believe that the death penalty was appropriate for a nation whose laws were founded on the principle of the inherent dignity of the individual. On 22 June 1987, he delivered a passionate speech before Parliament, pledging wholeheartedly to defend the current state of Canadian law. "I want to say ... , without reservation and without qualification, that I do not support the motion to reinstate." He continued, "I will resist with all my strength, all of my life, any action that would diminish that reality and would lessen that value."[38] Whether the speech had any effect on parliamentarians no one could say for sure. Two days before the final vote was to take place on 29 June, the *Globe and Mail* reported that the government was anticipating a tie in the House of Commons.[39]

As MPs assembled for the final session before the summer break, an air of nervous anticipation hung over the House. As had been the case in 1976, the debate had been polarized and highly charged. Proponents of reinstatement had repeated their claims that the death penalty was a necessary punitive measure for dealing with the most heinous crimes of violence and that bringing capital punishment back would restore public confidence in a criminal justice system low on credibility. They dismissed arguments that the death penalty promoted vengeance, contending instead that it offered a measure of protection and security to the public. Detractors, who were equally virulent, accused the other side of being willing to overlook the inequities and fallibility of the judicial system in their pursuit of retributive justice and countered that capital punishment was the moral equivalent of slavery.[40]

At 1:40 a.m., Parliament voted. Given the buildup and uncertainty, the outcome was anticlimactic. The motion was defeated by a healthy – but not overwhelming – margin of 148 to 127. The difference was that all but one of the seventy opposition MPs, Liberal George Baker of Newfoundland, had voted against it. The abolitionist side, both inside and outside Parliament, was ecstatic. Among the jubilant was the prime minister, boasting afterward to journalists, "it's an excellent day for Canada and an excellent day for parliamentary democracy."[41]

Following the vote, a dejected Domm was left to wonder what had gone wrong. In hindsight, he and his colleagues had not run a strong campaign. Perhaps they had believed that having public opinion on their side was enough to carry the day. But among their mistakes, they had devoted little effort to lobbying the Quebec caucus of the Conservative Party, most of whom were under little pressure from their constituents to support the motion. Instead, they had concentrated on drumming up support among their colleagues in Ontario and the West, areas where arguments in favour of reinstatement already had considerable backing. In the end, of the fifty-seven Conservative MPs from Quebec, only nine voted for reinstatement.[42]

One unexpected outcome of the motion was that AI Canada, through a combination of focused lobbying tactics and principled arguments, had solidified its reputation as one of the country's leading authorities on the death penalty. Its resolve would be tested a year later thanks to two violent fugitives from the United States.

Charles Chitat Ng was arrested at a downtown shopping centre in Calgary on 6 July 1985. The incident began after two security guards stopped him for attempted shoplifting. Panicked, Ng resisted, shooting one of the guards in the finger before being subdued. He was eventually sentenced to four and a half years in prison at the federal penitentiary in Prince Albert, Saskatchewan, on charges of armed robbery, aggravated assault, and illegal use of a firearm.[43] Ng was also one of the most dangerous fugitives from the United States. An alleged serial killer from California, Ng and his partner, Leonard Thomas Lake (who committed suicide by swallowing a cyanide capsule while being detained by police), were accused of having committed horrific crimes involving sexual assault, torture, and murder. Ng had fled to Canada to seek refuge from American authorities with his sister, who was living in Calgary at the time. As news of his capture spread, US prosecutors began preparing their case against him. On 17 November 1987, they made a formal extradition request to the Canadian government for Ng to face trial for the twenty-five charges levelled against him, twelve of which were for murders committed in Calaveras and San Francisco counties between July 1984 and June 1985. Little did they know at the time that Ng's case, along with that of American fugitive Joseph Kindler, would spark a debate about whether, in the *Charter* era, the Canadian state had the legal authority to send an individual to another country to face possible execution.

Extradition proceedings against Ng began on 17 February 1988. His hearing began, *in camera*, eight months later in the Alberta Court of Queen's Bench. The case against Ng was overwhelming. The prosecution submitted vast amounts of evidence, including ninety affidavits, twenty-one witnesses, and thirty-nine exhibits. At the conclusion of the hearing, the judge found little reason to doubt that Ng would be found guilty for the crimes he was accused of committing. She ruled that he could be surrendered to US authorities based on nineteen of the twenty-five charges against him, including the twelve for murder.[44]

Ng's lawyer, Donald MacLeod, challenged the decision before the same court by way of a writ of *habeas corpus ad subjiciendum*. His efforts were to no avail, as the court dismissed his request. MacLeod then filed an appeal with the Alberta Court of Appeal, contending that the ruling should be quashed on three separate grounds: capital murder could not be the subject of extradition; the judge had not heard evidence relating to ministerial discretion found in Article 6 of the Canada-US Extradition Treaty; and the judge had failed to permit cross-examination of a number of the witnesses.[45] Once again his efforts were rebuffed. On 2 May 1989, the Alberta Court of Appeal dismissed the appeal. MacLeod applied for leave to appeal to the Supreme Court of Canada, but it too refused to hear the case. Having exhausted all avenues available to his client during the committal stage of the extradition process, he petitioned federal Minister of Justice Doug Lewis not to surrender his client right away. At this stage in the proceedings, the only issue still up for debate was whether Canada would be a party to Ng's potential execution. MacLeod called on the minister not to extradite his client without first seeking assurances under Canada's extradition treaty with the United States that the death penalty would not be used should his client be found guilty.

Lewis was less than sympathetic. In a letter dated 26 October 1989, the minister rejected MacLeod's request, explaining that ministerial discretion was to be used sparingly, reserved only for cases that shocked the conscience of Canadians, which Ng's did not. Assurances, he wrote, were to be sought only "in circumstances where the particular facts of the case warrant that special exercise of discretion" and "are not to be sought routinely in every case in which the death penalty is applicable." Lewis continued that the federal government had to consider the potential harm that invoking ministerial discretion might cause to public safety. Moreover, Canada had obligations to the United States under its extradition treaty that it could not take lightly.[46]

Undeterred, MacLeod sought a declaration from the Federal Court (Trial Division) in the fall of 1989 stating that Lewis' decision violated the *Charter* and that his client was not to be surrendered to the United States.[47] Lewis' successor, Kim Campbell, responded by referring the case to the Supreme Court of Canada by way of an Order-in-Council. The case was to be heard concurrently with that of Joseph Kindler, a convicted murderer from Pennsylvania who had escaped from prison and fled to St. Adèle, Quebec, whose request for a conditional surrender had also been denied by the Canadian government and subsequently reversed by the Federal Court of Appeal in December 1988.[48] At issue were whether the two men's constitutional rights had been violated and whether the ministers of justice (John Crosbie in

Kindler's case) had erred in his use of the discretion available to him under Article 6 of the Canada-US extradition treaty. Meanwhile, anger toward Ng, and to a lesser extent Kindler, became more pronounced.

The man spearheading the backlash was none other than Bill Domm. Having failed in his attempt to bring back the death penalty in 1987, he now set his sights on reforming Canada's extradition laws, which he believed were far too generous. In his opinion, the law, with its many appeals, placed too much emphasis on the rights of the fugitive over those of the victims, and he believed that the entire system was inefficient and costly to taxpayers. Moreover, Domm feared that, if Canada's extradition laws were not streamlined, Canada would become a "safe haven" for other American fugitives hoping to escape execution.

There was considerable merit to Domm's criticism that Canada's extradition laws were overly cumbersome. The entire extradition process involved a two-track system, both tracks of which were extensive. The first track, the committal stage, involved the initial hearing to determine whether there were sufficient grounds to extradite the individual in question. If unsuccessful, he or she could then challenge the legitimacy of the extradition warrant by applying for a writ of *habeas corpus* to a superior court judge to be removed from prison, thus blocking the extradition. If this challenge was unsuccessful, the individual could request permission to file an appeal with the provincial or territorial Court of Appeal and then with the Supreme Court of Canada.

The second track, the surrender stage, was equally lengthy. After all of the available appeals in the committal stage were exhausted, the federal minister of justice would decide whether to issue a warrant of surrender. If the minister agreed to the surrender, the person could contest the decision, on the grounds that the minister had acted beyond his or her jurisdiction, by seeking permission to appeal the decision to the Federal Court, the Federal Court of Appeal, and, if still unsuccessful, the Supreme Court of Canada. Alternatively, the minister's surrender order could be reviewed by writ of *habeas corpus* to the appropriate provincial superior court, again with the possibility of appeals to the Provincial Court of Appeal and the Supreme Court of Canada.[49] In total, the system allowed for up to three judicial reviews and six possible appeals to Canada's provincial and federal courts, a situation that Domm believed was unnecessarily drawn out and expensive. MacLeod had taken advantage of all of them.

To expedite the process, Domm submitted two private member's bills to Parliament in April 1989. The first, Bill C-209, *An Act to Amend the Extradition Act (Appeal)*, proposed to streamline the first track by eliminating two of the appeals in the committal stage, the first being the ability to apply for a writ of *habeas corpus* to challenge the initial ruling, the second being the option to appeal to the Supreme Court of Canada. That would leave only one appeal to the appropriate provincial or territorial Court of Appeal.[50] The second, Bill C-210, *An Act to Amend the Criminal Code and the Supreme Court Act (Habeas Corpus)*, also directed at the committal stage, recommended that any individual facing extradition be allowed only one appeal by writ of *habeas corpus*, thereby eliminating both the appeals to the Provincial Court of Appeal and the Supreme Court of Canada.[51]

This time Domm showed considerably more savvy than he had the year before during his push to have capital punishment reinstated in the *Criminal Code*. Throughout Ng's and Kindler's various appeals, he had been relentless in his efforts to drum up support for his reforms. His office produced and distributed several flyers recounting the two men's crimes. In his own riding, he delivered a number of impassioned speeches on the dangers of the status quo, warning his constituents that Canada faced the harsh prospect of becoming "a killer's haven."[52] Domm held numerous press conferences with members of the families of Ng's victims, calling on Canadians to see that justice was not denied to them. The Canadian media were generally quite receptive to Domm's arguments and accepted that the two fugitives and their lawyers were not only abusing the generosity of Canada's legal system at considerable cost to taxpayers but also compromising public safety.[53]

Assisting Domm was a new organization, the Victims of Violence Society (VOV), a grassroots organization based in Edmonton and founded by Gary and Sharon Rosenfeldt, the parents of one of the victims of convicted serial killer Clifford Olson.[54] VOV's objectives were to see that violent criminals were held accountable for their crimes and that the victims and their families received support and counselling to help them cope with their pain and suffering. Retributive justice was a core component of the organization's mandate. A vocal backer of the Peterborough MP's efforts to have the death penalty reinstated in the *Criminal Code*, VOV believed that capital punishment was a just and proportional response to certain violent acts. And like Domm, VOV was equally frustrated with the current state of Canada's laws and treaty obligations, which it believed delayed justice at best and denied it altogether at worst.

For VOV, Ng and Kindler were proof that the system was in need of reform. Shortly after Ng's original ruling, it began to rally grassroots support for the fugitive's immediate extradition. In an opinion editorial in the *Toronto Star*, Gary Rosenfeldt argued that Canada's laws were too lenient and that, once "in Canada, these murderers are protected as though they were an endangered species."[55] Not only did the delays result in considerable legal costs (the editorial estimated that Ng had already cost the public purse $1.5 million), but also the longer the wait the greater the risk that evidence would become more difficult to obtain.

VOV also stressed the considerable human toll caused by the delays. It noted that friends and family of the victims were made to suffer further from the knowledge that the perpetrator had not been – nor might ever be – brought to justice. Together with Domm and other like-minded MPs, the organization amassed over 90,000 letters and gathered tens of thousands of signatures from Canadians across the country by the spring of 1989, a truly remarkable effort. All called for Ng's and Kindler's immediate extradition and for Canada's extradition laws to be reformed.[56]

The trial put Amnesty International Canada in an unenviable position. On principle, AI believed that extraditing any individual who could be put to death by the state was tantamount to being complicit in his or her execution. Staff at AI Canada accepted the appropriateness of this position. But given the vehemence of the public outcry against the two fugitives, the most fitting strategy for articulating this stance to the Canadian public was not obvious. AI's International Secretariat was sympathetic to the Canadian section's dilemma. Careful not to interfere, it left the decision to take an "active public stance" or a "quiet, behind-the-scenes" approach solely with its Canadian section.[57]

After much deliberation, AI Canada opted for the former, recognizing that the latter would likely not get it very far. Ultimately, it had little choice but to challenge openly the terms of Ng's and Kindler's extraditions. To abandon either man would be to sacrifice one of the cornerstones of the organization's mandate and open AI Canada to charges that it believed in abolition only in theory, not in practice. Convinced that it was the right thing to do, AI Canada applied for and was granted leave to intervene in the trial, which was to begin on 21 February 1991.[58]

As was feared, AI Canada quickly became a lightning rod for much of the anger that surrounded the case. Several journalists accused the organization of being unfaithful to its founding ideals. They questioned how the world-renowned human rights organization could make the leap from defending prisoners of conscience to defending fugitives such as Ng and Kindler. Even fewer were sympathetic to its contention that the Canadian government had violated either fugitive's rights. The *Calgary Sun* charged the organization with obstructing justice and diverging from its well-earned reputation as a defender of "civil rights for dissidents in evil dictatorships the world over."[59] Similarly, the *Toronto Sun* accused the organization of committing "a shameful denial of its own past – a past in which it won the Nobel Peace Prize and was so concerned about the absolute integrity of human rights campaigns that it never – to its credit – declared Nelson Mandela a prisoner of conscience because he advocated violence."[60] Gary Rosenfeldt told the Canadian Press that AI should focus its efforts on "countries that show no respect for human life, like Iran and Iraq."[61]

Coinciding with this external pressure was a swift and bitter outcry from AI Canada's own membership. Many of its supporters had been unaware of its position on capital punishment, and the news that AI opposed the use of the death penalty in all cases caught them by surprise. Many questioned the merits of participating in a trial in which the outcome could be to deny justice to the victims of heinous crimes.

The internal backlash was particularly fierce in Alberta. Prominent AI members in Edmonton and Calgary were outraged, calling the decision to intervene a "betrayal" and an "appalling mistake" that was not only "morally wrong" but also "not in conformity" with the organization's mandate.[62] Defending Ng and Kindler, they argued, violated the organization's original commitment to the defence of the non-violent POC whose cause was both righteous and just. Neither Ng nor Kindler fit the mould: they were the abusers, not the abused.[63] Members questioned whether the section's limited resources might be put to better use and warned that the public would only see an organization that had become an apologist for two violent killers.[64]

At the time, no one knew the extent of the damage to the credibility of AI Canada. Some within the organization wondered whether it was irreparable. In its newsletter to its members, *Amnesty International Bulletin*, staff conceded that they had lost the "popularity contest" on Ng and Kindler.[65]

In *Kindler*, the Supreme Court of Canada had to answer four questions. The first was whether surrendering individuals to the United States to face possible execution constituted a violation of their rights under the Constitution. The second was whether the Canadian government had committed an error in law in deciding not to employ the discretion available to the minister of justice under Article 6 of the Canada-US Extradition Treaty and seek assurances that Ng and Kindler would not be executed if convicted of the capital charges against them.[66] Similarly, the third and fourth questions considered whether section 25 of the *Extradition Act*, which granted the minister of justice the final decision to surrender an individual, violated sections 7 and 12 of the *Charter* and, if so, whether such a violation could be justified under section 1.[67] To determine the answer to the last question, the test before the court was whether Kindler's (or Ng's) unconditional surrender shocked the conscience of Canadians.

For the hearing, AI Canada turned to long-time supporter David Matas to represent the organization. A distinguished and well-respected human rights and refugee lawyer from Winnipeg, Matas was one of Canada's leading authorities on international law. He also knew the Supreme Court well, having been a clerk for Chief Justice John Robert Cartwright in the late 1960s.[68]

Predictably, there were a number of similarities between Matas' factum to the court and that of Kindler's counsel, Julius Grey of Montreal. Both believed that the answers to the questions before the court were yes, yes, yes, and no. On the first two questions, both agreed that the extraterritoriality of the *Charter* was a moot point since both sections 7 and 12 covered "everyone" physically present in Canada and Article 6 of the Canada-US Extradition Treaty allowed for Canadian interference in the American judicial system in cases involving the possibility of capital punishment. Consequently, the Canadian government had erred in not seeking to invoke "its own standards" of justice in the two cases.[69] Similarly, on the third question – whether the death penalty violated the right to life, the right not to be subjected to cruel and unusual punishment, and the principles of fundamental justice – both adopted an absolutist position that the inherent brutality of the death penalty, combined with the fallibilities of criminal justice systems (including the US criminal justice system), constituted sufficient grounds for the court to rule that the law was unconstitutional.[70]

Both Matas and Grey also downplayed the extent to which Canadians were angered by Ng's and Kindler's presence in Canada in the hope that the justices would not take into account events occurring outside the court, even though they had to gauge whether the Canadian government's actions shocked the conscience of Canadians.[71] Both also took aim at the safe haven argument, suggesting that it was little more than an "oratorical flourish" and a "speculative fear" based in a "factual vacuum."[72] Much of Grey's argument focused on administrative aspects of the decision not to seek assurances for his client, specifically John Crosbie's decision not to provide Kindler with an oral hearing that would have allowed his client to plead his case before the minister. Citing Justice Wilson in *Singh* (see Chapter 1), the counsel for Kindler implied that demanding assurances was a "procedural inconvenience" and suggested that any impairment that might come about as a result of removing the discretion available to the minister would be both minimal to the functioning of the Canada-US Extradition Treaty and speculative, since Crosbie had assumed that the State of Pennsylvania would have rejected his request that the death penalty not be used against Kindler.

Where the arguments of Matas differed significantly from those of Grey was on the fourth question, namely, section 1's applicability to Canada's extradition treaty. More specifically, Matas contended that the phrase "demonstrably justified in a free and democratic society" found in section 1 warranted a comparison with the practices of other countries that had similar legal and political values. His hope was to persuade the Supreme Court that the federal government, in agreeing to surrender the two men without conditions, had failed to live up to its duties as a responsible member of the international community. Given that much of Amnesty International's legitimacy came from its defence of international law, this strategy was neither surprising nor out of character. Matas contended that new developments in international law, which included equating the practice with torture, pointed to the conclusion that there was a credible movement within the international community toward the eventual global abolition of the death penalty and that Canada's actions were a clear violation of this new norm.[73]

The decision to place *Kindler* in the context of events within the international community was a gamble, albeit a well-calculated one.[74] Abolitionist forces around the world had seen many successes throughout the 1980s and early 1990s. During this time, twenty-three nations did away with the death penalty in either law or practice.[75] Moreover, there were significant advances in international law, all of which prohibited capital punishment. In 1980, the 12th Conference of European Ministers of Justice agreed to work toward abolition in all member states. The next year the Parliament for the European Community invited its member states to amend their respective national laws in favour of abolition, and in 1984 the Council of Europe announced that it was in favour of abolition for ordinary crimes, if not military ones.[76] Similarly, in 1989, the Vienna Concluding Document of the Conference on Security and Cooperation in Europe agreed to review its position on the death penalty, and the Parliament of the European Community denounced it as a clear violation of human rights.[77] At the United Nations, after nearly a decade at the drafting table, the General Assembly passed in 1989 the *Second Optional Protocol to the ICCPR Aiming at the Abolition of the Death Penalty*. In the Americas, the General Assembly of the Organization of American States (OAS) passed in 1990 the *Protocol to the American Convention on Human Rights to Abolish the Death Penalty*.[78]

The range of crimes for which states could employ the death penalty had also become more restrictive. Beginning in the 1960s, abolitionists had begun to "chip away at the death penalty rather than confront it head on" by attempting to limit its application to only the most serious crimes. According to William Schabas, this was part of a larger strategy to convince states – and courts – of the existence of emerging norms or "evolving standards of decency" relating to both the various methods of execution and the protected categories of individuals who, by virtue of their particular situation or circumstances, were exempted from being put to death by the state.[79]

Still, the argument that the world was becoming abolitionist was not without shortcomings. The most obvious one was that, at the time of the trial, more than half of the world's states still retained the death penalty for certain non-military crimes. Many of these states were Soviet-bloc nations in Eastern Europe or despotic and dictatorial regimes in Africa, Asia, Latin America, the Caribbean, and the Middle East. But there were also a handful of democratic nations that still employed the death penalty, notably regional and international powers such as India, Japan, South Korea, Turkey, and, of course, the United States.[80] None saw it as a violation of the "right to life."[81] Thus, though advocates of global abolition could claim with a great degree of certainty that momentum was on their side, there was little evidence to suggest that the world community saw capital punishment as an unjust punitive sentence. If there was an international norm against its use, in the early 1990s it was not obvious.

Of course, the Crown attempted to persuade the Supreme Court that extradition without assurances did not shock Canadian sensibilities. Represented by John C. Tait, the deputy attorney general of Canada, the federal government contended that there was no conclusive evidence that capital punishment was inherently cruel and unusual or that it constituted an automatic violation of either the right to life or the principles of fundamental justice. Instead, he suggested that the phrase was a qualifier that allowed for limits on the rights proscribed in section 7, provided that due process was followed, and not a justification for a categorical prohibition of the death penalty. Tait was equally dismissive of the arguments relating to the failings of the US criminal justice system. Building on his earlier argument relating to section 7, he argued that the American judicial system was not sufficiently different from that of Canada and that "numerous avenues for judicial review on both conviction and sentence" were very much in accordance with Canadian "standards of fundamental justice."[82]

Tait was not incorrect. There was little evidence to suggest that any of these deficiencies was relevant to the cases at hand. Although educating the court on the shortcomings and fallibilities of the US courts was an important component of the overall goal of establishing that the death penalty was cruel and unusual, there was no conclusive evidence to suggest that Kindler's sentence had been issued in an arbitrary manner by the Pennsylvania courts, and it was not yet known whether Ng would receive a fair trial once he returned to California. Nor was there consensus that the method of execution or other concerns, such as the "death row phenomenon" (the term used to describe the emotional anxiety that inmates often experience while awaiting execution), offered sufficient justification for obtaining conditions on the two fugitives' extraditions. And of course the question of innocence went beyond the mandate of the court, as its task was to determine the parameters of the two men's respective surrenders, not the merits of the cases against them.

Tait put little stock in the argument that Crosbie had mishandled Kindler's case. His central point was that the minister's role was executive, not judicial. His task was not to resolve legal issues that had already been examined in the committal stage of the extradition process. The only issue was whether his decision, not the process by which he came to that decision, violated the *Charter*. Tait believed that it did not. To require the minister to review the evidence against the individual being extradited was not only unrealistic but would also undermine the role of the courts in Canada and the United States. Moreover, such a requirement would "cripple the operation of our extradition arrangements and would undermine the good faith of this country in honouring its international obligations." Given that the minister was obliged to take into account public safety and that there were numerous judicial reviews available to Kindler in Pennsylvania and the possibility of executive clemency, Tait concluded that Crosbie had shown a "clear understanding" of the discretionary power available to him.[83]

On 26 September 1991, the Supreme Court of Canada sided with the Canadian government, issuing a four to three split decision in favour of extradition without assurances. It was a popular ruling among Canadians. Nonetheless, the closeness did little to stem the controversies surrounding the case, as neither side could claim a decisive victory. Although not apparent at the time, the ruling would come to be a significant victory for Amnesty International Canada.

The three dissenters were Chief Justice Lamer and Justices Sopinka and Cory. Both Lamer and Sopinka ruled that the decision not to seek assurances constituted a violation of the principles of fundamental justice found in section 7 of the *Charter* and equated the government's actions with giving "official blessing to the death penalty, despite the fact that the Canadian public policy stands firmly opposed to its use."[84] They ruled that section 25 of the *Extradition Act* did not constitute a reasonable limit within the meaning of section 1 of the *Charter*. Cory (with Lamer agreeing) was equally damning.[85] There was a strong correlation between his ruling and AI Canada's intervention. For him, what mattered was section 12. Citing emerging norms in international law (all the while emphasizing Canada's contribution to these developments at the UN), he criticized the Canadian government for its complicity in a practice that all in the Western world save the United States and Japan had abolished.[86] Believing that the government had been wrong to base its actions on the safe haven argument, he chastised it for not acting in accordance with Canadian conceptions of justice, which he believed were rooted in respect for human dignity, not retributive justice. For Cory, capital punishment was the ultimate punishment and was unacceptable regardless of the crimes committed or the individual who committed them. Like his fellow dissenters, he too ruled that no situation or no argument could constitute a reasonable limit on this principle. He even went so far as to compare the federal government's actions to those of Pontius Pilate, the Roman procurator who, when presented with the chance to acquit Jesus Christ and the two thieves, chose not to for fear of the repercussions.[87]

The majority of the court, however, found little wrong with the federal government's handling of *Ng* and *Kindler*, believing that the respective ministers had not acted unreasonably. As Schabas notes, both "cases involved brutal murders, and neither fugitive could lay claim to significant mitigating factors that might arouse the sympathy of bureaucrats, judges, or jurors."[88] Three of the justices – La Forest, L'Heureux-Dubé, and Gonthier – rejected the section 12 argument that the death penalty constituted cruel and unusual punishment, and they dismissed any suggestion that the Canadian government would somehow be complicit in the executions of these men should they take place. Writing for the group, La Forest noted that, though far from perfect, the US justice system was not so dissimilar to the Canadian system. He was confident that each man would receive due process if returned. Nor did he believe that the imperfections that Grey and Matas had raised – the "alleged arbitrariness," the cruelty of the method of execution, and the death row phenomenon – were sufficient to alter the final decision. For La Forest, the issue was section 7, whether the federal government had violated the principles of fundamental justice. Although he conceded that execution of Ng and Kindler would undoubtedly constitute a violation of section 12 had their crimes occurred in Canada, he maintained that, given the nature of the offences, neither Lewis nor Crosbie had acted improperly.

Conscious of the pressures on the state to deal with such cases expeditiously and provide security to the public, La Forest gave considerable weight to the safe haven argument. He suggested that deterring other fugitives from landing in Canada was a "compelling social goal": "It would be strange if Canada could keep out lesser offenders but be obliged to grant sanctuary to those accused or convicted of the worst crimes."[89] Moreover, he could not accept that, with the numerous appeals available to each fugitive throughout the extradition process, the state had committed a violation of fundamental justice. Nor, for that matter, was he convinced that returning Ng and Kindler to the United States shocked the conscience of Canadians, and he rejected the argument that capital punishment was synonymous with torture.[90] Given the animosity toward the two men and Parliament's rather tenuous commitment to abolition in 1976 and 1987, his assessment was not unreasonable.

La Forest also rejected Matas' estimation of the international context, at least in part. He recognized that international norms and international law mattered, but he remained unconvinced that much of the world viewed the death penalty as an inappropriate punitive measure.[91] Again, given that more than half of the world's states still practised capital punishment, this position was not unreasonable. Despite the shifts toward abolition that had been made in the 1980s, the world was simply not yet there.

Madam Justice McLachlin concurred with La Forest, though for different reasons. Conscious of the Supreme Court's standing as an institution, she favoured rulings that did not give the impression that the court was overstepping its authority.[92] For her, *Kindler* was not about the death penalty *per se*. Rather, it was about the relationship between the *Charter* and Canada's extradition laws and whether the Constitution should require the Canadian government to interfere in the sovereign affairs of another state. She ruled that "to apply s. 12 directly to the act of surrender to a foreign country where a particular penalty may be imposed is to overshoot the purpose of the guarantee and to cast the net of the *Charter* broadly in extraterritorial waters."

She continued, "effective relations between different states require that we respect the differences of our neighbours and that we refrain from imposing our constitutional guarantees on other states under the guise of refusing to assist them (and extradition is a form of assistance) unless they conform to our *Charter*."[93] Like La Forest, McLachlin agreed that there were no clear norms about the use of the death penalty in Canada and thus put little stock in the argument that section 25 of the *Extradition Act* violated section 7 of the *Charter*. She found no reason why the Supreme Court should overturn the ministers' decisions. Ng and Kindler could be extradited unconditionally.

Ottawa's reaction to the ruling was swift. Within hours of the decision, Kim Campbell ordered officers of the Royal Canadian Mounted Police to board the two men onto airplanes destined for California and Pennsylvania, respectively.[94] Neither man's attorney was notified. Campbell even ignored a request from the UN Human Rights Committee to postpone extradition until it could review the cases to determine whether the Canadian government's decision to extradite the men without seeking assurances that they would not be executed violated the *ICCPR*. For this, Campbell was unapologetic. From the perspective of the Canadian government, the extradition process had gone on long enough. Each man had received ample appeals. Any further delays would constitute an obstruction of justice.

Those who had been campaigning for the extradition of Ng and Kindler were elated. On the day of the verdict, Domm thanked the hundreds of thousands of Canadians who had supported him in his efforts to see that the two men were brought to justice. The Victims of Violence Society applauded the Canadian government for sending the "strongest message there is" that Canada does not welcome fugitives who wish to escape American justice.[95] In an interview with CBC's *The National,* Gary Rosenfeldt remarked, "it's the end of what has been a nightmare for I think all Canadians and victims of crime in the US who have been seeing alleged and convicted murderers coming to Canada and using this country as a haven."[96] The *Globe and Mail*'s editorial board concurred: "Canada cannot allow itself to become the final court of appeal for the United States criminal justice system."[97]

Only AI Canada voiced its opposition. Matas called the federal government's decision to ignore the UN's request a "callous disregard for human rights" and an "affront to international diplomacy."[98] Roger Clark, the secretary general for the Canadian section, agreed, telling reporters that, in light of the closeness of the ruling, Campbell's decision to extradite the men showed "inappropriate and unseemly haste" that was inconsistent with Canada's "national pattern of justice."[99]

But Matas and Clark were very much in the minority. For many Canadians, any claim that AI might once have had as a champion of justice was gone. Indeed, the organization had paid a heavy price for its intervention in the case.[100] Its arguments had had a limited influence on the Supreme Court. Had the makeup of the court been different, its ideas might have had more of an impact. Moreover, much of the organization's membership had been willing to separate the principle from the person. Although no exact figures were kept, staff at the Canadian section estimated that thousands of members and supporters left the organization over the section's decision to involve itself with Ng and Kindler.[101] Despite its best efforts, its message – that the death penalty is the ultimate violation of human rights – was lost on an uninterested public. The organization found itself on the defensive, forced to react to allegations that it was defending killers and obstructing justice, all at the expense of the safety of the public.

Kindler showed that "human rights" can be a fickle concept and that how it is applied depends not only on the punishment in question but also on the individual and the offences that he or she is accused of having committed. Charles Ng and Joseph Kindler were particularly reprehensible figures. Although Parliament had twice deemed capital punishment to be inconsistent with Canadian conceptions of justice, the Canadian public had not necessarily followed suit. For many, the injustice was not in the penalty that Ng and Kindler might face but in the delays that were forestalling such a fate. If, as Matas suggested, the trial was not about Ng and Kindler but about who Canadians are, then Canadians showed that they were not offended by the potential execution of the two fugitives. Nor, for that matter, was the Mulroney government. Despite the stand that it had taken in 1987, its handling of *Ng* and *Kindler* revealed that it was not prepared to face the wrath of angry voters or interfere with the American criminal justice system.

Shortly after the ruling, the federal government renewed its commitment to streamlining Canada's extradition laws. Neither of Domm's bills had been adopted (Bill C-209 was not selected for consideration by the Standing Committee on Privileges and Elections; Bill C-210 was selected but, thanks to NDP filibustering, was allowed to die on the order paper).[102] Shortly thereafter, the Canadian government introduced new legislation, Bill C-31, *Amendments to the Extradition Act*. Although still a two-track system, it proposed a number of reforms designed to reduce delays and protect Canada from becoming a safe haven for violent criminals. One was to allow extradition judges to consider *Charter* issues when determining whether there were sufficient grounds for extradition, the intention being that they could be addressed before the case made its way to the higher courts. Another was to permit the extradition ruling to be appealed directly to the appropriate provincial or territorial Court of Appeal, thus reducing the number of appeals available throughout the process.[103] A third involved granting the minister of justice the authority to make a decision on surrender while the case was still in the committal stage, thereby expediting the process. The result of these reforms would be that both stages could be heard simultaneously by the relevant provincial or territorial Court of Appeal, and any ruling in either the committal stage or the surrender stage could then be appealed to the Supreme Court of Canada. All of these steps contained strict deadlines limiting the time in which each stage could be completed. If the bill passed, three of the appeals would be removed: the *habeas corpus* review in the committal stage and the appeals to the Federal Court of Canada (Trial Division) and Federal Court of Appeal in the surrender stage.

AI Canada remained critical of the proposed new legislation. Appearing as a witness before the House of Commons Standing Committee on Justice and the Solicitor General, Clark explained that AI was not opposed to streamlining the extradition process to reduce delays, as long as due process was not compromised. For Clark, the reforms missed the mark. Because the law still permitted ministerial discretion in the surrender stage, individuals could still be returned to the United States to face execution. Bill C-31, he argued, did little to settle the issue. He warned that, given the divided court in *Kindler*, another constitutional challenge was by no means out of the realm of possibility.[104]

Kindler is by no means the end of the story. In the decade and a half since the trial, much has changed both in Canada and in the international community. Much has also changed for Amnesty International in Canada. It took its lumps but recovered shortly thereafter, convinced that its decision to intervene had ultimately been the right one. Indeed, it has even gone back to the Supreme Court of Canada, having intervened in several cases since, each time arguing that norms in international law and the international community offer important guidance for shaping human rights laws in Canada, a claim that the Supreme Court has since been far more willing to accept.[105]

Of these cases, *Burns v. United States* contained a number of parallels to *Kindler*. In July 1994, Glen Sebastian Burns and Atif Ahmad Rafay, two Vancouver men, were alleged to have committed triple homicide in Washington

State, murdering Rafay's parents and younger sister in the hope of collecting the money from the family's life insurance policy. They were eventually arrested in Vancouver after Burns confessed his crime to an undercover RCMP agent. Following the arrests, Washington State made a formal extradition request on the grounds that the two men were wanted on three counts of aggravated first-degree murder. Allan Rock, the minister of justice at the time, agreed to the request without first seeking assurances that the death penalty would not be used should the two men be convicted, as he was entitled to do under Article 6 of the 1976 Canada-US Extradition Treaty. Both Burns and Rafay challenged the decision, claiming that their rights under the *Charter* had been violated. This time the Supreme Court of Canada agreed – resoundingly so, in fact, ruling nine to zero in their favour. *Burns* was indicative of just how much had changed in the decade since *Kindler*.

Much of the shift had taken place at the international level. The July 1998 *Rome Statute of the International Criminal Court*, with a "life sentence" as its most stringent penalty, was definitive in its opposition to the death penalty, as were the terms for the independent international tribunals established in response to the genocide, ethnic cleansing, and crimes against humanity committed in Rwanda, the former Yugoslavia, and Sierra Leone in the 1990s.[106] Equally significant was that, by 2001, fewer than half of the states making up the international community still relied on the practice.

A second difference was that Amnesty International Canada was no longer alone in its unconditional opposition to the death penalty. Also intervening in *Burns* were the International Centre for Criminal Law and Human Rights, the Criminal Lawyers Association of Ontario, the Washington Association of Criminal Defense Lawyers, and, marking the first time that a foreign state was granted intervention in a Canadian court, the Senate of the Republic of Italy (in 1998, the Italian government had launched an international campaign to abolish the death penalty). In addition to Matas, who was once again representing AI Canada, the case featured prominent defence lawyers such as Edward Greenspan, Clayton Ruby, and James Lockyear. Ten years earlier such support had been non-existent. Now there was no shortage of it.

As Thomas Bateman argues, it was in the context of these international events that the Supreme Court of Canada reversed its position in *Burns*.[107] Granted, throughout the 1990s there had been a significant turnover in the Supreme Court, with six new justices on the bench (though the three remaining members from *Kindler* had all been part of the majority decision).[108] And Rafay and Burns were not Charles Ng and Joseph Kindler. They were two eighteen-year-old Canadians accused of triple homicide. Despite the horrendous nature of their crimes, they were not American serial killers responsible for cruel acts of torture and murder. As James Kelly notes, at the time of the ruling there were two significant debates taking place, the first in the United States concerning the use of capital punishment and the fallibilities of the US criminal justice system, the second in Parliament concerning the constitutionality of ministerial discretion in Canada's extradition and immigration laws.[109]

In *Burns*, the Supreme Court found that extradition without assurances did shock the conscience of Canadians, in large part because of AI Canada's defence of international norms in *Kindler*.[110] Although neither Rafay nor Burns was a minor at the time, their relative youth was also a mitigating factor in the court's decision. So too was the fallibility of the courts, the possibility of wrongful convictions, and the death row phenomenon. The court also rejected the safe haven argument, believing it to be no more of a deterrent than the possibility of a life sentence: "Elimination of a 'safe haven' depends on vigorous law enforcement rather than on infliction of the death penalty by a foreign state after the fugitive has been removed from this country." But most importantly, the court ruled that in seeking assurances Canada would be living up to its international obligations as an advocate of global abolition, its suggestion being that Canada had a duty to see that international customary law evolved such that prohibition of capital punishment would one day become a legitimate norm. It concluded that "a balance which tilted in favour of extradition without assurances in *Kindler* and *Ng* now tilts against the constitutionality of such an outcome."[111]

There was, however, a caveat to its decision. Seeking assurances against the death penalty was a constitutional requirement, except in "exceptional cases," though exactly what this meant was neither explained nor defined by the Supreme Court.[112] In the event of another Charles Ng – another individual who constitutes a clear threat to public safety and national security – it remains to be seen whether the Supreme Court of Canada would once again refrain from interfering with the federal government's discretionary powers.[113]

On 25 November 2005, the ministers of foreign affairs and justice, Pierre Pettigrew and Irwin Cotler, announced that Canada had acceded to the 1989 *Second Optional Protocol to the International Covenant on Civil and Political Rights*, its intentions being to "formalize" Canada's "long-standing support for the abolition of the death penalty" and to place the country "at the forefront of the international struggle toward abolition."[114] The news sparked little reaction. The norm of abolition has been firmly entrenched in Canadian law, and since *Burns* the question of whether capital punishment shocks the Canadian conscience has been settled.

Even so, Canadian support for abolition is not yet absolute. Responding to a bid for clemency by Ronald Smith, a Canadian facing execution in Montana for committing double homicide in the early 1980s, the Stephen Harper government announced that Ottawa would no longer automatically seek the commutation of death sentences for Canadians imprisoned abroad in democratic countries with criminal justice systems similar to Canada's. Smith's lawyers – supported by AI Canada – filed a motion in the Federal Court of Canada contending that the sudden shift in Canadian policy was not only a violation of Smith's *Charter* rights but also out of sync with the practices of other Western democracies that no longer employed the death penalty as a punitive sentence.[115] On 4 March 2009, the Federal Court ruled in Smith's favour. A month later the federal government announced, rather unexpectedly, that it would not appeal the decision and would seek clemency on Smith's behalf.[116] Anti-death penalty advocates hailed the news.

Smith's case offers a reminder that human rights norms – regardless of how seemingly far advanced they are – are rarely as entrenched as their supporters would like them to be. Norms favouring abolition restrict the discretion available to governments when forced to deal with difficult cases. In a Westminster liberal democracy, they limit Parliament's ability to respond to acts of violence that represent a threat to public safety, national security, and the country's external relations. Amnesty International Canada has been successful in securing greater constitutional prohibitions against use of the death penalty against both Canadians who have committed capital crimes abroad and non-citizens who face extradition and possible execution by a foreign government. It has done so by convincing the courts that the death penalty is in contravention of international norms and laws. Although the bar favouring abolition has been raised, the ban remains qualified, reserved for exceptional cases, and open to politicization. As long as there are violent individuals and democratic states that see capital punishment as a legitimate punitive sentence, a comprehensive ban in Canada that organizations such as AI Canada seek will undoubtedly remain elusive.

Conclusion
Principles in the Age of Rights

Without question, one of the most significant achievements of the post-Second World War international order has been an elevation in the status of rights norms. For Norberto Bobbio, the dawning of the age of rights is evidence of humanity's "moral progress," "one of the greatest inventions of our civilization."[1] He is by no means alone in his exaltation of the transformative power of rights. Philosopher Brian Orend eloquently describes them as a moral language "designed to be spoken universally" that, "when first introduced, went against the grain of history." In an equally laudatory manner, Alison Brysk suggests that rights are the "highest stage of liberalism," while Michael Ignatieff sees them as nothing less than the "expressions of our moral identity as a people."[2] Simply put, they are the ideas that define the constraints that limit the state's authority over the individual. They embody the spirit of a modern era of human history in which those in power are bound by the rule of law.

Although human rights undoubtedly enhance governance, they complicate it as well. The focus of this book is on the emergence, advancement, and defence of three particular norms through the activism and contributions of four particular interest groups, including their interventions at the Supreme Court of Canada in the *Charter* era. But it is not just about the transformation of "noble but vague aspirations and just but weak demands into legally established rights" in Canada.[3] It is also about the difficult cases – those involving the rights of non-citizens, hate-mongers, and violent individuals –

that test the resolve of democratic societies and their adherence to rights principles.

Despite the emergence of an international human rights law regime in the post-Second World War era, there is nothing inevitable about the adoption and protection of rights, even in a liberal parliamentary democracy such as Canada. Quite simply, human rights norms are context dependent. Their scope and application are both a product of and a response to specific historical events and experiences and the articulation of a moral claim to entitlement, often made by civil society actors, designed to push the state to rectify a particular injustice whether real or perceived.

In Canada, the transition from idea to law – or from "ought" to "is" – has been an uneven process. Changes have often come slowly, incrementally, and, at times, at great costs to the organizations championing them. The fate of any given human rights norm – be it the procedural rights for those fleeing persecution, limits on expression for the purposes of protecting vulnerable groups from hate speech, or prescriptions relating to the meaning of the "right to life" – has depended on whether individuals and organizations within a society – from an ecumenical sense of obligation, a fear of genocide or tyranny, or a personal commitment to the protection of the individual – are prepared to advance and defend it.

In the contest to define the parameters of the relationship between the state and its citizens, principled ideas and actors matter. In each of the three case studies featured in this book, principled ideas were championed by organizations that held a deep commitment to particular ideals – ideals that were simultaneously uncompromising and obdurate yet clumsy and even divisive. In each case, the NGOs featured were willing to defend principles, even at considerable costs to their well-being and reputation, all in the hope of raising the bar of the morally permissible. The Supreme Court of Canada, in permitting interest groups to help interpret the meaning of the *Charter of Rights and Freedoms*, has legitimized this process.

Canada is not alone in its struggles to govern in a way that respects both individual rights and collective security. Indeed, on the rights issues featured in this book, Canada has fared relatively well in comparison with other liberal democracies. Despite its stumbles, Canada has a reputation of having an open and generous refugee determination system, particularly when compared with those of the United States, Australia, and many European states that face far greater pressures as a result of their geographic proximity to states mired in political conflict and economic underdevelopment. On issues of free expression and the protection of minorities from hate, the conflicts that have arisen as a result of offensive materials have been largely restricted to the courts and not the streets, unlike in some European states that, for a variety of historical, political, and cultural reasons, have struggled to integrate their immigrant populations. And on matters of extradition to face potential execution, Canadian policy is much closer to the European Union's policy of conditional surrender than to that of the United States, which, of course, still practises capital punishment. As in other liberal democracies, Canada has seen advances on these issues in part because the authority of the judicial branch of the government has been augmented as a direct result of the proliferation and widespread adoption of rights norms among liberal democracies but also because civil society organizations such as the ones featured in this book have seen the judiciary as a viable means for securing a human rights-friendly jurisprudence.

Rhoda Howard argues that human rights "are nothing more than what human beings proclaim they ought to be," a "choice of a particular moral vision of human potentiality and the institutions for realising that vision."[4] The key insight here is that they are a choice. Human rights norms are ideals to which states are pressured to aspire. But they are just that: ideals. They may be palatable, even desirable, principles guiding state behaviour. But they are ambiguous, fluid, their "character and nature," to quote Abdul Said, "determined in the crucible of a specific socio-political culture."[5] Even when codified into law, they remain only as strong as the actors responsible for upholding them wish them to be, suggesting that internalization, the third and final stage of Finnemore and Sikkink's norm life cycle, is by far the most difficult to realize. When tested by real, complex, and trying circumstances – the difficult cases – principles are susceptible to being tempered, discarded, or even abandoned in the face of material constraints as in the case of *Singh*, competing rights claims as in the case of *Keegstra*, or competing obligations of the state as in the case of *Kindler*.

Robert Drinan writes that the "law teaches and deters. Law may be a feeble instrument, but sometimes it works and the human family becomes less barbarous and more civilized."[6] In Canada in the post-*Charter* era, interest groups, judicial activism, and domestic internalization of international law have all become important components of this "civilizing" process. Indeed, Canada's Constitution is a vague, ever evolving document. It lends itself to a multitude of different interpretations. It has become an important tool for interest groups that wish to establish a strong human rights jurisprudence in Canada.

But it is an imperfect tool. No interest group can have a moral claim imposed by the judiciary on an unwilling Parliament, at least not indefinitely. This lesson suggests that there is an inherent fragility to the age of rights. Scholars such as Todd Landman have aptly written of the "precarious triumph of human rights," "precarious ... since these same achievements can be reversed where politics and power have shaped the different ways in which such gains have been achieved."[7] Indeed, future scholars studying the first decade of the twenty-first century may come to identify a fourth era of the age of rights that began with the terrorist attacks of 11 September 2001 in New York and Washington and was, as some scholars and observers have contended, defined by a general weakening of human rights norms in the name of national security.

It is too soon to know the extent to which the events of that tragedy marked a watershed moment in the age of rights in Canada and internationally.[8] That there has been a regression in rights standards should not be surprising. Debates about the scope and legitimacy of human rights norms are, after all, often highly charged contests of ideas. This was certainly true of the three norms examined in this book. As Finnemore and Sikkink note, the process by which norms are advanced is not linear, nor is there anything inevitable about the result.[9] But as long as there are contests waged between civil society actors willing to defend a principle, the elusive search for human dignity that has come to characterize the age of rights for liberal parliamentary democracies will go on.

Notes

INTRODUCTION

1 Norberto Bobbio, *The Age of Rights*, trans. Allan Cameron (Cambridge, MA: Polity Press, 1996).
2 Micheline R. Ishay, *The History of Human Rights: From Ancient Times to the Globalization Era* (Berkeley: University of California Press, 2004), 2.
3 *Ibid*. For examples of early antecedents to the modern human rights system, see C.A. Macartney, "The League of Nations' Protection of Minority Rights," in *The International Protection of Human Rights*, ed. Evan Luard (New York: Frederick A. Praeger, 1967), 22-38; Paul Gordon Lauren, "Human Rights in History: Diplomacy and Racial Equality at the Paris Peace Conference," *Diplomatic History* 2 (1978): 257-78; and Paul Gordon Lauren, "First Principles of Racial Equality: History and the Politics and Diplomacy of Human Rights Provisions in the United Nations Charter," *Human Rights Quarterly* 5, 1 (1983): 1-26.
4 For a brief survey of some of the scholarly literature on the emergence of the international human rights regime and the legacy of the *UDHR*, see G. Alfredsson and Asbjorn Eide, *The Universal Declaration of Human Rights: A Common Standard of Achievement* (The Hague: Martinus Nijhoff, 1999); Jan Herman Burgers, "The Road to San Francisco: The Revival of Human Rights Ideas in the 20th Century," *Human Rights Quarterly* 14 (1992): 447-77; René Cassin, *La Declaration universelle et la mise en oeuvre des droits de l'homme* (Paris: Librarie du Recueil Sirey, 1951); Jack Donnelly, *International Human Rights*, 3rd ed. (Boulder, CO: Westview Press, 2007), 4-5; Asbjorn Eide, "The Historical Significance of the Universal Declaration," *International Social Science Journal* 50, 4 (1998): 475-97; John P. Humphrey, "The United Nations Charter and the Universal Declaration of Human Rights," in *The International Protection of Human Rights*, ed. Evan Luard (New York: Frederick A. Praeger,

1967), 39-58; John P. Humphrey, "The Universal Declaration of Human Rights: Its History, Impact, and Juridical Character," in *Human Rights: Thirty Years after the Universal Declaration*, ed. B.G. Ramcharan (The Hague: Martinus Nijhoff, 1979), 21-37; John P. Humphrey, *Human Rights and the United Nations: A Great Adventure* (Dobbs Ferry, NY: Transnational, 1984); and Johannes Morsink, "Cultural Genocide, the Universal Declaration, and Minority Rights," *Human Rights Quarterly* 21, 4 (1999): 1009-60.

5 Ross Lambertson, *Repression and Resistance: Canadian Human Rights Activists, 1930-1960* (Toronto: University of Toronto Press, 2005); Stephanie Bangarth, *Voices Raised in Protest: Defending North American Citizens of Japanese Ancestry, 1942-49* (Vancouver: UBC Press, 2008); Dominique Clément, *Canada's Rights Revolution* (Vancouver: UBC Press, 2009).

6 James W. St.G. Walker, *"Race," Rights, and the Law in the Supreme Court of Canada: Historical Case Studies* (Waterloo: Wilfrid Laurier University Press; Osgoode Society for Canadian Legal History, 1998); Constance Backhouse, *Colour-Coded: A Legal History of Racism in Canada, 1900-1950* (Toronto: University of Toronto Press; Osgoode Society for Canadian Legal History, 1999).

7 Lambertson, *Repression and Resistance*, 371.

8 Michael Ignatieff, *The Rights Revolution* (Toronto: Anansi, 2000), 1-2; Alan C. Cairns, "International Influences on the Charter," in *Charter versus Federalism: The Dilemmas of Constitutional Reform* (Montreal/Kingston: McGill-Queen's University Press, 1992), 15.

9 Jack Donnelly, "Human Rights: A New Standard of Civilization?" *International Affairs* 74, 1 (1998): 14. The covenants were first presented to the UN General Assembly in 1954 but not opened for signature until 1966. For a history of the negotiations around the covenants, see Howard Tolley Jr., *The UN Commission on Human Rights* (Boulder, CO: Westview Press, 1987), 24-29.

10 Akira Iriye, "A Century of NGOs," *Diplomatic History* 23, 3 (1999): 425-28; William Korey, *NGOs and the Universal Declaration of Human Rights: "A Curious Grapevine"* (New York: St. Martin's Press, 1998).

11 For a history of the 1960s, see Doug Owram, *Born at the Right Time: A History of the Baby Boom Generation* (Toronto: University of Toronto Press, 1997).

12 Pierre Elliott Trudeau, "Quebec and the Constitutional Problem," in *Federalism and the French Canadians* (Toronto: Macmillan, 1968), 11.

13 Pierre Elliott Trudeau, *Memoirs* (Toronto: McClelland and Stewart, 1993), 83. According to George Radwanski, Trudeau's handling of the reforms eventually "rocketed [him] toward the status of national hero." George Radwanski, *Trudeau* (Toronto: Macmillan, 1978), 96. See also John English, *Just Watch Me: The Life of Pierre Elliott Trudeau, 1968-2000* (Toronto: Random House, 2009), 112-15; Christina McCall and Stephen Clarkson, *Trudeau and Our Times*, vol. 1, *The Magnificent Obsession* (Toronto: McClelland and Stewart, 1990), 107; and Andrew S. Thompson, "Slow to Leave the Bedrooms of the Nation: Trudeau and the Modernizing of Canadian Law, 1967-1969," in *The Hidden Pierre Elliott Trudeau: The Faith behind the Politics*, ed. John English, Richard Gwyn, and P. Whitney Lackenbauer (Ottawa: Novalis, 2004), 117-33.

Notes to pages 4-5 123

14 James G. Snell and Frederick Vaughan, *The Supreme Court of Canada: History of the Institution* (Toronto: University of Toronto Press, 1985), 258. For an example of Trudeau's views on civil liberties and the function of a bill of rights, see Pierre Elliott Trudeau, "A Constitutional Declaration of Rights," in *Federalism and the French Canadians*, 54-55; and Pierre Elliott Trudeau, "The Values of a Just Society," in *Towards a Just Society: The Trudeau Years*, ed. Thomas S. Axworthy and Pierre Elliott Trudeau (Markham, ON: Viking, 1990), 358.

15 Section 94 of the *Indian Act* stated that "an Indian who (a) has intoxicants in his possession, (b) is intoxicated, or (c) makes or manufactures intoxicants off a reserve, is guilty of an offence and is liable on summary conviction to a fine of not less than ten dollars and not more than fifty dollars or to imprisonment for a term not exceeding three months or to both fine and imprisonment." *Indian Act*, R.S.C. 1952, c. 149. See *R. v. Drybones*, [1970] 9 D.L.R. (3d) 473.

16 Snell and Vaughn, *The Supreme Court of Canada*, 225. Ian Bushnell makes a similar point about Laskin's influence on the court. Ian Bushnell, *The Captive Court: A Study of the Supreme Court of Canada* (Montreal/Kingston: McGill-Queen's University Press, 1992), 401. For an excellent biography of Laskin, see Philip Girard, *Bora Laskin: Bringing Law to Life* (Toronto: University of Toronto Press for the Osgoode Society for Canadian Legal History, 2005).

17 Christopher P. Manfredi, *Feminist Activism in the Supreme Court: Legal Mobilization and the Women's Legal Education and Action Fund* (Vancouver: UBC Press, 2004), xii-xiii.

18 In their biography of Justice Brian Dickson, Robert J. Sharpe and Kent Roach reveal that by the early 1980s the Supreme Court – especially Dickson, who for a period in the 1980s would become one of the bench's most enthusiastic proponents of judicial review – had become increasingly sensitive to criticisms that its preference for restrictive interpretations of the law had "let the *Bill of Rights* die in the 1970s." They also suggest that by the mid-1980s "Dickson made no secret of his own determination to breathe life into [the *Charter*'s] vague and general language." Robert J. Sharpe and Kent Roach, *Brian Dickson: A Judge's Journey* (Toronto: University of Toronto Press for the Osgoode Society for Canadian Legal History, 2003), 25, 310, 336, 376.

19 In a 1967 speech to the Canadian Bar Association, Trudeau had indicated that he favoured a "bill that would guarantee the fundamental freedoms of the citizen from interference, whether federal or provincial." Trudeau, "A Constitutional Declaration of Rights," 54.

20 Cairns, "International Influences on the Charter," 17, 20, 21.

21 *Ibid.*, 29, 32.

22 John T. Saywell, *The Lawmakers: Judicial Power and the Shaping of Canadian Federalism* (Toronto: University of Toronto Press for the Osgoode Society for Canadian Legal History, 2002), 275.

23 Between 1976 and 1982, only thirty-five non-governmental organizations appeared before the court as interveners. Ian Brodie, *The Friends of the Court: The Privileging of Interest Group Litigants in Canada* (New York: SUNY Press, 2002), 27.

24 In *Attorney General of Canada v. Lavell*, the Supreme Court granted intervener status to the Six Nations Band of Indians of the County of Brant, the National Indian

Brotherhood, Aboriginal groups from all provinces and territories except Newfoundland and Prince Edward Island, University Women Graduates, the University Women's Club of Toronto, and a number of other women's organizations. *Attorney General of Canada v. Lavell* (1973), 38 D.L.R. (3d) 481. In the first *Morgentaler v. The Queen*, the Supreme Court heard from the Canadian Civil Liberties Association, the Foundation for Women in Crisis, the Alliance for Life, the Association des médécins du Québec pour la respect de la vie, the Front Commun pour la respect de la vie, and the Fondation pour la vie. *Morgentaler v. The Queen,* [1976] 1 S.C.R. 616.

25 Jillian Welch, "No Room at the Top: Interest Group Interveners and Charter Litigation in the Supreme Court of Canada," *University of Toronto Faculty of Law Review* 43, 2 (1985): 228, 230. See also Elizabeth J. Shilton, "Charter Litigation and the Policy Processes of Government: A Public Interest Perspective," *Osgoode Hall Law Journal* 30, 3 (1992): 653-60.
26 Brodie, *The Friends of the Court*, 32.
27 Sharpe and Roach, *Brian Dickson*, 386.
28 Ellen Anderson, *Judging Bertha Wilson: Law as Large as Life* (Toronto: University of Toronto Press for the Osgoode Society for Canadian Legal History, 2001), 16, 134.
29 Sharpe and Roach, *Brian Dickson*, 385.
30 *Ibid.,* 387-88.
31 John D. Whyte, "Legality and Legitimacy: The Problem of Judicial Review of Legislation," *Queen's Law Journal* 12, 1 (1987): 1-20; W.R. Lederman, "Democratic Parliaments, Independent Courts, and the Canadian Charter of Rights and Freedoms," *Queen's Law Journal* 11, 1 (1985): 1-25.
32 Not long into the *Charter* era, the Supreme Court became the focal point of a highly charged ideological debate. One fear was that it had become highly politicized, like its counterpart in the United States, an institution that has, since the Great Depression, played a prominent role in the politics of that nation. See C. Herman Pritchett, *The Roosevelt Court: A Study in Judicial Politics and Values, 1937-1947* (New York: Octagon Books, 1963). Since the 1980s, there has been an explosion of scholarship – largely by political scientists and legal analysts on both the right and the left of the political spectrum – on the effects of the new Constitution and the increased authority of the judicial branch of the government in Canadian federalism and democracy. The scholarship has been preoccupied with questions about the ideological leanings of the court and the legitimacy of judicial activism versus restraint in a parliamentary system of government. For works by conservative scholars who question the legitimacy of judicial review, see Marc Gold, "The Rhetoric of Rights: The Supreme Court and the Charter," *Osgoode Hall Law Journal* 25, 2 (1987): 375-410; and Robert Ivan Martin, *The Most Dangerous Branch: How the Supreme Court of Canada Has Undermined Our Law and Our Democracy* (Montreal/Kingston: McGill-Queen's University Press, 2003). On questions about the emergence of a *"Charter* dialogue" between the judiciary and the executive and legislative branches of the government and whether the *Charter* has had a centralizing effect on Canadian public policy and law, see Patrick J. Monahan and Marie Finkelstein, "The Charter of Rights and Public Policy in Canada," *Osgoode Hall Law Journal* 30, 3 (1992): 501-46; Mary Dawson, "The Impact of the Charter on the Public Policy Process and the Department of

Justice," *Osgoode Hall Law Journal* 30, 3 (1992): 595-603; F.L. Morton et al., "Judicial Nullification of Statutes under the Charter of Rights and Freedoms, 1982-1988," *Alberta Law Review* 28, 2 (1990): 396-426; James B. Kelly, "Reconciling Rights and Federalism during Review of the Charter of Rights and Freedoms: The Supreme Court of Canada and the Centralization Thesis, 1982-1999," *Canadian Journal of Political Science* 34, 2 (2001): 321-55; and James B. Kelly, *Governing with the Charter: Legislative and Judicial Activism and Framers' Intent* (Vancouver: UBC Press, 2005).
33 Monahan and Finkelstein, "The Charter of Rights and Public Policy in Canada," 508.
34 See Christopher P. Manfredi, *Judicial Power and the Charter: Canada and the Paradox of Liberal Constitutionalism* (New York: Oxford University Press, 2000), 187; Christopher P. Manfredi, *The Canadian Feminist Movement, Constitutional Politics, and the Strategic Use of Legal Resources* (Vancouver: SFU-UBC Centre for the Study of Government and Business, 2000); and Peter McCormick, *Canada's Courts: A Social Scientist's Ground-Breaking Account of the Canadian Judicial System* (Toronto: James Lorimer, 1994), 192. In his book *The Friends of the Court*, Brodie, a former student of Morton's, criticizes the politicization of the federal government's Court Challenges Program (CCP). Established in the late 1970s as an indirect means for the federal government to combat the language laws of the Parti Québécois, the program was expanded in 1985 to include equality rights litigation, once again on the grounds that funding litigation provided the state with an avenue for altering the political climate in favour of a more socially progressive agenda. In 1990, the program's budget was renewed, and the task of administering it was handed to the University of Ottawa's Human Rights Centre, a decision that meant that the federal government had effectively lost its ability to control which groups received funding. Two years later the Mulroney government announced its plan to cancel the program. Many of the groups that had benefited from the CCP protested the decision, so much so that the Chrétien Liberals reinstated it following their election victory in 1993. Their success, according to Brodie, was further proof of the "state working through interest groups," an "embedded state at war with itself in court." Brodie, *The Friends of the Court*, xiv, 15. See also Ian Brodie, "Interest Group Litigation and the Embedded State: Canada's Court Challenges Program," *Canadian Journal of Political Science* 34, 2 (2001): 357-76. In 2006, Brodie left academia to become chief of staff for the newly elected Conservative government under Stephen Harper. One of the first policy announcements was cancellation of the CCP.
35 Cairns calls the practice of advancing rights through the courts "constitutional minoritarianism." He argues that the "goal [of the *Charter*] is to find a new equilibrium between citizen and state, not to unleash a ruthless contest between atomistic pursuers of rights and their government opponents, who cynically manipulate rights rhetoric to keep the citizenry subservient." He continues, "interest group participation driven by a narrowly focused self-interest is insufficient, no matter how deserving and noble the goals of individual groups may be." Alan C. Cairns, "The Charter: A Political Science Perspective," *Osgoode Hall Law Journal* 30, 3 (1992): 617, 620, 622.
36 See F.L. Morton, "The Charter Revolution and the Court Party," *Osgoode Hall Law Journal* 30, 3 (1992): 627-52; and F.L. Morton and Rainer Knopff, *The Charter Revolution and the Court Party* (Peterborough: Broadview Press, 2000). For a rebuttal of

their ideas, as well as a more general critique of the *Charter* as a tool for promoting social justice, see Miriam Smith, "Ghosts of the Judicial Committee of the Privy Council: Group Politics and Charter Litigation in Canadian Political Science," *Canadian Journal of Political Science* 35, 1 (2002): 3-29; Miriam Smith, "Social Movements and Equality Seeking: The Case of Gay Liberation in Canada," *Canadian Journal of Political Science* 31, 2 (1998): 285-309; Miriam Smith, *Lesbian and Gay Rights in Canada: Social Movements and Equality-Seeking, 1971-1995* (Toronto: University of Toronto Press, 1999); Joel Bakan, *Just Words: Constitutional Rights and Social Wrongs* (Toronto: University of Toronto Press, 1997); and Michael Mandel, *The Charter of Rights and the Legalization of Politics in Canada* (Toronto: Wall and Thompson, 1989).

37 Beverley M. McLachlin, "The Charter: A New Role for the Judiciary?" *Alberta Law Review* 29, 3 (1991): 545.

38 Martha Finnemore and Kathryn Sikkink, "International Norm Dynamics and Political Change," *International Organization* 52, 4 (1998): 892.

39 Ted Hopf, "The Promise of Constructivism in International Relations Theory," *International Security* 23, 1 (1998): 176-77.

40 Thomas Risse and Kathryn Sikkink, "The Socialization of International Human Rights Norms into Domestic Practices: Introduction," in *The Power of Human Rights: International Norms and Domestic Change*, ed. Thomas Risse, Stephen C. Ropp, and Kathryn Sikkink (Cambridge: Cambridge University Press, 1999), 7, 9. Ann Marie Clark argues that civil society groups that tend to be most successful at advancing norms are those whose "principled commitment" to an issue is matched by "relatively high levels of information, expertise and, sometimes, resources to commit to issues." Ann Marie Clark, "Non-Governmental Organizations and Their Influence on International Society," *Journal of International Affairs* 48, 2 (1995): 510.

41 Michael Ignatieff, *The Lesser Evil: Political Ethics in the Age of Terror* (Princeton: Princeton University Press, 2004), 23; Finnemore and Sikkink, "International Norm Dynamics and Political Change," 900, 914.

42 Ann Marie Clark, *Diplomacy of Conscience: Amnesty International and Changing Human Rights Norms* (Princeton: Princeton University Press, 2001), 11. See also Donnelly, "Human Rights," 22. Several other scholars of human rights and international relations have made similar arguments about the importance of rights as a tool for the construction of identity. See Rhoda Howard, *Human Rights and the Search for Community* (Boulder, CO: Westview Press, 1995), 15; Risse and Sikkink, "Socialization of International Human Rights Norms," 5; and Mahmood Monshipouri et al., eds., *Constructing Human Rights in the Age of Globalization* (New York: M.E. Sharpe, 2003).

43 Finnemore and Sikkink, "International Norm Dynamics and Political Change," 916.

44 *Ibid.*, 895, 914.

45 Clark, *Diplomacy of Conscience*, 34.

46 Issues considered to fall under the realm of economic, social, and cultural and group rights, or second- and third-generation rights, respectively, fall outside the scope of this study.

47 Much has been written about Amnesty International's impact on the international human rights regime. For a survey of some of the scholarly literature on Amnesty International's contributions to the international human rights regime, see Peter R. Baehr, "Amnesty International and Its Self-Imposed Limited Mandate," *Netherlands Quarterly of Human Rights* 12, 1 (1994): 5-21; Tom Buchanan, "'The Truth Will Set You Free': The Making of Amnesty International," *Journal of Contemporary History* 37, 4 (2002): 575-97; Clark, *Diplomacy of Conscience*; Curt Goering, "Amnesty International and Economic, Social, and Cultural Rights," in *Ethics in Action: The Ethical Challenges of International Human Rights Nongovernmental Organizations*, ed. Daniel A. Bell and Jean-Marc Coicaud (New York: Cambridge University Press, 2007), 204-17; Stephen Hopgood, *Keepers of the Flame: Understanding Amnesty International* (Ithaca: Cornell University Press, 2006); Edy Kaufman, "Prisoners of Conscience: The Shaping of a New Human Rights Concept," *Human Rights Quarterly* 13, 3 (1991): 339-67; Korey, *NGOs and the Universal Declaration of Human Rights*, 159-80; Jonathan Power, *Like Water on Stone: The Story of Amnesty International* (Boston: Northeastern University Press, 2001); Ramesh Thakur, "Human Rights: Amnesty International and the United Nations," *Journal of Peace Research* 31, 2 (1994): 143-60; Claude E. Welch Jr., "Amnesty International and Human Rights Watch: A Comparison," in *NGOs and Human Rights: Promise and Performance*, ed. Claude E. Welch Jr. (Philadelphia: University of Pennsylvania Press, 2001), 85-118; and Morton E. Winston, "Assessing the Effectiveness of International Human Rights NGOs," in *NGOs and Human Rights: Promise and Performance*, ed. Claude E. Welch Jr. (Philadelphia: University of Pennsylvania Press, 2001), 25-54.

48 Bobbio, *The Age of Rights*, 11.

CHAPTER 1: MY BROTHER'S KEEPER

1 Its membership consisted of the Church of England in Canada, the United Baptist Convention of Maritime Provinces, the Baptist Convention of Ontario and Quebec, the Western Baptist Union, the Churches of Christ (Disciples), the Evangelical Church, the Presbyterian Church in Canada, the United Church of Canada, the Salvation Army, and the Society of Friends. Affiliated members included the National Council YWCA, the Student Christian Movement, and the National Council YMCA; also in attendance were delegates from the WCC Canadian Committee, the Christian Social Council of Canada, the Religious Education Council of Canada, and, informally, the Secretaries of the Mission Boards, Canadian Council of Churches. *Record of Proceedings of the First Meeting of the Canadian Council of Churches* [hereafter *Record of Proceedings of the First Meeting*], Yorkminster Baptist Church, Toronto, 26-28 September 1944, 39, Library and Archives Canada (LAC), MG28-I327, vol. 1, file 1, "Annual Meetings – Minutes, 1944-1947."

2 See C.B. Lumsden, "The Church and the Problem of Peace," in *Record of Proceedings of the First Meeting*, 86. See also E.A. Dale and W.J. Gallagher, "Commission on Peace and Reconstruction," in *Record of Proceedings of the Second Meeting*, St. Paul's Avenue Road, United Church, Toronto, 25-27 September 1945, 84, 107, LAC, MG28-I327, vol. 1, file 1, "Annual Meetings – Minutes, 1944-1947"; and W.J. Gallagher, "The

World Council of Churches Canadian Committee," in *Record of Proceedings of the First Meeting*, 52.

3 At the time, much of the international community shared this view. The Preamble to the 1951 UN *Convention Relating to the Status of Refugees* states, "*expressing* the wish that all States, recognizing the social and humanitarian nature of the problem of refugees, will do everything within their power to prevent this problem from becoming a cause of tension between States." *Convention Relating to the Status of Refugees*, Adopted 28 July 1951 by the UN Conference of Plenipotentiaries on the Status of Refugees and Stateless Persons Convened under General Assembly Resolution 429(V), 14 December 1950.

4 Gerald E. Dirks, "Canada and Immigration: International and Domestic Considerations in the Decade Preceding the 1956 Hungarian Exodus," in *Breaking Ground: The 1956 Hungarian Refugee Movement to Canada*, ed. Robert H. Keyserlingk (Toronto: York Lanes Press, 1993), 6.

5 Fred Poulton, "Committee on Immigration of Refugees: A Report to the Churches," October 1953, 4, LAC, MG28-I327, vol. 1, file 3, "Biennial Meetings – Minutes, 1954, 1956, 1958."

6 For a history of Canada's response to the crisis in Hungary, see Robert H. Keyserlingk, ed., *Breaking Ground: The 1956 Hungarian Refugee Movement to Canada* (Toronto: York Lanes Press, 1993).

7 J.W. Pickersgill, *Seeing Canada Whole: A Memoir* (Markham, ON: Fitzhenry and Whiteside, 1994), 436. See also Donald H. Avery, *Reluctant Host: Canada's Response to Immigrant Workers, 1896-1994* (Toronto: McClelland and Stewart, 1995), 174.

8 Other groups that assisted with the resettlement effort included the Canadian Catholic Conference, the Canadian Rural Settlement Society, the Canadian Jewish Congress, the Canadian Red Cross, the Canadian Hungarian Relief Committee, the Canadian Hungarian Protestant Ministerial Association, the Canadian Christian Council for the Rehabilitation of Refugees, the Canadian Welfare Council, and the Jewish Immigrant Aid Society. LAC, RG 26, vol. 117, file 3-24-34-1, vol. 1, "Meeting respecting Hungarian refugees," 27 November 1956, 1. See also Canadian Council of Churches, "Minutes of Immigration Conference," Ottawa, 19 March 1957, 2, LAC, MG28-I327, vol. 37, file 8, "Department of Ecumenical Affairs – Minutes, 1954-1964." See also Dirks, "Canada and Immigration," 9-10.

9 In 1957, the WCC was able to resettle 26,205 Hungarian refugees, of which roughly 20 percent came to Canada. Canadian Council of Churches, "Minutes of the Committee on Immigration of Refugees," 12 December 1957, 2. LAC, MG28-I327, vol. 37, file 8, "Department of Ecumenical Affairs – Minutes, 1954-1964." See also Canadian Council of Churches, "Memorandum of Interview with the Deputy Minister of Immigration," Ottawa, 13 December 1956, in "Department of Ecumenical Affairs – Minutes, 1954-1964." For an account of the CCC's contributions to the resettlement effort during the Hungarian refugee crisis, see Andrew S. Thompson and Stephanie Bangarth, "Transnational Christian Charity: The Canadian Council of Churches, the World Council of Churches, and the Hungarian Refugee Crisis, 1956-1957," *American Review of Canadian Studies* 38, 3 (2008): 295-316.

Notes to pages 18-20

10 In 1950 and 1952, the CCC passed resolutions to call on the federal government to make special arrangements for accepting British immigrants in addition to accepting refugees from Europe. See Canadian Council of Churches, "Resolution on British Immigration," in *Record of Proceedings, 7th Meeting of the Canadian Council of Churches*, Park Road Baptist Church, Toronto, 14-17 November 1950, 18; and Canadian Council of Churches, "Resolution on Immigration," in *Record of Proceedings, 9th Meeting of the Canadian Council of Churches*, Dundas Street Centre United Church, London, ON, 11-14 November 1952, 69, LAC, MG28-I327, vol. 1, file 2, "Annual Meetings – Minutes, 1948-1952."
11 Freda Hawkins argues that the program, operational from 1953 to 1958, was a "major concession" by the Canadian government in order to secure their participation in the resettlement process. Freda Hawkins, *Canada and Immigration: Public Policy and Public Concern* (Montreal/Kingston: McGill-Queen's University Press, 1972), 305.
12 World Council of Churches Central Committee, "General Statement on the Refugee Problem," Toronto, July 1950, 1, LAC, MG28-I327, vol. 37, file 7, "Department of Ecumenical Affairs – Minutes, 1950-1953." See also Canadian Council of Churches, "Notes on Immigration Conference," in "Department of Ecumenical Affairs – Minutes, 1950-1953."
13 Hawkins, *Canada and Immigration*, 306-7.
14 Gerald E. Dirks, "A Policy within a Policy: The Identification and Admission of Refugees to Canada," *Canadian Journal of Political Science* 17, 2 (1984): 280.
15 Canada, *White Paper on Immigration* (Ottawa: Queen's Printer, 1966), 6, 23.
16 Bill C-220, *The Immigration Appeal Board Act*, was passed on 1 March 1967. The minister of manpower and immigration and the solicitor general could intervene by "jointly presenting the Board with certification that the national interest requires the execution of a deportation order." See Canada, Department of Manpower and Immigration, *Annual Report, 1966-1967* (Ottawa: Government of Canada, 1967), 21. In the midst of these reforms, the Canadian government continued to respond with generosity to refugee crises around the world, albeit still on an *ad hoc* basis. In response to the Soviet invasion of Czechoslovakia on 20 August 1968 to put down the anti-communist uprisings that came to be known as the "Prague Spring," Canada accepted more than 11,000 Czechoslovakian exiles.
17 In October 1972, it did accept 7,000 Ugandans of Asian descent (who were not technically *Convention* refugees because they still resided within Uganda at the time of the crisis) following the Idi Amin regime's declaration that it intended to expel them from the country. Canadian Council of Churches, "Historical Precedents of Canadian Assistance to Foreign Refugees," Toronto, 1973, 2, LAC, MG28-I327, vol. 186, file 3, "Delegation to Ottawa, 3 October 1974 and 26 March 1974, Notes, Reports, Clippings, Memoranda, Correspondence, House of Commons Debates, Reprints, 1968-1974."
18 Christopher J. Wydrzynski, *Canadian Immigration Law and Procedure* (Aurora, ON: Canada Law Book, 1983), 59-63.
19 *Immigration Appeal Board Act*, S.C. 1966-67, c. 90, s. 15.
20 Wydrzynski, *Canadian Immigration Law and Procedure*, 63.

21 Gerald E. Dirks, *Canada's Refugee Policy: Indifference or Opportunism?* (Montreal/Kingston: McGill-Queen's University Press, 1977), 9.
22 *Hansard,* 21 January 1977, 7873. This was not a new concern. John Diefenbaker's Progressive Conservatives had earlier refused calls from the UN High Commissioner for Refugees to adopt the terms of the 1951 *Convention,* preferring instead to relax its selection criteria to permit certain unsponsored refugees from Europe who were healthy and capable of finding employment to seek entry into Canada.
23 Section 2 of the proposed *Immigration Act, 1976,* referred specifically to the refugee definition found in the *Convention* – anyone outside his or her country of origin with a well-founded fear that he or she will be persecuted "for the reasons of race, religion, nationality, membership in a particular social group or political opinion" if returned – but did not call for anything beyond this definition, despite its relatively limited scope. Sections 6(2), 115(1)(d) and (e), and 115(2) of the *Immigration Act, 1976,* allow the minister to make special allowances to admit internally displaced persons who fall outside the *Convention* definition. *Immigration Act,* S.C. 1976, c. 52, s. 46.
24 Christopher J. Wydrzynski, "Refugees and the Immigration Act," *McGill Law Journal* 25, 2 (1979): 156.
25 Dirks has argued that the *Immigration Act, 1976,* "established a process that most officials considered both judicious and administratively manageable, with appropriate appeal procedures for claims ruled invalid." The problem, however, was that "they did not anticipate large numbers availing themselves of the machinery." Gerald E. Dirks, *Controversy and Complexity: Canadian Immigration Policy during the 1980s* (Montreal/Kingston: McGill-Queen's University Press, 1995), 78-79.
26 Section 45 of the *Immigration Act, 1976,* states:

> (1) Where, at any time during an inquiry, the person who is subject of the inquiry claims that he is a Convention refugee, the inquiry shall be continued and, if it is determined that, but for the person's claim that he is a Convention refugee, a removal order or a departure notice would be made or issued with respect to that person, the inquiry shall be adjourned and that person shall be examined under oath by a senior immigration officer respecting his claim. (2) When a person who claims that he is a Convention refugee is examined under oath pursuant to subsection (1), his claim, together with a transcript of the examination with respect thereto, shall be referred to the Minister for determination. (3) A copy of the transcript of an examination under oath referred to in subsection (1) shall be forwarded to the person who claims that he is a Convention refugee. (4) Where a person's claim is referred to the Minister pursuant to subsection (2), the Minister shall refer the claim and the transcript of the examination under oath with respect thereto to the Refugee Status Advisory Committee established pursuant to section 48 for consideration and, after having obtained the advice of that Committee, shall determine whether or not the person is a Convention refugee. (5) When the Minister makes a determination with respect to a person's claim that he is a Convention refugee, the Minister shall thereupon in writing inform the senior immigration officer who conducted the examination under oath respecting the claim and the

person who claimed to be a Convention refugee of his determination. (6) Every person with respect to whom an examination under oath is to be held pursuant to subsection (1) shall be informed that he has the right to obtain the services of a barrister or solicitor or other counsel and to be represented by any such counsel at his examination and shall be given a reasonable opportunity, if he so desires and at his own expense, to obtain such counsel.

27 Section 4(2) of the *Immigration Act, 1976*, states:

Subject to any other Act of Parliament, a Canadian citizen, a permanent resident and a Convention refugee while lawfully in Canada have a right to remain in Canada except where (b) in the case of a Convention refugee, it is established that that person is a person described in paragraph 19 (1)(c), (d), (e), (f), or (g) or 27 (1)(c) or (d) or 27 (2)(c) or a person who has been convicted of an offence under any Act of Parliament for which a term of imprisonment of (i) more than six months has been imposed, or (ii) five years or more may be imposed.

28 Section 70 of the *Immigration Act, 1976*, states:

(1) A person who claims to be a Convention refugee and has been informed in writing by the Minister pursuant to subsection 45(5) that he is not a Convention refugee may, within such a period of time as is prescribed, make an application to the Board for the re-determination of his claim that he is a Convention refugee. (2) Where an application is made to the Board pursuant to subsection (1), the application shall be accompanied by a copy of the transcript of the examination under oath referred to in subsection 45(1) and shall contain or be accompanied by a declaration of the applicant under oath setting out (a) the nature of the basis of the application; (b) a statement in reasonable detail of the facts on which the application is based; (c) a summary in reasonable detail of the information and evidence intended to be offered at the hearing; and (d) such other representations as the applicant deems relevant to the application.

Section 71 states:

(1) Where the Board receives an application referred to in subsection 70(2), it shall forthwith consider the application and if, on the basis of such consideration, it is of the opinion that there are reasonable grounds to believe that a claim could, upon the hearing of the application, be established, it shall allow the application to proceed, and in any other case it shall refuse to allow the application to proceed and shall thereupon determine that the person is not a Convention refugee. (2) Where pursuant to subsection (1) the Board allows an application to proceed, it shall notify the Minister of the time and place where the application is to be heard and afford the Minister a reasonable opportunity to be heard. (3) Where the Board has made its determination as to whether or not a person is a Convention refugee, it shall, in writing, inform the Minister and the applicant of its decision. (4) The Board may, and at the request of the applicant or the Minister shall, give reasons for its determination.

Section 84 states:

> An appeal lies to the Federal Court of Appeal on any question of law, including questions of jurisdiction, from a decision of a Board on an appeal under this Act if leave to appeal is granted by that Court based on an application for leave to appeal filed with that Court within fifteen days after the day on which the decision appealed is pronounced, or within such extended time as a judge of that Court may, for special reasons, allow.

29 Wydrzynski, "Refugees," 163.
30 Section 72(2)(d), *Immigration Act, 1976*. See also W. Gunther Plaut, *Refugee Determination in Canada: Proposal for a New System, Report to the Honourable Flora MacDonald, Minister of Employment and Immigration* (Ottawa: Government of Canada, 1985), 28.
31 Dorothy Lipovenko, "Ottawa to Probe 75,000 Suspected of Being Aliens," *Globe and Mail*, 18 May 1984, M1.
32 Plaut, *Refugee Determination in Canada*, 26, 39, 45.
33 The "radical seventies" was the theme of the CCC's triennial meeting in 1969. See T.E. Floyd Honey, "Report of the General Secretary," in *Record of Proceedings*, Count Us In! Christians in the Radical Seventies, CCC First Triennial Assembly, Montreal, 24-28 November 1969, 7, LAC, MG28-I327, vol. 2, file 1, "Triennial Meetings – Minutes, 1969, 1972." See also Robert Bothwell, Ian Drummond, and John English, *Canada since 1945*, rev. ed. (Toronto: University of Toronto Press, 1989), 246.
34 Many of Canada's Protestant churches had approved of the federal government's swift decision to accept Czechoslovakian refugees in 1968 and Ugandans in 1972 yet were troubled by Trudeau's apparent ambivalence to the civil war in Nigeria over Biafran secession of the late 1960s. Indeed, the Nigerian/Biafran civil war caused considerable tension between the CCC and the Trudeau government. In hindsight, neither one handled the situation well. At times throughout the crisis, Trudeau seemed to be insensitive and uncaring. When asked about the conflict by reporters, his response was "where's Biafra?" which, according to Mitchell Sharp, did not go over well with those concerned about the situation. For its part, the CCC was swept up by the stories of mass starvation, most of which were part of an exaggerated propaganda campaign. The council was upset at Trudeau's refusal to direct Canadian relief aid to the Biafran refugees through the International Committee of the Red Cross (ICRC) and put little stock in the Canadian government's explanation that it could not "recognize a rebellion." To make matters worse, Trudeau later accused the CCC and WCC of co-operating with the ICRC "only when it suits them," a statement that caused considerable displeasure among CCC officials. See Mitchell Sharp, *Which Reminds Me ... A Memoir* (Toronto: University of Toronto Press, 1994), 207-8. See also World Council of Churches, "World Council of Churches General Secretary Reacts to Nigeria's U.N. Permanent Representative's Statement," Press Release No. 44-68, Geneva, 20 November 1968, LAC, MG28-I327, vol. 143, file 15, "GSO, WCC – Nigeria/Biafra (2), 1968-1969"; CCC Central Committee, "Report of Delegation to Ottawa re: Nigeria/Biafra," Ottawa, 14 February 1969, LAC, MG28-I327, vol. 143,

file 15, "GSO, WCC – Nigeria/Biafra (2), 1968-1969"; and Mitchell Sharp, "Statements and Speeches: The Conflict in Nigeria," No. 68/20, 26 November 1968, 2, LAC, MG28-I327, vol. 143, file 15, "GSO, WCC – Nigeria/Biafra (2), 1968-1969." See also Aaron Tolen, "Nigeria: The Basis of the Problem," *Christian Peace Conference*, Prague, 28 March 1969, 5, in LAC, MG28-I327, vol. 143, file 15, "GSO, WCC – Nigeria/Biafra (2), 1968-1969"; and Denis Smith, "Biafra: A Case against Trudeau's View," *Globe and Mail*, 30 October 1968, 7. See also C. Michael Lanphier, "Canada's Response to Refugees," *International Migration Review* 15, 1-2 (1981): 114-15; and Rhoda Howard, "The Canadian Government Response to Africa's Refugee Crisis," *Canadian Journal of African Studies* 15, 1 (1981): 105.

35 Bill Fairburn, "The Inter-Church Committee on Human Rights in Latin America," in *Coalitions for Justice*, ed. Christopher Lind and Joe Mihevc (Ottawa: Novalis, 1994), 169-72.

36 Ross, who during the coup referred to the human rights abuses committed by the junta as "all too reminiscent of Nazi methods," supported Salvador Allende's overthrow, believing that the military rule in Chile would be short-lived. The cables sent back and forth between Santiago and Ottawa were later leaked to the press and subsequently republished by the Latin American Working Group Chile-Canada Solidarity. See Andrew Ross, "Confidential Cable" 563 Sep24/73, Santiago, Chile, LAC, MG28-I327, vol. 186, file 1, "Documentation – Briefs, Reports, Memoranda, Newsletters, Correspondence, Reprints, Addresses, Publications, 1973-1974."

37 Robert Andras, Minister of Manpower and Immigration, "Letter to Reverend T.E. Floyd Honey," Ottawa, 7 February 1974, LAC, MG28-I327, vol. 185, file 14, "GSO, Chile – Information re: Refugees, 1974." See also J.W. Foster, United Church of Canada, "Notes on Consultation Held between the Minister of External Affairs, Mr. Mitchell Sharp, and a Delegation of Canadian Churchmen," Ottawa, 3 October 1973, 2, LAC, MG28-I327, vol. 185, file 14, "GSO, Chile – Information re: Refugees, 1974."

38 Canada, Department of Manpower and Immigration, *Annual Report, 1975-1976* (Ottawa: Government of Canada, 1976), 20.

39 Dirks, *Canada's Refugee Policy*, 258. Reg Whitaker argues that the Chilean refugee crisis revealed that "red and even shades of pink were still like the proverbial flag to the bull of the Ottawa security establishment and, it seemed, to the Trudeau government as a whole." Reg Whitaker, *Double Standard: The Secret History of Canadian Immigration* (Toronto: Lester and Orpen Dennys, 1987), 255. See also Rhoda Howard, "Contemporary Canadian Refugee Policy: A Critical Assessment," *Canadian Public Policy* 6, 2 (1980): 361-73.

40 Henriette Thompson, "The Inter-Church Committee for Refugees," in *Coalitions for Justice*, ed. Christopher Lind and Joe Mihevc (Ottawa: Novalis, 1994), 209.

41 Kathleen Ptolemy, "From Oppression to Promise: Journeying Together with the Refugee," in *Canadian Churches and Foreign Policy*, ed. Bonnie Greene (Toronto: James Lorimer, 1990), 145.

42 Dirks, "A Policy within a Policy," 291-92.

43 The members of the coalition were the Reverend Don Anderson, general secretary of the CCC and later founder of the Refugee Concerns Project; George Cram, Anglican

Church of Canada, chairman of the Inter-Church Committee on Human Rights in Latin America; Bernard Daly, Canadian Catholic Conference of Bishops; Bishop A. Proulx, Human Rights Commission of the Catholic Conference of Bishops and member of the Inter-Church Committee on Human Rights in Latin America; Elizabeth Loweth, Human Rights, United Church of Canada; Pierre Golberger, Église Unie du Canada and Comité Chrétien pour les Droits Humains en Amérique Latine; Jeanne Boisclair, Comité Chrétien; Dick Gathercole, professor, Faculty of Law, University of Toronto; Ian Morrison, law student, Toronto Community Assistance Services; Lorne Waldman, lawyer, Toronto; Taivi Lobu, Parkdale Community Legal Services; Thea Herman, Toronto Community Legal Assistance Services; Giuseppe Sciortino, lawyer, Montreal; Susan Devine, Legal Aid Services Society of Manitoba; Noel Sainte-Pierre, Services d'Aides aux Neo-Québécoise et Imigrants et Comité Chrétien; Dr. F. Allodi, psychiatrist, Toronto Western Hospital; Noel Gates, chairperson, Executive Committee, Amnesty International Canadian Section (English Speaking); Don Lee, Human Rights, Ontario Federation of Labour; and Charles Brabazon, Canadian Federation of Civil Liberties and Human Rights Association.

44 See Delegation of Concerned Church, Legal, Medical, Labour, and Humanitarian Organizations, "Recommended Changes in Canada's Refugee Status Determination Procedures: A Brief to the Honourable Bud Cullen," Ottawa, 13 March 1979, 8-10, Supreme Court Records Office, file nos. 18209, 17997, 17952, 17898, 18207, 18235, 17904.
45 *Ibid.*, 3, 7, 9.
46 *Ibid.*, 3, 6, 10, 11.
47 *Ibid.*, 17.
48 Delegation of Concerned Church, Legal, Medical, Labour, and Humanitarian Organizations, "The Refugee Determination Process: A Brief to the Honourable Lloyd Axworthy, Minister of Employment and Immigration," Ottawa, 9 May 1980, A14, Supreme Court Records Office, file nos. 18209, 17997, 17952, 17898, 18207, 18235, 17904.
49 Ptolemy, "From Oppression to Promise," 156.
50 W.G. Robinson, *The Refugee Status Determination Process: A Report of the Task Force on Immigration Practices and Procedures to the Honourable Lloyd Axworthy* (Ottawa: Government of Canada, 1982), 99.
51 *Hansard*, 2 May 1983, 25049.
52 Howard Adelman, "Canadian Refugee Policy in the Postwar Period: An Analysis," in *Refugee Policy: Canada and the United States*, ed. Howard Adelman (Toronto: York Lanes Press, 1991), 205-6.
53 Delegation of Concerned Church, Legal, Medical, Labour, and Humanitarian Organizations, "Recommendations for Changes in Canada's Refugee Status Determination Procedures: A Brief to the Honourable Lloyd Axworthy, MEI," December 1983, 4-4, Supreme Court Records Office, file nos. 18209, 17997, 17952, 17898, 18207, 18235, 17904.
54 Charles M. Campbell, *Betrayal and Deceit: The Politics of Canadian Immigration* (Vancouver: Jasmine Books, 2000), 71.
55 *Ibid.*, 72.

56 Ed Ratushny, *A New Refugee Status Determination Process for Canada: A Report to the Honourable John Roberts* (Ottawa: Government of Canada, 1983).
57 W. Gunther Plaut, *Asylum: A Moral Dilemma* (Westport, CT: Praeger, 1995), 19. See also Howard Adelman, "Rabbi W. Gunther Plaut's Contribution to Canadian Refugee Law and Practice," in *A Rabbi of Words and Deeds: Essays in Honour of the 90th Birthday of W. Gunther Plaut*, ed. John Moscowitz and Natalie Fingerhut (Toronto: Holy Blossom Temple, 2002), 69.
58 Campbell, *Betrayal and Deceit*, 72-73.
59 *Singh et al. v. Minister of Employment and Immigration [Singh]*, [1985] 1 S.C.R. 177.
60 Thompson, "The Inter-Church Committee for Refugees," 215.
61 The Federation of Canadian Sikh Societies was established in the early 1980s. Its members included Sri Guru Ravi Das Sabha, Nanaksar Isher Darbar Gursikh Temple of Toronto, the Sikh Youths Association of Scarborough, Khalsa Diwan Society of Vancouver, Sri Guru Singh Sabha of Toronto, Shrumani Sikh Society of Toronto, Sri Guru Singh Sabha Canada, Hindu Prarthana Samaj of Toronto, Sikh Sangat of Hamilton, the Golden Triangle Sikh Association of Waterloo, Ontario Khalsa Darbar Inc., the Sikh Association of Brantford, Sri Guru Singh Sabha of Waterloo County, and Sikh Association of Guelph. At the time, the federation represented approximately 72,300 Canadians of Sikh origin. Supreme Court Records Office, file nos. 18209, 17997, 17952, 17898, 18207, 18235, 17904.
62 Appellant's factum, *Singh*, 12.
63 Section 6(1) of the *Charter* states that "every citizen of Canada has the right to enter, remain in and leave Canada." *Canadian Charter of Rights and Freedoms*, Part I of the *Constitution Act, 1982*, being Schedule B to the *Canada Act 1982* (U.K.), 1982, c. 11.
64 Respondent's Factum, *Singh*, 13-14.
65 *Ibid.*, 20.
66 *Ibid.*, 23.
67 Intervener's Factum, *Singh*, 14.
68 *Ibid.*, 18. The cases that Jackman was referring to were *Re Hanna* (1957), 8 D.L.R. (2d) 566; and *Chan v. McFarlane*, [1962] O.R. 798 (C.A.).
69 Intervener's Factum, Singh, 22.
70 Appellant's Factum, *Singh*, 26.
71 Article 32(1) of the UN *Convention Relating to the Status of Refugees* states that "the Contracting States shall not expel a refugee lawfully in their territory save on grounds of national security or public order."

Article 33(1) prohibits the refoulement of any refugee: "No Contracting State shall expel or return *('refouler')* a refugee in any manner whatsoever to the frontiers of territories where his life or freedom would be threatened on account of his race, religion, nationality, membership of a particular social group or political opinion." Section 55 of the *Immigration Act, 1976*, states that "notwithstanding subsections 54(2) and (3), a Convention refugee shall not be removed from Canada to a country where his life or freedom would be threatened on account of his race, religion, nationality, membership in a particular social group or political opinion."
72 Intervener's Factum, *Singh*, 31.
73 *Ibid.*, 41-42.

74 Section 2(e) of the *Canadian Bill of Rights* states, "deprive a person of the right to a fair hearing in accordance with the principles of fundamental justice for the determination of his rights and obligations." *Canadian Bill of Rights* (1960, c. 44)
75 Scott argued that section 71(1) should be shortened to read "where the Board receives an application referred to in subsection 70(2), it shall forthwith consider the application." The result of such a change would be that all claimants would receive an oral hearing before the IAB. Appellants' Submission with Respect to the *Canadian Bill of Rights, Singh*, 19-20.
76 Intervenor's Submission with Respect to the *Canadian Bill of Rights, Singh*, 9.
77 Section 26 of the *Charter*, which states that "the guarantee in this Charter of certain rights and freedoms shall not be construed as denying the existence of any other rights or freedoms that exist in Canada," gives weight to the contention that the *Bill of Rights* had constitutional relevance to *Singh*.
78 Submissions of the Attorney General of Canada with Respect to the *Canadian Bill of Rights, Singh*, 2-10, 13.
79 Judgment, *Singh*, 207. Wilson also accepted Jackman's argument that distinguishing between those who make their claim once in Canada and those who make it at a port of entry encouraged abuse of the system. *Ibid.*, 211.
80 *Ibid.*, 218.
81 *Ibid.*, 231.
82 *Ibid.*, 235-36.
83 MacDonald tabled the report in the House of Commons on 17 June 1985.
84 Plaut, *Refugee Determination in Canada*, 109.
85 *Ibid.*, 119.
86 *Ibid.*, 34, 40, 83.
87 Victor Malarek, "Ottawa Won't Act on Portuguese Visas," *Globe and Mail*, 15 July 1986, A8.
88 Editorial Board, "Claims of Refuge," *Globe and Mail*, 5 January 1988, A6.
89 Victor Malarek, "Refugee Reform Proposals Criticized," *Globe and Mail*, 22 May 1986, A5.
90 Interview with Walter McLean, 24 August 2004; interview with Tom Clark, 17 June 2004.
91 Victor Malarek, *Haven's Gate: Canada's Immigration Fiasco* (Toronto: Macmillan, 1987), 74, 133, 142.
92 Susan Delacourt, "PM's Welcome to Castaways Hailed as Enlightened," *Globe and Mail*, 19 August 1986, A4.
93 John Douglas, "Lenient Refugee Policy Urged by Church Council," *Globe and Mail*, 25 August 1986, A13.
94 As Whitaker, *Double Standard*, 298, has argued, the proposed changes to the *Immigration Act, 1976*, "read as if the government [was] trying to roll back the implications of the Supreme Court *Charter* decision in the *Singh* case."
95 Sections 48.1(1)(a) and (b) of the *Immigration Act, 1976*, state the following:

> (1) A person who claims to be a Convention refugee is not eligible to have the claim determined by the Refugee Division if (a) the claimant has been recognized

by any country, other than Canada, as a Convention refugee and has been issued a valid and subsisting travel document by that country pursuant to Article 28 of the Convention; (b) the claimant came to Canada from a country that has been prescribed as a safe third country for all persons or for persons of a specified class of persons of which the claimant is a member and would be allowed to return to that country, if removed from Canada, or has a right to have the claim determined therein.

96 James C. Hathaway, "Selective Concern: An Overview of Refugee Law in Canada," *McGill Law Review* 33, 4 (1987-88): 708.
97 W. Gunther Plaut, "Bill Tilts Off Balance in Choosing Refugees," *Globe and Mail*, 25 June 1987.
98 *Hansard*, 18 June 1987, 7329.
99 Graham Fraser, "Seeking Refuge: Message Sent to World, Bouchard Says," *Globe and Mail*, 17 July 1987, A5. Sikh groups were outraged by the government's actions. They accused Ottawa of racism and questioned, albeit rhetorically, whether the reaction would have been the same had the ship been full of white Europeans. Deborah Wilson, "Detention Now 'Racism,' Sikh Leaders Charge," *Globe and Mail*, 17 July 1987, A5.
100 Section 2.1(b) and (c) of Bill C-84 state, "(b) to control widespread abuse of the procedures for determining refugee claims, particularly in light of organized incidents involving large-scale introduction of persons into Canada to take advantage of those procedures; and (c) to deter the smuggling of persons into Canada and thereby minimize the exploitation of and risks to persons seeking to come to Canada." *An Act to Amend the Immigration Act, 1976, and the Criminal Code in Consequence Thereof* [Bill C-84], 35-36-37 Elizabeth II, 1988, c. 36.
101 See Margaret Young, "Bill C-84: Emergency Bill to Deal with Refugee Claimants," Library of Parliament, Research Branch, Law and Government Division, 21 September 1987, 2-3.
102 Section 91.1, Bill C-84.
103 Young, "Bill C-84," 5.
104 Jean-Pierre Hocké, UN High Commissioner for Refugees, "Message to the Right Honourable Joe Clark, Secretary of State for External Affairs, and to the Right Honourable Benoît Bouchard, Minister of Employment and Immigration," 12 August 1987, 1. See also Benoît Bouchard, "Letter to Jean-Pierre Hocké, UN High Commissioner for Refugees," 18 August 1987, Appendix C in Young, "Bill C-84"; and "UN Fears Law Harms Refugees," *Globe and Mail*, 25 June 1987, A2.
105 *Hansard*, 14 August 1987, 8062.
106 Those representing the ICCR included Dr. Anne Squire, moderator of the United Church of Canada; Dr. Helga Kutz-Harder, Kathleen Ptolemy, and Dr. Fred Carruthers of the Anglican Church; Nancy Nichols, director of the Catholic Immigration Bureau; and Dr. Tony Clark of the Canadian Conference of Catholic Bishops. See House Minutes of Proceedings and Evidence of the Legislative Committee on Bill C-84, Bill C-84, vol. 1, 17 August 1987.
107 *Ibid.*, 61-62.

108 Those who appeared before the House committee on behalf of the ICCR were Dr. Helga Kutz-Herder, United Church of Canada; Nancy Nicholls, Catholic Immigration Bureau; Kathleen Ptolemy, Anglican Church; and Dr. Tom Clark, co-ordinator for the ICCR. House Minutes of Proceedings and Evidence of the Legislative Committee on Bill C-55, *An Act to Amend the Immigration Act, 1976, and to Amend Other Acts in Consequence Thereof* [Bill C-55], 35-36-37 Elizabeth II, 1988, c. 35. Others to appear before the committee on Bill C-55 included Amnesty International, B'nai Brith Canada, the Canadian Council for Refugees, Canada Employment and Immigration Union, the Canadian Ethnocultural Council, the Canadian Jewish Congress, the Coalition for a Just Immigration and Refugee Policy, the Department of Employment and Immigration, the Department of External Affairs, the Halifax Refugee Assistance Group, the Hispanic Congress, the Immigration Appeal Board, the International Air Transport Association, the Law Reform Commission of Canada, the Mennonite Central Committee, the Montreal Coalition, the Nanaimo Immigration Settlement Society and Reform Committee, the National Association of Women and the Law, Non-Governmental Groups Concerned with Immigration and Refugee Issues, the Refugee Status Advisory Committee, the Sikh Professional Association of Canada, the Task Force on Refugee Determination, the UN High Commission for Refugees, and the Vancouver Refugee Council. See the Legislative Committee on Bill C-55, Bill C-55, Index, 19 June 1985, 12.

109 ICCR delegates endorsed a proposal submitted by the Canadian Bar Association (at the time represented by Barbara Jackman) to amalgamate a number of the existing stages. Fearing that the new legislation failed to provide adequate safeguards against arbitrary decisions by senior immigration officers, it proposed an alternative two-step process. First, the senior immigration officer would be required to refer all refugee claimants to a "refugee status-determination hearing" involving a panel of two members from the refugee division. Included in this stage would be an oral hearing that would occur within the first ten days of arrival. Any negative decision would have to be made in writing. This, in turn, would lead to the second stage, which would involve an appeal to be carried out by a "specialized review body of the refugee division which [had] the power to require a hearing." In theory, the entire process would be completed within thirty days. *Ibid.*, 7-8, 53.

110 Although the opposition Liberals and NDP voted against it, only one Conservative MP, backbencher Fernand Jourdanais, broke party ranks and abstained from voting, citing for the record that his "conscience did not permit [him] to act otherwise." *Hansard*, 14 September 1987, 8928.

111 Jackman's assessment of the shortcomings of the new legislation was sweeping, and her aim was to see the entire determination process struck down. Scrutinizing ninety-one separate provisions of the new law, Jackman questioned the humaneness of a system that lacked procedural and substantive safeguards for refugee claimants at both the determination and the review stages as well as the virtues of a process that, among other things, discriminated against claimants based on the mode of arrival, relied on strict pre-screening measures to maintain efficiency, chanced refoulement by deporting claimants to safe third countries, and threatened to impose criminal sanctions on illegal smugglers and church workers alike should they be caught offering

assistance to aliens who lacked proper documentation. For the entire list of critiques, see Motion of Claim, *Canadian Council of Churches v. The Queen and the MEI*, Federal Court (Trial Division), 3 January 1989.

112 The decision to challenge the constitutionality of the new law was made in the autumn of 1988 at the urging of a number of member churches. See Ptolemy, "From Oppression to Promise," 158-59.
113 See Order of Mr. J. Rouleau, *Canadian Council of Churches v. Canada (Minister of Employment and Immigration)*, Federal Court, Trial Division, 26 April 1989.
114 *Ibid.*, 135.
115 The four points in Jackman's submission allowed to stand were point 3(c), which criticized sections 30(3) and 51(1)(b) of Bill C-55, which allowed designated counsel to represent a claimant without his or her consent; point 6(a), which took issue with sections 45(4) and 86(1)(b)(ii) of Bill C-55 and sections 20(2) and 23(4) of Bill C-84, which permitted the government to return any claimant coming from the United States to the United States without a hearing; point 10(a) covering section 51(1)(b) of Bill C-55, which allowed refugee claimants to be removed from Canada while their claims were pending in the courts; and point 14(c), which attacked section 51 of Bill C-55 for some of the potential criminal sanctions that church workers could face for assisting individuals in making a claim. Judgment, *Canadian Council of Churches v. Canada (Minister of Employment and Immigration)*, [1990] Federal Court of Appeal, A-223-89, 12 March 1990, 163, 164, 168.
116 In his factum to the court, John Tait, the deputy attorney general, offered a subtle yet compelling critique of the CCC and its arguments. He questioned the "seriousness" of any claim that found fault with an entire regulatory system using abstract and theoretical scenarios that were "premature, too remote and non-justiciable." Attacking the legitimacy of the CCC's standing with the court, he dismissed concerns about procedural failings or the lack of safeguards against refoulement that could arise as a result of the safe third country provisions. Tait argued that, since the federal government had not yet indicated which nations were listed as safe third countries, any fears that a claimant could eventually be returned to the country from which he or she was fleeing were speculative, and he suggested that the CCC should concern itself instead with "real" cases. Factum of the Respondents, *Canadian Council of Churches v. Canada (Minister of Employment and Immigration)*, [1992] 1 S.C.R. 236, 11.
117 Other interest groups that intervened in the case were the Coalition of Provincial Organizations of the Handicapped, Quebec Multi Ethnic Association for the Integration of Handicapped People, League for Human Rights of B'nai Brith Canada, Women's Legal Education and Action Fund, and Canadian Disability Rights Council.
118 *Canadian Council of Churches v. Canada (Minister of Employment and Immigration)*, [1992] 1 S.C.R. 236, 238, 254-55.
119 *Ibid.*, 252.
120 *Ibid.*, 237.
121 Prior to 1992, the refugee determination process involved two stages, the first to determine the credibility of the claim, the second to determine its validity. As Dirks

notes, since "95% of claims had passed through the first stage," Bill C-86 did away with it altogether. Dirks, *Controversy and Complexity,* 161.

122 James C. Hathaway and R. Alexander Neve, "Fundamental Justice and the Deflection of Refugees in Canada," *Osgoode Hall Law Journal* 34, 2 (1996): 230. Section 46.01(1) of the *Immigration Act* states that

> A person who claims to be a Convention refugee is not eligible to have the claim determined by the Refugee Division if the person (a) has been recognized as a Convention refugee by a country, other than Canada, that is a country to which the person can be returned; (b) came to Canada, directly or indirectly, from a country, other than a country of the person's nationality or, where the person has no country of nationality, the country of the person's habitual residence, that is a prescribed country under paragraph 114(1)(s).

According to section 114(8), cabinet had to consider the following criteria when determining whether another state could be prescribed as a "designated country":

> (a) Whether the country is a party to the Convention; (b) the country's policies and practices with respect to Convention refugee claims; (c) the country's record with respect to human rights; and (d) whether the country is a party to an agreement with Canada concerning the sharing of responsibility for examining refugee claims, notwithstanding that this factor is not a requirement for a country to be prescribed.

An Act to amend the Immigration Act and other Acts in consequence thereof, R.S. 1992, c. 49.

123 Section 53(1)(b) of Bill C-86 states:

> Notwithstanding subsections 52(2) and (3), no person who is determined under this Act or the regulations to be a Convention refugee, nor any person who has been determined to be not eligible to have a claim to be a Convention refugee determined by the Refugee Division on the basis that the person is a person described in paragraph 46.01(1)(a), shall be removed from Canada to a country where the person's life or freedom would be threatened for reasons of race, religion, nationality, membership in a particular social group or political opinion unless (b) the person is a member of an inadmissible class described in paragraph 19(1)(e), (f), (g), (j), (k) or (l) and the Minister is of the opinion that the person constitutes a danger to the security of Canada.

Section 19(1) states:

> (e) Persons who there are reasonable grounds to believe (iii) will engage in terrorism, or (iv) are members of an organization that there are reasonable grounds to believe will (C) engage in terrorism; (f) people who there are reasonable grounds to believe (ii) have engaged in terrorism, or (iii) are or were members of an organization that there are reasonable grounds to believe is or was engaged in (B) terrorism, except persons who have satisfied the Minister that their admission would not be detrimental to the national interest.

124 OAS Inter-American Commission on Human Rights, "Press Communiqué," No. 14/97, Washington, DC, 17 October 1997.
125 The report also found fault with the provisions in the *Immigration Act* that allowed for the prolonged detention of claimants (in some cases months) and did not allow for sufficient judicial review of the legality of the detention. Finally, it objected to measures that separated Canadian-born children from their alien parents and forced successful claimants to wait five years before their families could join them in Canada. OAS Inter-American Commission on Human Rights, "Report on the Situation of Human Rights of Asylum Seekers within the Canadian Refugee Determination System," OEA/Ser.L/V/II.106 Doc. 40 rev., Washington, DC, 28 February 2000, paras. 70, 73, 76,, 105, 110, 122, 142, 154.
126 Section 110 of the *Immigration and Refugee Protection Act* states:

> (1) A person or the Minister may appeal, in accordance with the rules of the Board on a question of law, of fact or of mixed law and fact, to the Refugee Appeal Division against a decision of the Refugee Protection Division to allow or reject the person's claim for refugee protection, or a decision of the Refugee Protection Division rejecting an application by the Minister for a determination that refugee protection has ceased or an application by the Minister to vacate a decision to allow a claim for refugee protection.

Immigration and Refugee Protection Act [Bill C-11] (2001, c. 27). See also Inter-Church Committee for Refugees, "Letter to Certain Senators for Hearings on Bill C-11, March 30, 2001," http://www.web.net/~iccr/docs/.
127 Michael Bossin, "Bill C-31: Limited Access to Refugee Determination and Protection," *Refuge* 19, 4 (2001): 55. Section 115(2) of Bill C-11 makes an exception to the principle of non-refoulement for any person

> (a) who is inadmissible on grounds of serious criminality and who constitutes, in the opinion of the Minister, a danger to the public in Canada; or (b) who is inadmissible on grounds of security, violating human or international rights or organized criminality if, in the opinion of the Minister, the person should not be allowed to remain in Canada on the basis of the nature and severity of acts committed or of danger to the security of Canada.

128 ICCR, "Letter to Certain Senators."
129 ICCR, "Two Changes to Bill C11," Brief for the Standing Committee on Citizenship and Immigration Hearing, Ottawa, 4 April 2001.
130 Canada, Department of Citizenship and Immigration, "Refugee Appeal Division Implementation Delayed," news release, Ottawa, 29 April 2002. Shortly after the attacks of 9/11, Howard Adelman argued that the threat of terrorism, though serious, had provided the Canadian government with the "cover" it needed to pass legislation that would serve its larger interest in restricting "the entry of claimants coming to Canada." Howard Adelman, "Refugee and Border Security Post-September 11," *Refuge* 20, 4 (2002): 11. For a similar argument, see Reg Whitaker, "Refugee Policy after September 11: Not Much New," *Refuge* 20, 4 (2002): 29-33; Michelle Lowry, "Creating Human Insecurity: The National Security Focus in Canada's Immigration System,"

Refuge 21, 1 (2002): 28-40; and Anna Pratt, *Securing Borders: Detention and Deportation in Canada* (Vancouver: UBC Press, 2005).
131 Canada, Department of Citizenship and Immigration, "Safe Third Country Agreement: Proposed Regulations Pre-Published," news release, Ottawa, 25 October 2002, http://www.cic.gc.ca/.
132 Adelman, "Canadian Refugee Policy in the Postwar Period," 208.
133 David Matas and Ilana Simon, *Closing the Doors: The Failure of Refugee Protection* (Toronto: Summerhill Press, 1989), 124, 126.
134 Michael Mandel, *The Charter of Rights and Freedoms and the Legalization of Politics in Canada* (Toronto: Wall and Thompson, 1989), 183.
135 Jeffrey Simpson, "Suckers for a Sob Story," *Globe and Mail*, 22 November 2003, A25. See also Jeffrey Simpson, "Can Paul Martin Do the Right Thing?" *Globe and Mail*, 4 December 2003, A23.
136 F.L. Morton and Rainer Knopff, *Charter Politics* (Toronto: Nelson Canada, 1992), 23; see also Peter H. Russell, *The Judiciary in Canada: The Third Branch of Government* (Toronto: McGraw-Hill Ryerson, 1987), 359.
137 Daniel Stoffman, *Who Gets In: What's Wrong with Canada's Immigration Program – and How to Fix It* (Toronto: Macfarlane Walter and Ross, 2002), 7, 10, 48-75, 161.
138 Other cases involving procedural fairness that the CCC has intervened in include *Baker v. Canada (Minister of Citizenship and Immigration)*, [1999] 2 S.C.R. 817; and *Chieu v. Canada (Minister of Citizenship and Immigration)*, [2002] 1 S.C.R. 84, 2002 SCC 3.
139 *Suresh v. Minister (Citizenship and Immigration)*, [2002] 1 S.C.R. 3.
140 *Ibid.*, para. 2.
141 *Ibid.*, para. 16.
142 The other interveners in the case were the United Nations High Commissioner for Refugees, Amnesty International, the Canadian Arab Federation, the Canadian Council for Refugees, the Federation of Associations of Canadian Tamils, the Centre for Constitutional Rights, the Canadian Bar Association, and the Canadian Council of Churches. David Matas represented the Canadian Bar Association; Audrey Macklin of the University of Toronto represented the Canadian Arab Federation and the Canadian Council for Refugees; and Michael Battista and Michael Bossin represented Amnesty International.
143 *Ibid.*, para. 129.
144 That same day the court handed out a second ruling, this time in the case of an Iranian by the name of Mansour Ahani (who had also been represented by Jackman), who was believed to be an assassin with the Iranian Ministry of Intelligence and Security. Although Ahani argued that he would be persecuted if returned to Iran, the Supreme Court ruled that Ahani, who had been allowed to respond to the case against him, had been granted procedural fairness since he had not made a *prima facie* case to the minister that he would be tortured if returned to Iran, as was required by *Suresh*. From there, the court sided with the federal government, agreeing with its conclusion that "the serious risk to Canadian security was outweighed against the minimal risk of harm to Ahani if returned to Iran." *Ahani v. Canada*

(Minister of Citizenship and Immigration), [2002] 1 S.C.R. 72, para. 20. Audrey Macklin, who participated in *Suresh*, has been critical of the interveners in *Suresh* for not pursuing similar interventions in Ahani's defence. Audrey Macklin, "Mr. Suresh and the Evil Twin," *Refuge* 20, 4 (2002): 15-22.
145 "The Church as Sanctuary," *CBC News Online*, 14 February 2005, http://www.cbc.ca/news/background/immigration/sanctuary.html.
146 Canadian Council for Refugees, "Safe Third Country Decision Welcomed by Rights Organizations and John Doe," news release, 30 November 2007.
147 Howard Adelman, "An Immigration Dream: Hungarian Refugees Come to Canada – An Analysis," in *Breaking Ground: The 1956 Hungarian Refugee Movement to Canada*, ed. Robert H. Keyserlingk (Toronto: York Lanes Press, 1993), 30.
148 Dirks, "A Policy within a Policy," 306.

CHAPTER 2: THE "MISUSE" OF FREEDOM?

1 In 1934, the CJC joined forces with the Anti-Defamation League of B'nai Brith to form the National Joint Public Relations Committee (NJPRC, later renamed the Joint Community Relations Committee). One purpose of the NJPRC was to co-ordinate the many voices of Canada's Jewish community, especially on issues involving antisemitism. Canadian Jewish Congress, *Fifty Years of Service, 1919-1969* (Montreal: CJC, 1970), 46.
2 Irving Abella and Harold Troper, *None Is Too Many: Canada and the Jews of Europe, 1933-1948* (Toronto: Lester and Orpen Dennys, 1982), 10.
3 Arnold Ages has argued that antisemitism in its most "diabolical" form "sees Jews not as human beings suffering from the foibles that characterize men and women in their weaknesses but as agents of an international conspiracy, as bacteriological pollutants allied with unnamed sinister forces to dominate the world," and that "only for a brief time in the 1930s was there a lapse into the more virulent phase, occasioned by the spread of fascist ideology and the general economic and political turbulence of that period." Arnold Ages, "Antisemitism: The Uneasy Calm," in *The Canadian Jewish Mosaic*, ed. M. Weinfeld, W. Shaffir, and I. Cotler (Toronto: John Wiley and Sons, 1981), 384. For a survey of antisemitism in Canada in the 1930s and early 1940s, see Irving Abella, *A Coat of Many Colours: Two Centuries of Jewish Life in Canada* (Toronto: Lester and Orpen Dennys, 1990), particularly Chapter 8. For an account of the CJC's failed attempts to combat the antisemitism of the Social Credit Party in the 1930s, see Janine Stingel, *Social Discredit: Anti-Semitism, Social Credit, and the Jewish Response* (Montreal/Kingston: McGill-Queen's University Press, 2000).
4 For a history of antisemitism in Canada, see Alan Davies, ed., *Antisemitism in Canada: History and Interpretation* (Waterloo: Wilfrid Laurier University Press, 1992).
5 Although the sustained campaign for a hate propaganda law did not get under way until after the Second World War, Joshua MacFadyen argues that the campaign's intellectual origins can be traced back to the libel suit launched against J.E. Plamondon for antisemitic remarks that he made to a "Catholic youth group" in Quebec in March 1910. See Joshua D. MacFadyen, "'Nip the Noxious Growth in the Bud': *Ortenberg v. Plamondon* and the Roots of Canadian Anti-Hate Activism," *Canadian Jewish Studies* 12 (2004): 73-96.

6 Philip Girard, *Bora Laskin: Bringing Law to Life* (Toronto: University of Toronto Press, 2005), 247.
7 Canadian Jewish Congress, "Submission of the Canadian Jewish Congress to the House of Commons Special Committee on the Criminal Code," Ottawa, 3 March 1953, 2, LAC, RG 125, vol. 3822, file 21118F, *R. v. Keegstra*, [1990] 3 S.C.R. 697.
8 Section 166 of the *Criminal Code of Canada* stated that "everyone who wilfully publishes a tale or news that he knows is false and that causes or is likely to cause injury or mischief to a public interest is guilty of an indictable offence and is liable to imprisonment for two years." Similarly, section 62 stated that "everyone who (a) speaks seditious words, (b) publishes a seditious libel, or (c) is party to a seditious conspiracy, is guilty of an indictable offence and is liable to imprisonment for fourteen years." As quoted in Canadian Jewish Congress, "Submission of the Canadian Jewish Congress to the House of Commons Special Committee on the Criminal Code," Ottawa, 3 March 1953, 4, LAC, RG 125, vol. 3822, file 21118F, *R. v. Keegstra*, [1990] 3 S.C.R. 697.
9 The CJC recommended two supplementary subsections to sections 166 and 62. For the former, it proposed 166(2): "Injury or mischief to a public interest shall include promoting disaffection among or ill-will or hostility between different classes of persons in Canada." For the latter, it suggested 62(A): "Everyone who publishes or circulates, or causes to be published or circulated, orally or in writing, any statement, tale or news, intended or calculated to incite violence or provoke disorder against any class of persons or against any person as a member of any class in Canada shall be guilty of an indictable offence and liable to imprisonment for two years." Canadian Jewish Congress, "Submission to the House of Commons Special Committee," 4.
10 The committee's decision was consistent with the common law at the time. In *Boucher v. The King* (1950), a case involving a Jehovah's Witness from Quebec who had been convicted of seditious libel for distributing an anti-Catholic pamphlet titled "Quebec's Burning Hate for God and Christ and Freedom Is the Shame of All Canada," the Supreme Court of Canada ruled that fostering ill will between different groups did not constitute an illegal offence. *Boucher v. The King*, [1951] 1 S.C.R. 265, 288.
11 Franklin Bialystok, *Delayed Impact: The Holocaust and the Canadian Jewish Community* (Montreal/Kingston: McGill-Queen's University Press, 2000).
12 *Report to the Minister of Justice of the Special Committee on Hate Propaganda in Canada* (Ottawa: Queen's Printer, 1966), 253-56.
13 For examples of this type of antisemitic material, see *ibid.*, "Appendix IIIC: Samples of Hate Propaganda in Canada," 260-71.
14 Bialystok, *Delayed Impact*, 110.
15 Michael Garber, Sydney Harris, and Saul Hayes, "Letter to the Honourable Guy Favreau, the Honourable John R. Nicholson, and the Honourable John R. Garland," 12 March 1964, 6-7, LAC, RG 125, vol. 3822, file 21118F, *R. v. Keegstra*, [1990] 3 S.C.R. 697. Of the three men, Hayes would come to play the most prominent role in the CJC's campaign. A long-time spokesperson for Canada's Jewish community, he had first joined the organization in 1939, becoming executive director of the Canadian

Jewish Committee for Refugees. A year later the congress made him its national executive director, his main task being to lobby the Mackenzie King government, both publicly and privately, on behalf of Europe's Jewish refugees. Abella and Troper, *None Is Too Many*, 57. After the war, Hayes remained the recognizable face of the CJC, representing the organization abroad at the 1945 UN assembly in San Francisco and the 1946 Paris Peace Conference while directing the organization's ill-fated public relations efforts against the antisemitism of Alberta's Social Credit government at home. See Stingel, *Social Discredit*, 207.

16 Garber, Harris, and Hayes, "Letter," 2.
17 *Ibid.*, 1.
18 Cohen had been active with the CJC throughout much of the 1950s and 1960s. He was chair of the Public Relations Committee from 1952 to 1965, and in 1965 he became the chair of the Foreign Affairs Committee, a position that he held until 1967. Throughout 1964 and 1965, a number of private members' bills were introduced in the House of Commons, all of which were designed to address the "deficit" in the law in some capacity or another, be it to criminalize the promotion of genocide, bar the delivery of hate materials through the mail, or forbid so-called group libel. As is the fate of many private members' bills, not much ever came of them. Their lack of success was a reflection, in part, of just how poorly they were conceived, as none offered any meaningful safeguards against undue encroachments of freedom of expression. More sober reflection was needed. The bills in question were Bill C-21, *An Act Respecting Genocide*; Bill C-43, *An Act to Amend the Post Office Act (Hate Literature)*; Bill C-16, *An Act to Amend the Criminal Code (Disturbing the Public Peace)*; and Bill C-117, *An Act to Amend the Criminal Code (Group Defamatory Libel)*. See *Report ... of the Special Committee on Hate Propaganda in Canada*, 273-75. See also Canadian Jewish Congress, "Submission to the House of Commons Standing Committee on External Affairs Respecting the Subject Matter of Bills C21 and C43 – Hate Literature," Ottawa, n.d., LAC, RG 125, vol. 3822, file 21118F, *R. v. Keegstra*, [1990] 3 S.C.R. 697.
19 "Preface," in *Report ... of the Special Committee on Hate Propaganda in Canada*, xiii.
20 See William Kaplan, "Maxwell Cohen and the Report of the Special Committee on Hate Propaganda," in *Law, Policy, and International Justice: Essays in Honour of Maxwell Cohen*, ed. William Kaplan and Donald McRae (Montreal/Kingston: McGill-Queen's University Press, 1993), 247.
21 Trudeau and Cohen had worked together back in January 1962 as members of *Le Devoir* editor André Laurendeau's "informal committee on French-English relations." According to historian Jack Granatstein, Laurendeau's informal committee was a response not only to the nationalist threat in Quebec following the end of the Duplessis era but also to Prime Minister Diefenbaker's refusal to support his call for an inquiry "into the condition of bilingualism in Canada." Jack L. Granatstein, *Canada, 1957-1967: The Years of Uncertainty and Innovation* (Toronto: McClelland and Stewart, 1986), 246. For a collection of Trudeau's writings on a variety of issues related to the civil liberties of Canadians, see Pierre Elliott Trudeau, "A Constitutional Declaration of Rights," in *Federalism and the French Canadians* (Toronto: Macmillan, 1968).

22 See Ross Lambertson, *Repression and Resistance: Canadian Human Rights Activists, 1930-1960* (Toronto: University of Toronto Press, 2005), specifically Chapters 1-4.
23 Canadian Civil Liberties Association, "History." See http://www.ccla.org/his/.
24 Standing Senate Committee on Legal and Constitutional Affairs, *Seventh Proceedings on Bill S-21: An Act to Amend the Criminal Code*, vol. 7, Ottawa, 22 April 1969, 136-37, LAC, R9833, vol. 35, file 24, "Fundamental Freedoms – Hate Propaganda – Briefs to Government on Amendments to Criminal Code – Hate Propaganda, 1966-1969." Hundreds soon joined the association. By 1969, membership in the CCLA ranged somewhere between 300 and 400 individuals, many of whom were prominent Canadian lawyers, journalists, and academics. Prominent members included, among others, Professor H.W. Arthurs, Faculty of Law, Osgoode Hall; activist June Callwood; Professor G. Horowitz, Faculty of Political Science, University of Toronto; Rev. Donald Gillies; Julian Porter; Dr. Martin O'Connell; Professor D.P. Gauthier; and Dr. Wilson Head. Standing Senate Committee on Legal and Constitutional Affairs, *Seventh Proceedings on Bill S-21*, 142.
25 The quotation is attributed to "Junius," the pseudonym of an unidentified writer who submitted letters to the *London Public Advertiser* throughout the late 1760s and early 1770s.
26 "The Problem: Stifle Hate while Preserving Freedom," *Globe and Mail*, 12 January 1965.
27 Senate Standing Committee on the Criminal Code, "Second Proceedings on Bill S-5: An Act to Amend the Criminal Code, Testimony of Dean Maxwell Cohen," Second Session, Twenty-Seventh Parliament, 1967-1968, Ottawa, 29 February 1968, 55. See also Ralph Hyman, "Race Hate Afflicts Minority in Canada, Professor Says," *Globe and Mail*, 3 June 1965, 3.
28 Three years later Cohen would tell the Senate Standing Committee on the Criminal Code that "the democratic processes did not require any group to stand idly by and be vilified in the name of free speech when the effects of such vilification were, under our modern understanding of propaganda, likely to be much more severe than often was assumed two or three generations ago." Senate Standing Committee on the Criminal Code, "Second Proceedings on Bill S-5," 43.
29 Beattie, a twenty-three-year-old customs clerk at a surgical supply store, was a relatively recent convert to the party, having been recruited the previous year by former Nazi Party leader David Stanley. Beattie had also crossed paths with notorious Nazi sympathizers such as Jack DeCock, leader of the Canadian Youth Corps, a self-described "Nazi front outfit." Douglas Glynn, "Nazi Lived in an Anti-Nazi Home, Leaving Hate and an Unpaid Bill," *Globe and Mail*, 2 June 1965, 5. Another friend and Nazi Party member was the Reverend Charles Thompson, a twenty-eight year old who had broken his ties with the Apostolic Church in Saskatchewan. Beattie considered Thompson to be his spiritual adviser. The two met while at a meeting of the Social Credit Party. Michael Valpy, "Beattie's Adviser," *Globe and Mail*, 5 June 1965, 5.
30 According to an article in the *Globe and Mail*, Bylaw 21379 for the City of Toronto only authorized the parks commission to determine the time and place of a public rally, not to bar it altogether. "City Moves to Halt Nazi Park Meetings," *Globe and Mail*, 1 June 1965, 1-2. Three weeks after the Allan Gardens Riot, Toronto City

Council voted thirteen to ten in favour of denying Beattie a permit to hold another rally in Allan Gardens on the grounds that he was applying for a "license to riot." They also passed an amendment that required the city parks commissioner to forward any "contentious" applications for permits to the Parks and Recreation Committee, which would make a recommendation to council on whether to grant the permit. "Council Refuses Permit to Nazis," *Globe and Mail*, 22 June 1965, 5.

31 Bialystok, *Delayed Impact*, 132-33.
32 Surprisingly, one of the staunchest critics of the riot was the *Globe and Mail*, its editorial board offering a sharp, if perhaps melodramatic, analysis by suggesting that Canadians had not fought against the brutalities of Nazism so that others could carry out mob justice. See "Freedom Carried a Club," *Globe and Mail*, 1 June 1965, 6.
33 It later became known that, prior to the rally, these "self-appointed leaders" of the Jewish community had exploited the confusion surrounding an earlier and unrelated incident in which a group of Jewish youth had been beaten up on Toronto Island so that they might "whip up some groups within the Jewish community to the pitch of fear and frenzy that assisted in creating the atmosphere that led to the mob violence." Moreover, these individuals also used the rally to demand legislation that would grant specific protections to the Jewish community, such as making it a criminal offence to strike anyone who was Jewish. "Congress Leader Decries Mob Action," *Globe and Mail*, 2 June 1965, 5; see also W. Gunther Plaut, "The Riot at Allan Gardens," *Globe and Mail*, 5 June 1965, 6; "Jewish Congress Blames Jews for Fomenting Mob Violence," *Globe and Mail*, 9 June 1965, 1-2. See also *Report ... of the Special Committee on Hate Propaganda in Canada*, 32-33.
34 "Reason in the Wake of Folly," *Globe and Mail*, 10 June 1965, 6. One month later, in July 1965, Beattie once again staged a rally in Allan Gardens despite having his request for a permit turned down by Toronto City Council. This time little came of it. Despite calls from certain segments of Canada's Jewish community to once again meet Beattie with force, the CJC was able to convince most of the community to stay away from the event. See "Legion Urges Jews to Avoid Nazi Speech in Allan Gardens," *Globe and Mail*, 9 July 1965, 5; and "Allan Gardens Guarded by Police as Non-Nazi Assails Park Curbs," *Globe and Mail*, 12 July 1965, 17.
35 Another legacy of the Allan Gardens Riot was the creation of the Community Anti-Nazi Committee to co-ordinate future responses – with survivors – to any incidents involving neo-Nazis. Franklin Bialystok, "Neo-Nazis in Toronto: The Allan Gardens Riot," in "New Perspectives on Canada, the Holocaust, and Survivors," special issue, *Canadian Jewish Studies* 4-5 (1996-97): 2, 25-27.
36 The committee concluded that there were approximately fourteen organizations involved in spreading hate propaganda, which included "splinter groups derived from now expelled elements of the Social Credit movement," "outright Nazi-type parties," and a few "indigenous Canadian-fascist associations." *Report ... of the Special Committee on Hate Propaganda in Canada*, 14, 24.
37 In their introduction to the report, the committee members wrote:

> The successes of modern advertising, the triumphs of impudent propaganda such as Hitler's, have qualified sharply our belief in the rationality of man. We know that

under strain and pressure in times of irritation and frustration, the individual is swayed and even swept away by hysterical, emotional appeals. We act irresponsibly if we ignore the way in which emotion can drive reason from the field.

Ibid., 8-9.
38 Ibid., 24.
39 Ibid., 45-46.
40 Ibid., 47-48.
41 Regulation 5(1)(b) of the *Broadcast Act* states that "no station or network operator shall broadcast any abusive comment [or abusive pictorial representation in the case of television] on any race or religion." *Ibid.*, 51.
42 The Cohen committee proposed the following amendments:

> (1) Every one who advocates or promotes genocide is guilty of an indictable offence [and] is liable to imprisonment for five years. (2) Every one who, by communicating statements in any public place, incites hatred or contempt against any identifiable group, where such incitement is likely to lead to a breach of the peace, is guilty of (a) an indictable offence and is liable to imprisonment for two years, or (b) an offence punishable on summary conviction.

The committee's third recommendation stated that "every one who by communicating statements, wilfully promotes hatred or contempt against any identifiable group is guilty of (a) an indictable offence and is liable to imprisonment for two years or (b) an offence punishable on summary conviction." *Ibid.*, 69-71.
43 The Cohen committee's fourth qualifier for its third proposed amendment stated that "no person shall be convicted of an offence under subsection 3 (a) where he proves that the statements communicated were true, or (b) where he proves that they were relevant to any subject of public interest, the public discussion of which was for the public benefit, and that on reasonable grounds he believed them to be true." *Ibid.*, 69.
44 *Ibid.*, 66. For a critique of the Cohen committee's conclusions, see Joseph Magnet, "Hate Propaganda in Canada," in *Free Expression: Essays in Law and Philosophy*, ed. W.J. Waluchow (Oxford: Oxford University Press, 1994), 223-50.
45 "A Stick for the Neo-Nazis Is a Stick for All," *Globe and Mail*, 18 May 1966, 17. During the height of the anti-communist witch hunts of the 1950s, Pearson and his colleagues at the Department of External Affairs had attempted to protect Canadian diplomat Herbert Norman from accusations by the US Senate Subcommittee on Internal Security that he was a Soviet spy. Succumbing to the pressure of McCarthyism, Norman would eventually take his own life. The episode left a deep impression on Pearson, who, in refusing to co-operate with the subcommittee, was subsequently accused of being an agent of the USSR and dubbed by the *Chicago Tribune* as the "most dangerous man in the western world." John English, *The Worldly Years: The Life of Lester Pearson*, vol. 2, *1949-1972* (Toronto: Alfred A. Knopf Canada, 1992), 88.

For Pearson, the incident revealed the dangers associated with arbitrary curtailments of civil liberties and the potential for abuse that can arise when the state attempts to ban or censor ideas deemed to be dangerous or subversive. For accounts of the Norman affair, see Lester B. Pearson, *Mike: The Memoirs of the Rt. Hon. Lester B. Pearson*, vol. 3, *1957-1968* (Toronto: University of Toronto Press, 1975), 168-73; English, *The Worldly Years*, 164-81, 190-91; and Reg Whitaker and Gary Marcuse, *Cold War Canada: The Making of a National Insecurity State, 1945-1957* (Toronto: University of Toronto Press, 1994), 402-25.

46 "Foundation for a Prison," *Globe and Mail*, 6 April 1966, 6.
47 According to Kaplan, Cohen, MacGuigan, and Harvey Yarosky, Cohen's executive assistant wrote the initial draft of the report, which each member agreed to sign. Also, the committee had been divided on the question of whether to include a defence of truth in the section on group defamation. Hayes did not want such a provision written into the law; however, MacGuigan insisted that it be included and even threatened not to sign the report were it not. Kaplan, "Maxwell Cohen and the Report of the Special Committee on Hate Propaganda," 255-56.
48 Canadian Civil Liberties Association, "Position of the Canadian Civil Liberties Association on Hate Propaganda," n.d., 1, LAC, R9833, vol. 38, file 26, "Special Committee on Hate Propaganda (Federal), 1965, 1969." See also Sidney B. Linden, "Letter to James E. Walker," 2 August 1966, 1, LAC, R9833, vol. 38, file 26, "Special Committee on Hate Propaganda (Federal), 1965, 1969."
49 Canadian Civil Liberties Association, "Statement of the Canadian Civil Liberties Association: Hate Literature," n.d., 1, LAC, R9833, vol. 38, file 26, "Special Committee on Hate Propaganda (Federal), 1965, 1969."
50 Canadian Jewish Congress, "Hatemongers and the Mass Media," 13 November 1968, 3-4, LAC, MG28 V133, vol. 36, files 20-21, "Joint Community Relations Committee: Correspondence and Memoranda, 1968."
51 Canadian Jewish Congress, "Letter from Louis Herman, Chairman, Special Planning Committee, and Meyer W. Gasner, Chairman, Central Region," Toronto, 20 January 1967, 1-2, LAC, MG28 V133, vol. 36, file 19, "Joint Community Relations Committee: Correspondence and Memoranda, 1966-1967." Also, in 1968, members of John Beattie's Canadian National Socialist Party began distributing "pro-white" newsletters and flyers to workers at a General Motors plant in Oshawa. Beattie warned of the apparent dangers of inter-racial marriages between blacks and whites and accused Jews of profiting off the backs of Canadian workers and securing special privileges from the federal government while simultaneously orchestrating the rise of militant separatist activity in Quebec. See John Beattie, "Letter to the Editorial Staff of the *Oshaworker*," Toronto, 16 October 1968; and John Beattie, "Special Rights for Jews?" flyer from the Canadian National Socialist Party, Toronto, n.d., LAC, MG28 V133, vol. 36, files 20-21, "Joint Community Relations Committee: Correspondence and Memoranda, 1968."
52 Von Thadden was not the first racist to appear on the CBC. Throughout the 1960s, the station had conducted a number of feature interviews with known neo-Nazis, among them George Lincoln Rockwell of the American Nazi Party (25 October 1964), Nazi sympathizer David Stanley, and fascist John Ross Taylor of the Western Guard Party (17 January 1965), all of whom had appeared at one point or another on the news show *This Hour Has Seven Days*. Canadian Jewish Congress, "Hatemongers and the Mass Media," 2. See also Bruce Lawson, "Neo-Nazi on CBC's *Sunday* Stirs

Opposition," *Globe and Mail*, 11 January 1967, 10. See also W. Gunther Plaut, "Germany's Neo-Nazis: They Are Unimportant but Bear Watching," *Globe and Mail*, 21 September 1967, 7.

53 "Urged CBC to Alter von Thadden Plans, LaMarsh Tells MPs," *Globe and Mail*, 15 November 1967, 9.

54 When asked about the CJC's complaint about Mosley's participation in CBC's *Front Page Challenge*, Berton replied:

> I think they're wrong to do it. First of all, I think it's perfectly legitimate for a program which delves into the news stories of the past to bring on anybody and it clearly doesn't have to approve of him. Mosley isn't the first wrong-o on that program and if you confine it only to right-o's, it would not only be a dull program but it would not be serving its purpose of reminding people of what happened in the past.

Transcript of "Dialogue: Pierre Berton and Charles Templeton," CFRB, Toronto, 27 December 1968, 1, LAC, MG28 V133, vol. 36, files 20-21, "Joint Community Relations Committee: Correspondence and Memoranda, 1968."

55 Canadian Jewish Congress, "Hatemongers and the Mass Media," 1.

56 James Walker has argued that, for much of the postwar era, the CJC adopted a "universalist" approach to advancing racial equality in Canada. However, the "mid-1960s demonstrations of antisemitism taught some the lesson that antisemitism was not just one example of prejudice but a unique problem that needed individual and detailed attention in its own right." James W.St.G. Walker, "The 'Jewish Phase' in the Movement for Racial Equality in Canada," *Canadian Ethnic Studies* 34, 1 (2000): 18.

57 Canadian Jewish Congress, "Summary of Minutes, Meeting of Regional Council, Central Region," Associated Hebrew Schools, Toronto, 10 March 1966, 7, LAC, MG28 V133, vol. 34, file 14, "Canadian Jewish Congress: Correspondence, 1965-1966."

58 The bill originally defined "identifiable group" (section 267B(5)(b) of the *Criminal Code of Canada*) as "any section of the public distinguished by colour, race or ethnic origin," whereas the Cohen Report defined the phrase as "any section of the public distinguished by religion, colour, race, language, ethnic or national origin." "Religion" was initially left out because of fears that discussion about religious matters might fall under the purview of the law; however, it was reinserted on the request of delegates from the Canadian Jewish Congress, who argued that, without the term, Jews would not be protected by the law, the reason being that the Jewish community was defined principally along religious affiliation and not "colour, race or ethnic origin" as a result of its members' varied cultural and national backgrounds. Senate of Canada, Bill S-5, *An Act to Amend the Criminal Code*, Second Session, Twenty-Seventh Parliament, 1967-68, 29 February 1969, 2. See *Report ... of the Special Committee on Hate Propaganda in Canada*, 70.

59 The nervousness that accompanied Bill S-49 was not restricted to politicians. True to form, the *Globe and Mail* remained highly dubious of the bill, believing once again that, if passed, it could be used to curtail freedom of the press. In December 1967, just as Parliament was ending for the year, its editorial board offered a pessimistic, if perhaps overstated, assessment of the new legislation. The board compared it

Notes to pages 65-67

to an overly potent yet indiscriminate pharmaceutical that, in the process of attacking those cells that are cancerous, proved "deadly" to those that are "healthy" and "normal." The newspaper's hope was that the session's end would also spell the end of the bill. Resolute in its view that little good could come of Bill S-49, the paper warned that "the safest safeguard would be to abandon the legislation before it has a chance to erode our freedom." "A Law that Could Kill More than Hate," *Globe and Mail*, 21 December 1967, 6.

60 The delegation representing the Canadian Jewish Congress and B'nai Brith consisted of Michael Garber, QC, national president, CJC; Louis Herman, QC, national chairman and chairman, Joint Committee on Community Relations, B'nai Brith; Sydney Harris, vice-chairman, Central Region, CJC; John A. Geller, chairman, Committee on Bill S-5, CJC; Saul Hayes, QC, executive vice-president, CJC; F.M. Catzman, QC, chairman, Legal Committee, Central Region, CJC; B.G. Kayfetz, national executive director, Joint Community Relations, and national executive director, Joint Community Relations Committee, B'nai Brith; Minerva Rosenthal, national president, National Council of Jewish Women; and Jacob Egit, executive director, United Organizations for Histadrut. Also appearing before the Senate committee was Dean Maxwell Cohen, who appeared immediately after the congress. Senate Standing Committee on the Criminal Code, "Second Proceedings on Bill S-5."

61 *Ibid.*, 18. See also "Joseph Goebbels, 1897-1945," in *Who's Who in Nazi Germany*, http://www.thirdreich.net/.

62 Senate Standing Committee on the Criminal Code, "Second Proceedings on Bill S-5," 40. See also 28-29, 54.

63 *Ibid.*, 31.

64 Canadian Jewish Congress, "Brief of the Canadian Jewish Congress to the Senate Special Committee on the Criminal Code (Hate Propaganda)," Ottawa, 22 February 1968, 15, LAC, RG 125, vol. 3822, file 21118F, *R. v. Keegstra*, [1990] 3 S.C.R. 697.

65 *Ibid.*, 16.

66 Senate Standing Committee on the Criminal Code, "Second Proceedings on Bill S-5," 24. See also "Senator Says Anti-Hate Bill May Be a Slur," *Globe and Mail*, 29 March 1968.

67 During deliberations, Trudeau had told the committee, "I am not as certain now that the sheer size of the problem is the crucial consideration. We must consider the effects of hate propaganda on those people who are being insulted. Even if there are fewer people affected than we might have thought, this still might be something significant to be dealt with by law." Quoted in Kaplan, "Maxwell Cohen and the Report of the Special Committee on Hate Propaganda," 255. See also National Joint Community Relations Committee, "Letter re: Legislative Campaign for Bill S-5," 24 October 1968, 1-2, LAC, MG28 V133, vol. 36, files 20-21, "Joint Community Relations Committee: Correspondence and Memoranda, 1968."

68 According to Tom Axworthy, Trudeau's principal secretary from 1981 to 1984,

> Trudeau's ultimate goal was to expand the degrees by which individuals could have real choices, and in one case it meant taking the state away and the other meant using it as a mechanism for change. I think that he was rather agnostic about the use of the state, except as a means to try to expand human freedom: restricting [it]

in one case, but allowing it to exercise some measure of regulation on the market on the other.

Quoted in "Discussion," in *The Hidden Pierre Elliott Trudeau: The Faith behind the Politics*, ed. John English, Richard Gwyn, and P. Whitney Lackenbauer (Ottawa: Novalis, 2004), 150. See also Pierre Elliott Trudeau, "The Values of a Just Society," in *Towards a Just Society: The Trudeau Years*, ed. Thomas S. Axworthy and Pierre Elliott Trudeau (Markham, ON: Viking, 1990), 359.

69 Standing Senate Committee on Legal and Constitutional Affairs, *Seventh Proceedings on Bill S-21: An Act to Amend the Criminal Code*, no. 7, First Session, Twenty-Eighth Parliament, Ottawa, 22 April 1969, LAC, R9833, vol. 35, file 24, "Fundamental Freedoms – Hate Propaganda – Briefs to Government on Amendments to Criminal Code – Hate Propaganda, 1966-1969." See also H.W. Arthurs, "Hate Propaganda – An Argument against Attempts to Stop It by Legislation," *Chitty's Law Journal* 18, 1 (1970): 1-5.

70 MacGuigan believed that the bill found the proper balance between protection of minorities and freedom of expression. See Mark R. MacGuigan, "Proposed Anti-Hate Legislation," *Chitty's Law Journal* 15, 9 (1967): 302-6. Interview with Professor Harry Arthurs, 5 March 2005.

71 Standing Senate Committee on Legal and Constitutional Affairs, *Seventh Proceedings on Bill S-21*, 136-37.

72 Ibid., 137.

73 Ibid., 138.

74 See "Alternatives to Repression," *Globe and Mail*, 24 April 1969, 6; and "A Plan to Stifle Hate without the Law," *Globe and Mail*, 24 April 1969, 7.

75 Stefan Braun, *Democracy Off Balance: Freedom of Expression and Hate Propaganda Law in Canada* (Toronto: University of Toronto Press, 2004), 13. See also *Hansard*, 13 April 1970, 5807; and Clyde Sanger, "Government Hate Propaganda Bill Gets Third Reading with 89 to 45 Vote," *Globe and Mail*, 14 April 1970, 1-2.

76 "How Free Speech Becomes a Crime," *Globe and Mail*, 28 April 1970, 6.

77 See "Hate Propaganda Bill Sparks Major Debate," *Globe and Mail*, 29 April 1970, 8.

78 Of course, hate propaganda still existed in Canada. In 1978, Don Andrews and David Zarytshansky of the Western Guard Party were both sentenced to prison for violating Canada's hate propaganda law. Two years later John Ross Taylor, also of the Western Guard Party, was taken to court by the Canadian Human Rights Commission for violating a court order to cease sending antisemitic messages over the telephone, which was prohibited under the 1977 *Canadian Human Rights Act*. However, the JCRC was of the opinion that, by and large, the few incidents brought to its attention were insufficient to warrant legal action. Canadian Jewish Congress, "Central Region Report, 1971-1974," Toronto, n.d., 1, LAC, MG28 V133, vol. 37, file 1, "Joint Community Relations Committee: Correspondence and Minutes of Meetings, 1971." See also Joint Community Relations Committee, "Minutes," Montreal, 21 June 1971, 2, LAC, MG28 V133, vol. 37, file 1, "Joint Community Relations Committee: Correspondence and Minutes of Meetings, 1971." See also Joint Community Relations Committee, "Minutes," Toronto, 2 May 1978, 5; and "Minutes," Toronto, 26 September

circa 1981, LAC, R9833, vol. 214, file 3, "Civil Liberties – General [Correspondence] – Canadian Jewish Congress, 1976-1977."
79 Joint Community Relations Committee, "Minutes," Toronto, 20 January 1971, 2, LAC, MG28 V133, vol. 37, file 1, "Joint Community Relations Committee: Correspondence and Minutes of Meetings, 1971." See also Joint Community Relations Committee, "Minutes," Toronto, 27 October 1976, 2-3, LAC, R9833, vol. 214, file 4, "Civil Liberties – General [Correspondence] – Canadian Jewish Congress, 1976-1977."
80 Bialystok, *Delayed Impact*, 161.
81 In *Drybones*, the Supreme Court of Canada ruled that section 94 of the *Indian Act*, which prohibited Aboriginal people from consuming alcohol off reserve lands, contravened the "right of the individual to equality before the law and the protection of the law" found in section 1(b) of the 1960 *Bill of Rights*. Indian Act, R.S.C. 1952, c. 149. See *R. v. Drybones*, [1970] 9 D.L.R. (3d) 473.
82 Joint Community Relations Committee, "Minutes," Montreal, 21 June 1971, 2, LAC, MG28 V133, vol. 37, file 1, "Joint Community Relations Committee: Correspondence and Minutes of Meetings, 1971."
83 A. Alan Borovoy, "Freedom of Speech or Freedom of Soliloquy? Some Recent and Impending Canadian Problems," Toronto, circa 1968, 10.
84 The article was part of a special issue on the effects of the Trudeau government's decision to enact the *War Measures Act* on 16 October 1970, following the kidnappings of British diplomat James Cross and Quebec Minister of Labour Pierre Laporte by the Front de libération du Québec. A. Alan Borovoy, "Rebuilding a Free Society," *Canadian Forum* (January 1971): 349-55.
85 Borovoy's fear was not unfounded. In 1975, Toronto police arrested a number of demonstrators for distributing pamphlets at the Shriners' Day parade that read "Yankee Go Home." All were charged with violating Canada's hate propaganda law. The Crown attorney eventually dropped the charges; however, as Borovoy noted in a speech in 1984, "these young activists suffered the suppression of their free speech rights and some of them spent up to two days in jail." A. Alan Borovoy, "Freedom of Expression – Some Recurring Impediments," paper presented at the 1984 Conference of the Canadian Institute for the Administration of Justice, Ottawa, 25 October 1984, 21, LAC, R9833, vol. 29, file 10, "Fundamental Freedoms – Free Speech – Alan Borovoy Article 'Freedom of Expression – Some Recurring Impediments,' 1984." For other examples of the law "catching" more than the hate-monger, see A. Alan Borovoy, *When Freedoms Collide: The Case for Our Civil Liberties* (Toronto: Lester and Orpen Dennys, 1988), 42-43.
86 Joint Community Relations Committee, "Minutes," Toronto, 2 May 1978, 1, LAC, R9833, vol. 214, file 3, "Civil Liberties – General [Correspondence] – Canadian Jewish Congress, 1976-1977." See also Mark Bonokoski, "Neo Nazi Leads Toronto Protest," *Toronto Sun*, 19 April 1978, 16.
87 Section 41 of the *Canada Post Corporation Act* grants the minister the authority to revoke mailing privileges for an individual if the minister believes that "1. that person is committing an offence by means of the mail; 2. that by some means other than the mail the person is aiding someone who is committing an offence by means

of the mail; or 3. that the person intends to commit any offence and uses the mail to accomplish that object." As quoted in Canadian Civil Liberties Association, "Re: Civil Liberties Association – and Samisdat Publishers," draft factum, circa 1982, 5, 13, LAC, R9833, vol. 36, file 6, "Fundamental Freedoms – Hate Propaganda – Ernst Zundel – Samisdat Publications, Ltd., 1981-1990."

88 *Criminal Code of Canada*, R.S.C. 1970, c. C-34. To its credit, the CCLA appeared before the Postal Board of Review's hearing in 1982, raising two arguments in Zundel's defence. First, it submitted that section 41 should be deemed inoperative on the grounds that Samisdat Publishers had not been convicted of any crime, so the law contravened his right to be "presumed innocent until proven guilty," as outlined in sections 2(f) of the 1960 *Bill of Rights* and 11(d) of the new *Charter of Rights and Freedoms*. Specifically, it contested the wisdom of a law that granted the minister responsible for Canada Post the authority to impose a penalty without a trial or hearing, specifically since section 281.2 required that any charges be first brought by either the federal attorney general or a provincial attorney general. Second, the CCLA argued that section 281.2 violated the freedom of expression guarantees found in sections 1(d) of the 1960 *Bill of Rights* and 2(b) of the *Charter*, so the order against Zundel should be revoked. Canadian Civil Liberties Association, "Re: Civil Liberties Association – and Samisdat Publishers," 5, 13.

89 In a rather brazen move, Zundel accused the CCLA of being complicit in the Canadian government's "unjust actions" toward him, contending that it did not do more to publicize his case. Citing Voltaire, he chastised Borovoy directly, accusing him of adopting a policy of "self-imposed censorship," the result of which would be nothing less than the eventual destruction of "liberty under the cloak of secrecy." Predictably, he believed that fault lay with the "many members of the CCLA [who] are not only of the Jewish, but of the Zionist persuasion." Ernst Zundel, "Letter to Alan Borovoy," 4 November 1982, 2, LAC, R9833, vol. 36, file 6, "Fundamental Freedoms – Hate Propaganda – Ernst Zundel – Samisdat Publications, Ltd., 1981-1990."

In November 1982, Zundel wrote a letter to the Canadian Jewish Congress in which he asked its executive to "resume our initiation of discussions towards the defusing of the danger implicit in the rapidly-eroding Holocaust Legend which can no longer be used to absolve Israeli crimes and aggression by pointing to alleged crimes and aggression committed by Germans over 40 years ago." Ernst Zundel, "Letter to the Directors, Canadian Jewish Congress," 4 November 1982; see also Ernst Zundel, "Letter to Alan Borovoy," 17 February 1983, LAC, R9833, vol. 36, file 6, "Fundamental Freedoms – Hate Propaganda – Ernst Zundel – Samisdat Publications, Ltd., 1981-1990."

90 Keegstra taught his students that Jews were atheistic and anti-Christian, dishonest, and obsessed with power, that they were murderers and anarchists, members of secret societies, and manipulators of governments. Moreover, he believed that they were revolutionaries and warmongers and were responsible for both socialism and, of all things, the Irish Republican Army. For an account of the historical origins of Keegstra's conspiracy theories, see Alan Davies, "The Keegstra Affair," in *Antisemitism in Canada: History and Interpretation*, ed. Alan Davies (Waterloo: Wilfrid Laurier University Press, 1992), 227-47.

Notes to pages 70-71

91 Factum of the Appellant, *R. v. Keegstra*, [1990] 3 S.C.R. 697, 1-3.
92 There was considerable evidence to suggest that his teachings had a deep impression on his students. In one essay, a pupil wrote, "since the time before Christ, the Jews have been involved in all kinds of underhanded dealings. In 1783, they joined hands with the Communists to establish a one-world order." Another concluded, "I have also shown that where ever the communists rule it was set up by the Jews. In my opinion this must come to a dead halt. We must get rid of every Jew in existence so we may live in peace and freedom." Quoted in Steve Mertl and John Ward, *Keegstra: The Trial, the Issues, the Consequences* (Saskatoon: Western Producer Prairie Books, 1985), 3-8. A third stated, "you take the Jews. They hate Christ. They have set out to destroy us." Quoted in Robert Lee, "Teaching Hate in Alberta Schools," *Maclean's*, 18 April 1983: 24-25.
93 David Bercuson and Douglas Wertheimer, *A Trust Betrayed: The Keegstra Affair* (Toronto: Doubleday Canada, 1985).
94 The original name for Western Canada Concept was Committee for Western Independence. The party was a product of the growing western dissatisfaction with the language and interventionist economic policies of the Trudeau government. Doug Collins, "Independence for the West? Don't Laugh," *Toronto Star*, 2 December 1976. See also Olivia Ward, "Idealist Has a Western Mission," *Toronto Star*, 8 March 1981, B4.
95 Claude Adams, "Through the Fingers," *Canadian Lawyer* (April 1985): 17-18; Gabriel Weimann and Conrad Winn, *Hate on Trial: The Zundel Affair, the Media, Public Opinion in Canada* (Oakville, ON: Mosaic Press, 1986), 26-27. For an excellent feature story on Christie, see Paula Kulig, "Doug Christie: Counsel for the Damned," *Canadian Lawyer* (November 1990): 14-19. See also Shona McKay, "The Unpopular Defender," *Maclean's*, 11 March 1985: 49.
96 See Canadian Jewish Congress, "Brief Submitted to the Special Committee on Visible Minorities," Ottawa, October 1983, LAC, RG 125, vol. 3822, file 21118F, *R. v. Keegstra*, [1990] 3 S.C.R. 697.
97 The recommendations were that

> 1. Justice Canada should prepare amendments to Section 281.2(2) of the Criminal Code so that it is no longer necessary to show that an accused specifically intended to promote hatred, in order to obtain a conviction; 2. Justice Canada should prepare amendments to S. 281.2(6) of the Criminal Code so that the consent of the provincial attorneys general is no longer required for a prosecution in cases of public incitement of hatred.

Canada, House of Commons, *The First Report to the House of the Special Committee on Participation of Visible Minorities in Canadian Society*, Second Session of the Thirty-Second Parliament, 1983-84 (March 1984), 69-70.
98 One of the groups was the League for Human Rights of B'nai Brith Canada. Believing at the time that the law as it was written "may have had some intimidation effect," but had thus far "proven to be almost totally inadequate in application," it presented Mark MacGuigan, who was now the minister of justice, with a brief in September 1983, "proposing a number of changes" to the law. Alan Shefman, *The*

Review of Anti-Semitism 1983 (Downsview, ON: League for Human Rights of B'nai Brith Canada, 1984), 27-28.
99 Borovoy, "Freedom of Expression," 22.
100 Keegstra finished last in the election, receiving only 691 of the 55,276 votes cast in the riding of Red Deer or approximately 0.01 percent. Despite his best efforts, Keegstra remained a peripheral figure with limited appeal. After his conviction in 1985, he made an ill-fated run for leader of the Social Credit Party in 1986 but lost to the Reverend Harvey Lainson. Although Keegstra was briefly named interim leader in July 1987, after Lainson was asked to step down during a period of intense fighting within the party, his time as leader lasted only a few months. Borovoy, *When Freedoms Collide*, 50. See also Stingel, *Social Discredit*.
101 Borovoy, "Freedom of Expression," 24-25.
102 *Criminal Code*, R.S.C., 1985, c. C-46, s. 181. The basis for the charges was the content of two of Zündel's pamphlets, *Did Six Million Really Die?* and *The West, War, and Islam*. Roy McMurty, the attorney general of Ontario at the time, had opted against charging Zündel with violating the hate propaganda law because his advisers believed that there would be both "significant legal hurdles, given the very broad defences provided by the legislation," and "a real danger of what could be a highly publicized acquittal that could have the effect of encouraging other potential hatemongers." See Roy McMurty, "Law and Antisemitism: The Role of the State in Responding to Hatred," in *Contemporary Antisemitism: Canada and the World*, ed. Derek J. Penslar, Michael R. Marrus, and Janice Gross Stein (Toronto: University of Toronto Press, 2005), 30.
103 Ernst Zündel, "Holocaust Trial," *Samisdat News* (Winter 1984): 1-2.
104 Ibid., 3.
105 Manuel Prutschi, "The Zündel Affair," in *Antisemitism in Canada: History and Interpretation*, ed. Alan Davies (Waterloo: Wilfrid Laurier University Press, 1992), 251.
106 Hal Quinn, "The Holocaust Trial," *Maclean's*, 11 March 1985: 42-43; Kirk Makin, "Media Distorted Teachings, Keegstra Tells Zundel Trial," *Globe and Mail*, 15 February 1985, M1, M3.
107 Adams, "Through the Fingers," 19.
108 Kirk Makin, "Zundel Guilty, but Unrepentant," *Globe and Mail*, 1 March 1985, 1-2.
109 The trial also had the unexpected benefit of raising awareness of the Holocaust within Canadian society. Weiman and Winn, *Hate on Trial*, 163.
110 Interview with A. Alan Borovoy, Toronto, 8 February 2005.
111 Canadian Civil Liberties Association, "CCLA Statement on Zundel Case," Toronto, 25 March 1985, 2, LAC, R9833, vol. 36, file 14, "CCLA Statement on Zundel Case, 1985."
112 A. Alan Borovoy, "Is Prosecution Right Way to Handle People Like Zundel?," *Toronto Star*, circa March 1985, A5.
113 *R. v. Keegstra* (1984), 19 C.C.C. (3d) 254.
114 Joint Community Relations Committee, "Memorandum re: Upcoming Keegstra Trial," 2 April 1985, 1-3, 5, LAC, MG28 V133, vol. 37, file 12, "National Joint Community Relations Committee: Correspondence and Reports, 1982-1985."

115 Keegstra was a keynote speaker along with Paul Fromm of the Western Canada Separatist Party at a "Freedom of Speech" conference in Calgary sponsored by various right-wing organizations. Joint Community Relations Committee, "Minutes," Toronto, 28 May 1984, 4, LAC, MG28 V133, vol. 37, file 12, "National Joint Community Relations Committee: Correspondence and Reports, 1982-1985."
116 A. Alan Borovoy, "Law Used to Prosecute Keegstra Is Dangerously Vague," *Toronto Star*, 29 July 1985, A8.
117 Ibid.
118 Joint Community Relations Committee, "Minutes," Toronto, 28 May 1984, 5, LAC, MG28 V133, vol. 37, file 12, "National Joint Community Relations Committee: Correspondence and Reports, 1982-1985."
119 Ibid., 6.
120 Makin, "Zundel Guilty, but Unrepentant."
121 Irving Abella, "The State of the Jews: Canada 1986," address to the plenary session of the Canadian Jewish Congress, circa 1986, LAC, R9833, vol. 36, file 18, "Fundamental Freedoms – Hate Propaganda – Articles, n.d. 1984-1986." In 1993, Evelyn Kallen and Lawrence Lam attempted to quantify the psychological impact that the 1985 Zündel and Keegstra trials had on Canada's Jewish community and the Canadian public at large. They found that even "Jews who do *not* define themselves as survivors can experience Holocaust-related trauma." Many respondents in their survey reported "psychic harm" and "mental anguish" throughout the trials. Interestingly, despite the "great pain and stress," most respondents "strongly endorsed criminal trials as necessary means of curbing the spread of hate by publicly-identified hatemongers and also as serving an educative and preventative function for other hate propagandists." Evelyn Kallen and Lawrence Lam, "Target for Hate: The Impact of the Zundel and Keegstra Trials on a Jewish-Canadian Audience," *Canadian Ethnic Studies* 25, 1 (1993): 21-22.
122 The Zündel trial drew attention from around the world, including from the Australian Civil Liberties Union, which was deeply disturbed by the outcome of the case, claiming that Holocaust "revisionism" was "freely debated on all major TV networks in Australia, most university libraries carry copies of revisionist books ... and information is available in most newsagents setting out the claims of the so-called 'revisionists.'" Australian Civil Liberties Union, "Letter to CCLA," 15 September 1986, LAC, R9833, vol. 36, file 17, "Fundamental Freedoms – Hate Propaganda – Articles, 1968-1987." See also Canadian Civil Liberties Association, "Letter to the Australian Civil Liberties Union," 27 November 1986, LAC, R9833, vol. 36, file 17, "Fundamental Freedoms – Hate Propaganda – Articles, 1968-1987"; Euro-American Alliance, "Letter to Alan Borovoy," 29 July 1986; and Canadian Resistance Movement, "Letter to Mr. Borovoy," 25 July 1986, LAC, R9833, vol. 36, file 6, "Fundamental Freedoms – Hate Propaganda – Ernst Zundel – Samisdat Publications, Ltd., 1981-1990."
123 According to Borovoy's letter, Christie had been quoted in the *Canadian Jewish News* as saying, "every day a representative of the Canadian Jewish Congress sits in court and walks in and out of the prosecutor's office at the breaks, as well as advises the media, showing us who is the real power in the land." He had also told the CBC

that "I can't believe it [accounts of the gas chamber at Auschwitz]. I'm sorry, I am an unbeliever." A. Alan Borovoy, "Letter to Douglas Christie," 28 July 1986, 2-3, LAC, RG 125, vol. 3822, file 21118F, *R. v. Keegstra*, [1990] 3 S.C.R. 697.

124 *Ibid.*, 1-2. This was not the first time that the CCLA had sought clarification on Christie's beliefs. Following an address that Christie had given in Calgary in April 1985, a lawyer for the organization, Sheldon Chumir, challenged Christie to reveal whether he shared his client's views. Christie declined, responding, "I do not answer questions of that kind with respect to my personal opinion because I have concluded I do not live in a society that tolerates freedom of opinion." Quoted in Joan Bryden, "Christie's Personal Views under Fire during Speech," *Calgary Herald*, 1 May 1985.

125 See D.H. Christie, "Letter to Alan Borovoy," 8 August 1986; and Ernst Zundel, "Letter to Doug Christie from A. Alan Borovoy," 28 July 1986, LAC, R9833, vol. 36, file 6, "Fundamental Freedoms – Hate Propaganda – Ernst Zundel – Samisdat Publications, Ltd., 1981-1990."

126 Paul Lungen, "No Intervention Allowed," *Canadian Jewish News*, 28 August 1986, 1.

127 Interview with A. Alan Borovoy, Toronto, 8 February 2005.

128 *R. v. Zundel*, [1987] 18 O.A.C. 161, 1; A. Alan Borovoy, "The Zundel Appeal," *Criminal Reports*, 56 C.R. (3d), 77-81, LAC, R9833, vol. 36, file 19, "Fundamental Freedoms – Hate Propaganda – Articles, n.d., 1988."

129 CCLA Factum, *R. v. Keegstra*, Appeal before the Alberta Court of Appeal (1985), 19 C.C.C. (3d) 254, 1-4, LAC, R9833, vol. 38, file 21, "Fundamental Freedoms – Hate Propaganda – Articles re: Jim Keegstra, 1985-1986."

130 Judgment (Kerans), *R. v. Keegstra*, Appeal before the Alberta Court of Appeal (1985), 19 C.C.C. (3d) 254, 1-4.

131 "Keegstra Conviction Struck Down," *Globe and Mail*, 7 June 1988, A1, A4.

132 "The Hate Law and the Charter of Rights," *Globe and Mail*, 8 June 1988, A6.

133 *R. v. Andrews and Smith*, [1988] 28 O.A.C. 161. See also Stanley Oziewicz, "Evangelist Wins Socred Leadership, Attacked as a Racist by Keegstra," *Globe and Mail*, 23 June 1986, A1-A2.

134 Judgment (Cory), *R. v. Andrews and Smith*, [1988] 28 O.A.C. 161.

135 "Appeal Will Be Allowed on Hate Law," *Globe and Mail*, 9 June 1988, A1.

136 See *R. v. Oakes*, [1986] 1 S.C.R. 103. Knopff and Morton have argued that the Oakes test offers "a veil of legalism over the unavoidably political business of section 1 analysis" that allows the courts to "second-guess the political judgments of legislatures." Rainer Knopff and F.L. Morton, *Charter Politics* (Scarborough, ON: Nelson Canada, 1992), 153.

137 Shannon Ishiyama Smithey sees the interventions in *Keegstra* as an example of a "liberal/post-liberal" debate. Shannon Ishiyama Smithey, "Cooperation and Conflict: Group Activity in *R. v. Keegstra*," in *The Myth of the Sacred: The Charter, the Courts, and the Politics of the Constitution in Canada*, ed. Patrick James, Donald E. Abelson, and Michael Lusztig (Montreal/Kingston: McGill-Queen's University Press, 2002), 191.

138 Elizabeth J. Shilton, "Charter Litigation and the Policy Process of Government: A Public Interest Perspective," *Osgoode Hall Law Journal* 30, 3 (1992): 653.

139 Factum of the Canadian Jewish Congress, 9-10; Factum of InterAmicus, 6-7; Factum of the Women's Legal Education Action Fund, 1, *R. v. Keegstra*, [1990] 3 S.C.R. 697.
140 Article 4(a) of the *ICEFRD* states that state parties "shall declare an offence punishable by law all dissemination of ideas based on racial superiority or hatred, incitement to racial discrimination, as well as all acts of violence or incitement to such acts against any race or group of persons of another colour or ethnic origin, and also the provision of any assistance to racist activities, including the financing thereof." *ICEFRD*, adopted and opened for signature and ratification by General Assembly Resolution 2106 (XX), 21 December 1965, entry into force 4 January 1969. Factum of the Canadian Jewish Congress, 15; Factum of InterAmicus, 12; Factum of B'nai Brith, 13, *R. v. Keegstra*, [1990] 3 S.C.R. 697. Canada ratified the *ICEFRD* on 14 October 1970.
141 Factum of the Canadian Jewish Congress, 17; Factum of B'nai Brith, 3; Factum of InterAmicus, 10, *R. v. Keegstra*, [1990] 3 S.C.R. 697. LEAF offered a similar defence, although its arguments were based not on the experiences of Canada's Jewish community but on the historical discrimination faced by women. Factum of the Women's Legal Education Action Fund, *R. v. Keegstra*, [1990] 3 S.C.R. 697, 7.
142 Factum of the Canadian Jewish Congress, *R. v. Keegstra*, [1990] 3 S.C.R. 697, 18.
143 *Ibid.*, 19; Factum of InterAmicus, 14; Factum of B'nai Brith, 15, *R. v. Keegstra*, [1990] 3 S.C.R. 697.
144 See also Factum of the Attorney General of Canada, Factum of the Attorney General for Ontario, Factum of the Attorney General for New Brunswick, Factum of the Attorney General for Manitoba, and Memoire du Procureur Général du Quebec, *R. v. Keegstra*, [1990] 3 S.C.R. 697.
145 Factum of the Appellant, *R. v. Keegstra*, [1990] 3 S.C.R. 697, 30.
146 *Ibid.*, 33, 38-39.
147 Factum of the Canadian Civil Liberties Association, *R. v. Keegstra*, [1990] 3 S.C.R. 697, 3-4.
148 *Ibid.*, 8.
149 Factum of the Canadian Civil Liberties Association, *R. v. Keegstra*, [1990] 3 S.C.R. 697, 14.
150 Factum of the Respondent, *R. v. Keegstra*, [1990] 3 S.C.R. 697, 5-12, 20.
151 Transcript of Oral Presentations, *R. v. Keegstra*, [1990] 3 S.C.R. 697, 6 December 1989, 54.
152 *Ibid.*
153 Factum of the Respondent, *R. v. Keegstra*, [1990] 3 S.C.R. 697, 14-15.
154 *Ibid.*, 14-15, 22.
155 *Ibid.*, 21-22.
156 *Ibid.*, 14.
157 Transcript of Oral Presentations, *R. v. Keegstra*, [1990] 3 S.C.R. 697, 57.
158 *Ibid.*, 90.
159 Factum of the Respondent, *R. v. Keegstra*, [1990] 3 S.C.R. 697, 35.
160 *Ibid.*, 95-96.

161 In addition to Dickson, the majority consisted of Justices Wilson, L'Heureux-Dubé, and Gonthier; the minority consisted of McLachlin and Justices Sopinka and La Forest.
162 Judgment (Dickson), *R. v. Keegstra*, [1990] 3 S.C.R. 697, 13 December 1990, 39, 53, 55-56, 64.
163 *Ibid.*, 100, 104.
164 In justifying her position, McLachlin wrote that "if the guarantee of free expression is to be meaningful, it must protect expression which challenges even the very basic conceptions about our society. A true commitment to freedom of expression demands nothing less." Judgment (McLachlin), *R. v. Keegstra*, [1990] 3 S.C.R. 697, 13 December 1990, 59.
165 *Ibid.*, 49, 53, 55.
166 *Ibid.*, 81.
167 *Ibid.*, 74. Upon hearing of the ruling, Keegstra told journalists, "this is the end of freedom in Canada. We have become a Communist country." Offering a more measured perspective, Borovoy lamented that the "casualties are likely to include very legitimate dissenters." See Graham Fraser and Miro Cernetig, "Supreme Court Upholds Curbs on Free Expression," *Globe and Mail*, 14 December 1990, A1, A8; and Rob Ferguson, "Reaction Varies on Decision," *Saint John Telegraph Journal*, 14 December 1990. See also Joscelyn Proby, "Welcome Soviet Republic of Canada," *Red Deer Advocate*, 14 December 1990; and "Ruling on Anti-Hate Laws Produces Mixed Reaction," *Lethbridge Herald*, 14 December 1990.
168 Ferguson, "Reaction Varies on Decision." See also Proby, "Welcome Soviet Republic of Canada"; and "Ruling on Anti-Hate Laws Produces Mixed Reaction."
169 *R. v. Keegstra*, [1995] 2 S.C.R. 381, 383.
170 *R. v. Keegstra*, [1996] 1 S.C.R. 458.
171 *R. v. Zundel*, [1992] 2 S.C.R. 731.
172 The other three justices who made up the majority included La Forest, L'Heureux-Dubé, and Sopinka. Those dissenting were Justices Gonthier, Cory, and Iacobucci. Although they agreed that section 181 of the *Criminal Code* violated section 2(b) of the *Charter*, they differed from the majority on the question of whether the law could be saved under section 1, which they believed could be justified on the grounds that it encourages "racial and social tolerance, which is so essential to the successful functioning of a democratic and multicultural society," and is consistent with the aims outlined in sections 15 and 27 of the *Charter. Ibid.*, 734, 736-37.
173 Despite the outcome, Borovoy took little solace in the decision. For him, it was a trial that could produce no winners. Had the prosecution won, it would have created another "bad" legal precedent; because it had not, Zündel was handed another opportunity to promote himself as a champion of civil liberties. Interview with A. Alan Borovoy, Toronto, 8 February 2005.
174 Joel Bakan, *Just Words: Constitutional Rights and Social Wrongs* (Toronto: University of Toronto Press, 1997), 94-95.
175 Warren Kinsella, *Web of Hate: Inside Canada's Far Right Network* (Toronto: HarperCollins, 2001), 437.

176 One of the most common examples cited is section 13 of the *Canadian Human Rights Act*, which prohibits the promotion of hate yet lacks safeguards such as those included in the 1970 hate propaganda law. The hate messages provisions of the *Human Rights Act* state that

> 13. (1) It is a discriminatory practice for a person or a group of persons acting in concert to communicate telephonically or to cause to be so communicated, repeatedly, in whole or in part by means of the facilities of a telecommunication undertaking within the legislative authority of Parliament, any matter that is likely to expose a person or persons to hatred or contempt by reason of the fact that that person or those persons are identifiable on the basis of a prohibited ground of discrimination.

Human Rights Act, R.S. 1985, c. H-6, s. 13; 2001, c. 41, s. 88.

177 Interview with A. Alan Borovoy, Toronto, 8 February 2005. See also A. Alan Borovoy, *The New Anti-Liberals* (Toronto: Canadian Scholars Press, 1999). Like Borovoy, Braun argues that the left has also looked to the judiciary to place prohibitions on certain types of pornography and other forms of discrimination. On the question of whether to criminalize hateful materials, he suggests that "hate censorship is a dated, failed, authoritarian relic of a pre-democratic past resuscitated by progressive censoring theorists for postmodern needs." Braun, *Democracy Off Balance*, 262.

178 Magnet, "Hate Propaganda in Canada," 242-43.

179 L.W. Sumner, *The Hateful and the Obscene: Studies in the Limits of Free Expression* (Toronto: University of Toronto Press, 2004), 62-63.

180 Derek J. Penslar, "Introduction," in *Contemporary Antisemitism: Canada and the World*, ed. Derek J. Penslar, Michael R. Marrus, and Janice Gross Stein (Toronto: University of Toronto Press, 2005), 10. Of course, antisemitism has not been eliminated in Canada. David Ahenakew, the former head of the Federation of Saskatchewan Indian Nations, told a crowd of three hundred in 2002 that Jews were a "disease" that Hitler had tried to "clean up." Katherine Harding, "Medicine, Wine Blamed for Anti-Semitic Tirade," *Globe and Mail*, 7 April 2005, A8. In November of the same year, twenty-two-year-old Yousef Sandouga pleaded guilty and was convicted of the October 2000 firebombing of the Beth Shalom Synagogue in Edmonton. In a similar but unrelated event, nineteen-year-old Sleiman Elmerhebi admitted to police in December 2004 that he was responsible for the firebombing of the United Talmud Torah School in Montreal on 5 April 2004. "Man Admits to Firebombing Montreal Jewish School," *CBC News Online*, 17 December 2004, http://www.cbc.ca/.

181 After Zündel, probably the most infamous Holocaust denier is British historian David Irving, who in April 2000 sued American historian Deborah Lipstadt and her publisher, Penguin Books, for libel after she wrote that Irving was "one of the most dangerous spokespersons for Holocaust denial. Familiar with historical evidence, he bends it until it conforms with his ideological leanings and political agenda." In response, Irving contended that Lipstadt had damaged his reputation as a historian. The court sided with Lipstadt, agreeing with her that there was considerable evidence to suggest that Irving had "deliberately misrepresented and manipulated

historical evidence in order to portray Hitler in 'an unwarrantedly favourable light.'" Quoted in Wendie Ellen Schneider, "Past Imperfect: *Irving v. Penguin Books Ltd.*," *Yale Law Journal* 110 (2001): 1532.

182 Manuel Prutschi, "The New Antisemitism: Not All that New," Canadian Jewish Congress, 25 October 2002, http://www.cjc.ca/. See also Canadian Jewish Congress, "The United Nations Conference against Racism, Racial Discrimination, Xenophobia, and Related Intolerance (WCAR)," 17 October 2001; and Canadian Jewish Congress, "Submission on Antisemitism in Canada to the Senate's Standing Committee on Human Rights Re: Resolution Encapsulating the 2002 Berlin OSCE (PA) Resolution," Ottawa, 19 April 2004. http://www.cjc.ca/2004/04/19/antisemitism-in-canada/.

One of the most pronounced examples in recent years in which new antisemitism came to the fore was at the September 2001 United Nations Conference against Racism, Racial Discrimination, Xenophobia, and Related Intolerance (WCAR), in which the overall agenda was "ground to a halt" by efforts among participants sympathetic to the Palestinians who sought to see Israel singled out as an "apartheid" state. For a firsthand account of the hostilities directed toward Israel during the civil society forum of the Durban conference, see David Matas, *Aftershock: Anti-Zionism and Antisemitism* (Toronto: Dundurn Group, 2005), 13-29. Other examples include the anti-Israeli divestment campaigns and boycotts that have become increasingly popular strategies for activists on the left.

183 Morton Weinfeld, "The Changing Dimensions of Contemporary Canadian Antisemitism," in *Contemporary Antisemitism: Canada and the World*, ed. Derek J. Penslar, Michael R. Marrus, and Janice Gross Stein (Toronto: University of Toronto Press, 2005), 44. For similar assessments of the nature of contemporary antisemitism and its relation to the Israeli-Palestinian question, see the other chapters in the volume: Steven J. Zipperstein, "Historical Reflections on Contemporary Antisemitism," 52-63; Todd M. Endelman, "Antisemitism in Western Europe Today," 64-79; Derek J. Penslar, "Antisemitism and Anti-Zionism: A Historical Approach," 80-95; and Mark Tessler, "The Nature and Determinants of Arab Attitudes towards Israel," 96-119.

184 In *The New Anti-Liberals,* Borovoy criticizes the CJC for becoming "pro-censorship" and "imperiling legitimate speech" through its efforts to broaden the scope of the law. See 47-51.

CHAPTER 3: SHOCKING THE CONSCIENCE?

1 According to the organization's official history, Benenson had been angered by the Salazar government's arrest of two students in Lisbon for openly drinking a toast to liberty while in a restaurant. He wrote an article for *The Observer* titled "The Forgotten Prisoners" and then approached two friends, Eric Baker and Louis Blom, with an idea: to launch a one-year letter-writing campaign called the Appeal for Amnesty, 1961. For a biography of Benenson, see http://www.amnesty.org.uk/. The definition of a POC was later expanded to include people "imprisoned, detained or restricted for their political, religious or other conscientiously held beliefs, their ethnic origin, sex, color or language who have not used or advocated violence." See also Appeal for Amnesty, 1961, "Action to Free Political Prisoners, International Movement Formed,

Secretariat in London," press release, London, 8 February 1961, Archives of the International Secretariat of Amnesty International, International Institute for Social History (IISH), Amsterdam, vol. "International Council Meeting," files 1-3. See also Jonathan Power, *Amnesty International: The Human Rights Story* (Oxford: Pergamon Press, 1981).

2 Appeal for Amnesty, 1961, "Draft Resolutions," London, 20 July 1961, Archives of the International Secretariat of Amnesty International, International Institute for Social History (IISH), Amsterdam, vol. "International Council Meeting," files 1-3.

3 Tom Buchanan, "'The Truth Will Set You Free': The Making of Amnesty International," *Journal of Contemporary History* 37, 4 (2002): 575-97.

4 Stephen Hopgood, *Keepers of the Flame: Understanding Amnesty International* (Ithaca: Cornell University Press, 2006), 54, 62.

5 *Ibid.*, 588-89. Initial support for the Appeal for Amnesty, 1961, came from human rights advocates in France, Switzerland, Germany, Belgium, Eire, the United Kingdom, and Luxembourg, as well as from the Council of Europe Strasbourg, the International Commission of Jurists, the International Press Institute, the Congress for Cultural Freedom, and Pax Romana. Appeal for Amnesty, 1961, International Planning Meeting, Luxembourg, 22 July 1961. By the end of that year, the list grew to include supporters from Australia, Denmark, Greece, India, Israel, Italy, Jamaica, Mexico, New Zealand, Nigeria, Norway, Sweden, the United States, and Ceylon. Appeal for Amnesty, 1961, Second International Meeting, London, 8 October 1961. Archives of the International Secretariat of Amnesty International, IISH, vol. "International Council Meeting," files 1-3.

6 Hopgood, *Keepers of the Flame*, 60. For an account of the problematic nature of the violence/non-violence framework and the POC concept, see Edy Kaufman, "Prisoners of Conscience: The Shaping of a New Human Rights Concept," *Human Rights Quarterly* 13, 3 (1991): 339-67.

7 For instance, prior to 1968, AI only sought the right not to be subjected "to torture or to cruel, inhuman or degrading treatment or punishment (Article 5 of the Universal Declaration of Human Rights)" in cases involving POCs. Amnesty International, "Meeting on Violence Working Paper," prepared for the 1973 International Council Meeting in Vienna, 14-16 September 1973, 2, Archives of the International Secretariat of Amnesty International, IISH, vol. "International Council Meeting," files 8, 13. Buchanan contends that the position on violence was not a significant issue for Benenson at the time of AI's founding; nevertheless, it made a great deal of sense for the nascent organization. According to Peter Baehr, it was a calculated way for the organization to remain politically impartial and distinguish political acts from those that were criminal, while simultaneously appealing to a broad spectrum of members, many of whom were of the "pacifist persuasion." Peter R. Baehr, "Amnesty International and Its Self-Imposed Limited Mandate," *Netherlands Quarterly of Human Rights* 12, 1 (1994): 13-14.

8 Richard Reoch, Development Office, International Secretariat, Amnesty International, "Memo: Expediency as an Excuse for Brutality Is Unacceptable," 25 August 1973, 3, Archives of the International Secretariat of Amnesty International, IISH, vol. "International Council Meeting," files 8, 13.

9   For an account of the divisions within AI on the question of whether to adopt unconditional opposition to the death penalty, see Andrew S. Thompson, "Beyond Expression: Amnesty International's Decision to Oppose Capital Punishment, 1973," *Journal of Human Rights* 7, 4 (2008): 327-40.
10 In December 1977, AI hosted a Conference on the Abolition of the Death Penalty in which it passed a declaration calling for "total and unconditional opposition to the death penalty." Quoted in James J. Megivern, *The Death Penalty: An Historical and Theological Survey* (New York: Paulist Press, 1997), 359. For a copy of the "Stockholm Declaration," see Amnesty International, *The Death Penalty* (London: Amnesty International Publications, 1979), 199.
11 Between 1955 and 1962, the death penalty had been used over twenty-five times, ending with the 11 December 1962 dual executions of Ronald Turpin and Arthur Lucas. Turpin, a member of the Mafia, was found guilty in the murder of a police officer; Lucas, a fifty-four year old from Detroit with a long history of criminal activity, was charged with the murders of "pimp-turned-drug-informant" Therland Carter and prostitute Carolyn Newman on 11 November 1961 in Toronto. See Betty Lee, "Murder? Arthur Lucas and the Dreadful Ultimate: Puzzling Aspects of a Sordid Case," *Globe and Mail*, 28 October 1963, 7. From 1951 to 1959, 111 death sentences were issued by Canadian courts; 50 were later pardoned. See United Nations, *Capital Punishment* (New York: UN Department of Economic and Social Affairs, 1962), 48.
12 For a summary of the various arguments for and against abolition of the death penalty that were raised in the House of Commons, see David Ballantine Chandler, "Capital Punishment and the Canadian Parliament: A Test of Durkheim's Hypothesis on Repressive Law" (PhD diss., Cornell University, 1970), 36-41.
13 Section 642 of the *Criminal Code* stated that "the sentence to be pronounced against a person who is sentenced to death shall be that he shall be hanged by the neck until he is dead." The intent behind Bill C-28 was to provide a "more humane method of execution of the sentence." Bill C-28, *An Act to Amend the Criminal Code (Capital Punishment, Form of Sentence)*, Second Session, Twenty-Seventh Parliament, first reading, Ottawa, 11 May 1967, 2.
14 Bill C-93, *An Act to Amend the Criminal Code (Punishment for Murder)*, Second Session, Twenty-Seventh Parliament, first reading, Ottawa, 11 May 1967; Bill C-141, *An Act to Amend the Criminal Code (Abolition of Capital Punishment) and the Parole Act (Persons Convicted of Murder or Treason)*, Second Session, Twenty-Seventh Parliament, first reading, Ottawa, 28 June 1967.
15 *Act to Amend the Criminal Code*, S.C. 1967, c. 15.
16 *Criminal Law Amendment Act*, S.C. 1973-74, c. 38.
17 *Criminal Law Amendment Act* (No. 2), S.C. 1976, c. 105.
18 *Hansard*, 3 May 1976, 13089.
19 *Hansard*, 15 June 1976, 14499, 14501.
20 In total, thirty-seven Liberal MPs voted against Bill C-84, and sixteen Tories voted in favour of it. As for the other parties, the sixteen NDP members were unanimous in their support, while the eleven Social Credit MPs were unanimous in their opposition.

21 *Hansard*, 3 May 1976, 13097-99, 13210, 13212; *Hansard*, 18 May 1976, 13609; *Hansard*, 4 June 1976, 14172, 14174.
22 The MP was Bill Kempling. *Hansard*, 15 June 1976, 14504.
23 *Ibid.*, 14499.
24 *Hansard*, 18 May 1976, 13609.
25 The three men were Réal Chartrand, René Vaillancourt, and John Connearney.
26 According to a Gallup poll conducted on 3 March 1976, 48 percent of Canadians said that they wanted Canada to retain the death penalty, even if the federal government was able to "achieve better law and order"; 41 percent indicated that they would be "satisfied with better law and order"; and 11 percent were undecided. "48% Want Capital Punishment: Better Law and Order Not Enough," *Gallup Report*, 3 March 1976, 1-2.
27 "Six-Vote Margin Carries Bill to Abolish Death Penalty for All Civilian Offences," *Globe and Mail*, 15 July 1976, 1.
28 Article 6 of the treaty states:

> When the offense for which extradition is requested is punishable by death under the laws of the requesting State and the laws of requesting State do not permit such punishment for that offense, extradition may be refused unless the requesting State provides such assurances as the requested State considers sufficient that the death penalty shall not be imposed, or, if imposed, shall not be executed.

> *Extradition Treaty between Canada and the United States of America* (amended by an exchange of notes), Treaty Series 1976, No. 3, Washington, DC, 3 December 1971, 8; instruments of ratification exchanged 22 March 1976; in force 22 March 1976.

29 Bill Domm, "Why I as a Christian Support Capital Punishment," sermon remarks at Northminster United Church, Peterborough, 25 January 1987, 7, LAC, MG32-C93, vol. 13, file 16, "Northminster United Church, Peterborough – Sermon on Capital Punishment, Correspondence, 1987."
30 *Ibid.* Also, according to a survey that he conducted of his constituents in January 1981, Domm claimed that 87.2 percent of those who responded favoured the reinstatement of capital punishment for crimes of premeditated first-degree murder. Bill Domm, "Tory MP's Poll Shows Overwhelming Majority in Favour of the Death Penalty," news release, 14 January 1981, LAC, MG32-C93, vol. 2, file 10, "News Releases, 1979-1988." Groups that supported Domm's push for reinstatement included Citizens Responding to You, Canadian Association of Chiefs of Police, Canadian Police Association, Canadian Resistance Movement, Citizens for Capital Punishment and Justice, Citizens United for Safety and Justice, Guelph Police Wives Auxiliary, Heritage Canada, Metropolitan Toronto Police Association, Nepean Police Association, Niagara Police Association, Ontario Provincial Police Association, Ottawa Police Association, Return Capital Punishment, Evangelical Fellowship of Canada, Fellowship of Evangelical Baptist Churches in Canada, Pentecostal Assemblies of Canada, and Victims of Violence Society. Domm, "Why I as a Christian Support Capital Punishment," 10.

31 According to the surveys, 61 percent of respondents favoured reinstatement, and 62 percent believed that it helped to protect society against violent crime. "Fewer Today Would Reinstate Death Penalty," *Gallup Report*, 7 May 1987, 1-3; "Majority View Execution as Protection for Society," *Gallup Report*, 11 May 1987, 1-2.

32 AI first established a presence in Canada in the early 1960s when letter-writing groups were formed first in Toronto and Montreal and then across the country. In May 1973, representatives from these groups travelled to St. Lambert, Quebec, to meet with Canadian Richard Reoch, the public information officer and "all-purpose general" at AI's International Secretariat in London. They also met with a number of prominent human rights activists in Canada, one of whom was Dr. John Humphrey, whose credentials included professor of human rights law at McGill University, former director of the Division of Human Rights at the United Nations, and member of the UN committee responsible for drafting the *UDHR* in 1947-48; Humphrey was elected president. There, they founded a national section, its primary purpose being to boost the organization's presence within Canada.

Drawn to the organization was a veritable "who's who" of the academic, legal, church, and government communities. Joining Humphrey on the executive board were notable Canadians such as Senator Thérèse Casgrain; Laing Ferguson, professor of geology at Mount Allison University; Mary Beattie, formerly of the World Health Organization; John E. Robbins, Canada's first ambassador to the Vatican and former president of Brandon University; senator and constitutional expert Eugene Forsey; Vernon Nichols, minister of First Unitarian Congregation of Ottawa; Jetty Robertson, widow of Norman Robertson, former Department of External Affairs mandarin and ambassador to Great Britain and the United States; Nathalie Barton of the first AI community group in Canada; and David Golden, president of Telesat Canada and former deputy minister of industry in the early 1960s. Robert Inch, who had recently retired from life as an academic at Brandon University, was named the first national executive director. Other notable members included George Ignatieff, former ambassador to the UN; Hugh Keenleyside, another former Ottawa mandarin and director general of the UN Technical Assistance Administration; Guy Belanger, Roman Catholic bishop of Valleyfield, Quebec; M.J. Coldwell; publisher Maynard Gertler; James A. Gibson, president emeritus, Brock University; Gustav Gingras, Montreal; Noel Kinsella; W.R. Lederman; Dorothy Livesay; George Lockwood; Ronald St. J. MacDonald, dean, Faculty of Law, Dalhousie University; Joe Morris, president of the Canadian Labour Congress; Claude de Montigny; E.W. Scott, primate, Anglican Church of Canada; vocal civil libertarian Frank R. Scott; T.H.B. Symons; George J. Wesley; and Carl Zurbrigg of the Dominion Chalmers United Church in Ottawa.

See Peter Warren, "Memorandum," St. Lambert, 20 March 1973; Judith Bishop, "Letter to Richard Reoch," Hamilton, 23 January 1973, LAC, R8298, vol. 71, file 15, "Setting Up the Canadian National Section: Correspondence, 1972-1973." See also Amnesty International Canada, "Early Roots of the Canadian National Section," n.d., 6, 8, LAC, R8298, vol. 94, file 4, "Amnesty International Canadian Section History, 1974-1979." See also Stephen Scott, "Amnesty International Going Canada-Wide," *Ottawa Citizen*, 26 May 1973, LAC, R8298, vol. 71, file 15, "Setting Up the Canadian

Notes to pages 97-99

National Section: Correspondence, 1973-1974." See also Amnesty International Canada, "Executive Committee Report," 11 May 1974, LAC, R8298, vol. 72, file 10, "First Annual Meeting, 11 May 1974, University of Ottawa: Minutes."
33 Amnesty International Canadian Section (English Speaking), "Letter to the Right Honourable Brian Mulroney from Bob Goodfellow, President AICS(ES)," 26 August 1986; see also Amnesty International Canadian Section (English Speaking), "Letter to the Right Honourable Brian Mulroney from Marilyn Wilson, Executive Director," 7 October 1986, LAC, R8298, vol. 66, file 9, "Action 503-508 Death Penalty, 1985-1987."
34 Amnesty International Canadian Section (English Speaking), "Survey of Members of Parliament," Ottawa, 30 May 1986, LAC, R8298, vol. 66, file 9, "Action 503-508 Death Penalty, 1985-1987."
35 Amnesty International Canadian Section (English Speaking) joined forces with the other members of CARDP in the fall of 1985. Amnesty International International Secretariat, "Letter to Ian Heide, Death Penalty Coordinator re: Coalition against the Return of the Death Penalty," 16 September 1985, LAC, R8298, vol. 66, file 8, "Action 500-502 Death Penalty, 1985-1987."
36 Also working in AI's favour was that the pro-death penalty lobby in Canada was, according to the organization, "both few in number and relatively unorganized," perhaps because Canadians' support for capital punishment remained high. AI estimated that vocal proponents of capital punishment consisted of only about 80 to 100 people, who, despite their numbers, were able to keep the issue alive. Paul J. LaRose-Edwards, Amnesty International, Ottawa, "Death Penalty Consultant's Report: AICS(ES) Campaign against the Return of the Death Penalty to Canada, August 1986 to July 1987," 9-10, internal file.
37 According to his memoirs, it was the execution of Wilbert Coffin in Quebec in the late 1950s, and later the sentencing of Steven Truscott, that first caused Mulroney to question the merits of capital punishment. Brian Mulroney, *Memoirs* (Toronto: McClelland and Stewart, 2007), 557.
38 *Hansard*, 22 June 1987, 7475-76. See also Patricia Poirier, "Capital Punishment a Repugnant Act, PM Tells Commons," *Globe and Mail*, 23 June 1987, A1-A2.
39 Patricia Poirier, "Speaker Braces for Tie on Death Penalty," *Globe and Mail*, 27 June 1987, A1-A2.
40 *Hansard*, 29 June 1976, 7720, 7721, 7723, 7727, 7729, 7732, 7753, 7755-56, 7764, 7767.
41 Tom Milburn, "Commons Vote Kills Death Penalty," *Peterborough Examiner*, 30 June 1987.
42 The eight MPs from Quebec who supported the motion were Treasury Board President Robert de Cotret (Berthier-Maskinongé-Lanaudière), Jean-Pierre Blackburn (Jonquière), Vincent Della Noce (Duvernay), Gabriel Fontaine (Lévis), Darryl Gray (Bonaventure-Îles-de-la-Madelaine), Charles Hamelin (Charlevoix), Fernand Jourdenais (La Prairie), and Ricardo Lopez (Châteauguay). Patricia Poirier, "Quebec Tories Key to Defeat of Noose," *Globe and Mail*, 1 July 1987, A1, A4.
43 For a detailed account of Ng's crimes, see Stephen Magagnini, "The Calaveras County Murders," *Sacramento Bee Magazine*, 22 May 1988: 6-9, 14-16.

44 *Reasons for the Decision of the Honourable Madam Justice Marguerite J. Trussler,* in the Court of the Queen's Bench of Alberta, Judicial District of Edmonton, in the Matter of the Extradition Act, R.S.C. 1970, Chapter E-21 and Amendments Thereto, and in the Matter of Charles Chitat Ng, and in the Matter of a Request by the United States of America for Extradition of Charles Chitat Ng from Canada to the United States of America, (1988), 93 A.R. 204, 29 November 1988, 17.

45 Memorandum of Judgment, *Her Majesty the Queen in the Right of Canada and the Attorney-General for Canada, Representing the United States of America v. Charles Chitat Ng,* in the Court of Appeal of Alberta, (1989), 97 A.R. 241, appeal #8903-0169-A, 5 May 1989, 2-5.

46 Doug Lewis, Minister of Justice and Attorney General of Canada, to Donald W. MacLeod, Ottawa, 26 October 1989, 3, internal file, AICS(ES), Ottawa.

47 Minister of Justice and Attorney General of Canada, "Extradition of Charles Ng Referred to Supreme Court," communiqué, 8 June 1990, internal file, AICS(ES), Ottawa.

48 On 30 August 1985, Justice Pinard of the Quebec Superior Court had ordered him to be held in detention pending the decision of Minister of Justice John Crosbie to surrender him to US authorities. In January 1986, Crosbie agreed to extradite Kindler without seeking assurances that the death penalty would not be used against him. Kindler sought leave to appeal the decision on the grounds that Crosbie had not agreed to a request from his lawyer for an oral hearing with the minister to review the merits of the evidence against Kindler. Justice Hugessen of the Federal Court of Appeal sided with the federal government and ruled that Crosbie had not committed an error in law according to Article 6 of the Canada-US Extradition Treaty; however, Justices Marceau and Pratte determined that Crosbie had violated Kindler's constitutional rights under section 12 of the *Charter.* See John C. Crosbie, Minister of Justice, "Letter to Julius Grey," Ottawa, 17 January 1986, internal file, AICS(ES), Ottawa. Judgment (Hugessen J.), *Kindler v. Canada (Minister of Justice),* Federal Court of Appeal, no. A-81-87, 20 December 1988; Judgment (Marceau J.), *Kindler v. Canada (Minister of Justice),* Federal Court of Appeal, no. A-81-87, 20 December 1988. See also Judgment (Cory J.), *Kindler v. Canada (Minister of Justice),* [1991] 2 S.C.R. 779, 26 September 1991, 2-6.

49 "Proposed Extradition Process: Background Information, Minister of Justice and Attorney General of Canada," Ottawa, September 1991, LAC, MG32-C93, vol. 14, file 13, "Briefing Book on Extradition (1), 1985-1992."

50 Bill C-209 also proposed that the minister of justice be allowed the discretion to determine whether to surrender an individual prior to completion of his or her sentence for crimes committed while in Canada.

51 Bill C-209, *An Act to Amend the Extradition Act (Appeal),* Second Session, Thirty-Fourth Parliament, first reading, Ottawa, 10 April 1989; Bill C-210, *An Act to Amend the Criminal Code and the Supreme Court Act (Habeas Corpus),* Second Session, Thirty-Fourth Parliament, first reading, Ottawa, 10 April 1989. See also Bill Domm, "Domm to Introduce Extradition Bills," news release, 10 April 1989, 1-2, LAC, MG32-C93, vol. 2, file 13, "News Releases Concerning Ng Extradition, 1988-1990."

52 Bill Domm, "Extradition: 'Canada May Become a Killer's Haven,'" speech delivered to the Eastport Lions Club, Peterborough, 11 May 1989; see also Bill Domm, "Private Member's Bill on Canada's Extradition Process," speech delivered to the Kiwanis Club of Peterborough, 2 March 1989, LAC, MG32-C93, vol. 14, file 13, "Briefing Book on Extradition (1), 1985-1992."
53 See "Kidnap, Sexual Abuse Plot Cited in Extradition Bid," *Winnipeg Free Press*, 18 October 1988, 14; Matthew Ingram, "Returning Ng to Justice," *Alberta Report*, 12 December 1988, 47-45; Drew McAnulty, "American Families of Sex Slaying Victims Seek: JUSTICE," *Ottawa Sunday Sun*, 23 April 1989, 18; Norm Ovenden, "Send Ng Home to Answer Jury, U.S. Victims Sob," *Edmonton Journal*, 18 May 1989, A3; "Victim's Mothers Plead for Return of Murder Suspect," *Peterborough Examiner*, 18 May 1989, 13; Sean Durkan, "Send Ng Back, They Cry," *Toronto Sun*, 18 May 1989, 28; and Geoff White, "Families Support Domm in Ng Case," *Calgary Herald*, 18 May 1989, A9.
54 A less prominent group that supported Domm in his efforts to see Ng's expeditious extradition was British Columbia's Citizens United for Safety and Justice. Citizens United for Safety and Justice, "Letter to Bill Domm re: Deportation, Extradition of Criminals to U.S.A.," 8 December 1988; and Citizens United for Safety and Justice, "Letter to the Right Honourable Brian Mulroney re: Criminal Fugitives in Canada and Specifically Charles Ng," 29 November 1988, LAC, MG32-C93, vol. 15, file 13, "Ng, Charles, Speeches, Clippings, Petitions, 1988-1989."
55 Gary Rosenfeldt, "Should Ng Be Extradited? Justice Will Be Served Only by Extraditing Ng," *Toronto Star*, 6 December 1988.
56 Other MPs to support Domm were Bill Attewell, Pauline Browes, Terry Clifford, Chuck Cook, Bob Corbett, Stan Darling, Doug Fee, Gabriel Fontaine, Girve Fretz, Bob Horner, Al Horning, Ken Hughes, Al Johnson, David Kilgour, Alex Kindy, Willie Littlechild, John A. MacDougall, Brian O'Kurley, Steve Paproski, André Plourde, Bob Porter, John Reimer, Lee Richardson, Jean-Marc Robitaille, Geoff Scott, Jack Shields, Barbara Sparrow, Scott Thorkelson, Walter Van de Walle, Bill Vankoughnet, and Robert Wenman. Bill Domm, "The Role of the Victims of Violence Society," April 1989, MG32-C93, vol. 15, file 3, "Handouts."
57 Amnesty International International Secretariat, "Letter re: Charles Ng – Extradition to California," London, 4 December 1989, internal file, AICS(ES), Ottawa.
58 See Amnesty International Canadian Section (English Speaking), "Amnesty International Opposes 'Unconditional' Extradition of Charles Ng and Joseph Kindler to the United States at Hearing before the Supreme Court of Canada," news release, 21 February 1991; and Amnesty International Canadian Section (English Speaking), "Questions and Answers: On Amnesty International's Opposition to the 'Unconditional' Extradition of Charles Ng and Joseph Kindler," n.d., internal file, AICS(ES), Ottawa.
59 "No to Amnesty," *Calgary Sun*, 19 February 1991, 10.
60 Lorrie Goldstein, "Opinion Editorial," *Toronto Sun*, 22 February 1991, 12.
61 "Extradition Cases Set to Go before Top Court," *Peterborough Examiner*, 20 February 1991, 7.

62 There were six reasons for their opposition to AI's intervention:

1. [AI] work[s] only for those persons who have neither used nor advocated violence ([AI] did not even adopt Nelson Mandela). 2. [AI] work[s] for torture victims not torturers. 3. [AI] work[s] for [a] fair and speedy trial, [it does] not oppose [a] fair trial. 4. [AI sections] do not work for prisoners in [their] own country. 5. [AI does] not presume guilt, [it] presume[s] innocence. In fact, in this case, if [it does] publicly presume his guilt by suggesting the death penalty is a certainty, [it] may compromise any future trial of Mr. Ng. 6. [AI does] oppose the Death Penalty, but Charles Ng has not yet been tried and so is not subject to the Death Penalty. [AI] can appeal the penalty if that is his sentence.

"Letter to President, and All Executive Members of AICS(ES)," 25 February 1991, 1-2, internal file, AICS(ES), Ottawa.

63 On 21 February 1991, AI Community Groups 2 and 57 sent an emergency motion to the Executive Committee:

WHEREAS it has always been the policy of Amnesty International to work only for those persons who have neither used nor espoused violence; AND WHEREAS it is not the policy of Amnesty International to obstruct justice, but rather to ask for speedy and fair trials; AND WHEREAS Amnesty International holds to the established principle of justice that anyone accused of a crime is presumed innocent until found guilty at trial: BE IT RESOLVED that Amnesty International not intervene at the hearings of any person to be deported for trial, in any case where those persons are accused of any violent crime, because it presumes guilt and commits Amnesty International to work for violent people contrary to its own Statute. However, if such a person should be found guilty and if the sentence should be the Death Penalty, then Amnesty International should appeal to the appropriate authorities for commutation of the Death Penalty according to its policy of opposition to this punishment under any circumstances.

Amnesty International Community Groups 2 and 57, "Emergency Motion," 21 February 1991, internal file, AICS(ES), Ottawa.

64 "Letter to Amnesty International," 18 February 1991, internal file, AICS(ES), Ottawa.
65 Amnesty International Canadian Section (English Speaking), *AI Bulletin*, December 1990–January 1991: 3.
66 The two referred by the governor in council were

1. Would the surrender by Canada of an extradition fugitive to the United States of America, to stand trial for wilful or deliberate murder for which the penalty upon conviction may be death, constitute a breach of the fugitive's rights guaranteed under the *Canadian Charter of Rights and Freedoms*?
2. Did the Minister of Justice, in deciding pursuant to Article 6 of the *Extradition Treaty between Canada and the United States of America*, to surrender the fugitive Charles Chitat Ng without seeking assurances from the United States of America that the death penalty would not be imposed on the said Charles Chitat Ng, if imposed, that it would not be executed, commit any of the errors

of law and jurisdiction alleged in the Statement of Claim filed in the Federal Court of Canada (Trial Division) by the said Charles Chitat Ng on October 30, 1989, having regard to the said Statement of Claim, the reasons given by the Minister of Justice for the said decision and to any other material which the Court, in its discretion, may receive and consider?

Judgment (Cory) *Kindler v. Canada (Minister of Justice)*, [1991] 2 S.C.R. 779, 1.

67 According to section 25 of the *Extradition Act*,

Subject to this Part, the Minister of Justice, on the requisition of the foreign state, may, under his hand and seal, order a fugitive who has been committed for surrender to be surrendered to the person or persons who are, in the Minister's opinion, duly authorized to receive the fugitive in the name and on behalf of the foreign state, and the fugitive shall be so surrendered accordingly.

Extradition Act, R.S.C., 1985, c. E-23. Supreme Court Justice Peter Cory later added two more questions for the court to examine:

1. Is s. 25 of the *Extradition Act*, R.S.C. 1985, c. E-23, to the extent that it permits the Minister of Justice to order the surrender of a fugitive for a crime for which the fugitive may be or has been sentenced to death in the foreign state without first obtaining assurances from the foreign state that the death penalty will not be imposed, or, if imposed, will not be executed, inconsistent with ss. 7 or 12 of the *Canadian Charter of Rights and Freedoms*?
2. If the answer to question 1 is in the affirmative, is s. 25 of the *Extradition Act*, R.S.C. 1985, c. E-23, a reasonable limit of the rights of a fugitive within the meaning of s. 1 of the *Canadian Charter of Rights and Freedoms*, and therefore not inconsistent with the *Constitution Act, 1982*?

Ibid., 2.

68 For Matas' bio, see Edmond Y. Lipsitz, ed., *Who's Who in Canadian Jewry: Canadian Jewry at Year 2000 and Beyond*, 3rd ed. (Toronto: JESL Educational Products, 2000), 107.
69 Factum of the Appellant, *Kindler v. Canada (Minister of Justice)*, [1991] 2 S.C.R. 779, 21 February 1991, 5; Factum of Amnesty International, *Kindler v. Canada (Minister of Justice)*, [1991] 2 S.C.R. 779, 21 February 1991, 3-4.
70 In their respective critiques of the US criminal justice system, both Matas and Grey focused on the possibility of error, the seemingly arbitrary application of the death penalty in the United States, the suffering caused by both the method of execution (electrocution for Kindler, the gas chamber for Ng) and the death row phenomenon, and the finality of capital cases. See Factum of the Appellant, *ibid.*, 30; and Factum of Amnesty International, *ibid.*, 13-16.
71 Matas suggested that neither public opinion polls nor Parliament's decision in 1987 to reject reinstatement bore much relevance to the case since "human rights must never be dependent on public opinion" and the free vote in the House of Commons said nothing about whether capital punishment was constitutional. David Matas, "Oral Remarks on Behalf of Amnesty International to the Supreme Court of Canada

in the Case of Ng and Kindler," *Kindler v. Canada (Minister of Justice)*, [1991] 2 S.C.R. 779, 21 February 1991, 5.

72 Factum of the Appellant, *Kindler v. Canada (Minister of Justice)*, [1991] 2 S.C.R. 779, 21 February 1991, 28; Matas, "Oral Remarks," 5.

73 Matas equated the death penalty to the ultimate form of torture and suggested that returning Kindler (and Ng) to the United States without seeking assurances was tantamount to participating in an "arbitrary gratuitous killing."

Matas also argued that Crosbie's decision violated Article 3 of the UN *Convention against Torture and Other Cruel, Inhuman, or Degrading Treatment or Punishment* (which Canada had ratified in 1987), which forbids the extradition of individuals in cases where they might be subjected to torture. Article 16 of the same document, he suggested, could be interpreted to extend this principle to other forms of "cruel, inhuman or degrading treatment or punishment pursuant to national law," the implication being that the decision in 1976 to become abolitionist meant that capital punishment fell into this category. Factum of Amnesty International, *Kindler v. Canada (Minister of Justice)*, [1991] 2 S.C.R. 779, 21 February 1991, 5-6.

According to Matas, the decision also violated the following articles in international human rights law: Article 3 of the *UDHR*: "Everyone has the right to life, liberty and security of the person"; Article 1 of the *ICCPR*: "Every human being has the inherent right to life. This right shall be protected by law. No one shall be arbitrarily deprived of his life"; Article 6 of the *ICCPR*: "Nothing in this article shall be invoked to delay or to prevent the abolition of capital punishment by any State Party to the Covenant"; Article 4.1: "Every person has the right to have his life respected. This right shall be protected by law and, in general, from the moment of conception. No one shall be arbitrarily deprived of his life"; Article 4.3 of the *American Convention on Human Rights*: "The death penalty shall not be re-established in states that have abolished it"; Article 1.1 of the *Second Optional Protocol to the ICCPR Aiming at the Abolition of Death Penalty*: "No one within the jurisdiction of a State party to the present Optional Protocol shall be executed"; and Article 1.2 of the *Second Optional Protocol to the ICCPR Aiming at the Abolition of Death Penalty*: "Each State party shall take all necessary measures to abolish the death penalty within its jurisdiction." See *American Convention on Human Rights*, OAS Official Records, OEA/Ser.K/XVII.1, Doc 65 Rev./Con.1 (1970); *Second Optional Protocol to the ICCPR Aiming at the Abolition of Death Penalty*, GA Res. 44/128, open for signature 15 December 1989.

Matas also cited Article 3 of UN General Assembly Resolution 2857(XXVI): "*Affirms* that, in order fully to guarantee the right to life, provided for under Article 3 of the *Universal Declaration of Human Rights*, the main objective to be pursued is that of progressively restricting the number of offences for which capital punishment may be imposed, with a view to the desirability of abolishing this punishment in all countries." UN General Assembly Resolution 2857(XXVI), 2027 plenary, 20 December 1971; and UN ECOSOC Resolution 1574(L) of 20 May 1971, UN ECOSOC Resolution 1745(LIV) of 16 May 1973, and UN ECOSOC Resolution 1930(LVIII) of 6 May 1975. *Ibid.*, 11.

74 In 1989, Amnesty International published a book titled *When the State Kills ... The Death Penalty v. Human Rights*. In it, AI argued, among other things, that capital punishment and human rights were incompatible, that the death penalty was tantamount to torture, and that a norm was starting to emerge within the international community favouring abolition. A copy of the book was submitted to the Supreme Court. See Amnesty International, *When the State Kills ... The Death Penalty v. Human Rights* (London: Amnesty International, 1989), 1-8.

75 According to Amnesty International, of these twenty-three nations, thirteen had become abolitionist for all crimes, four for non-military crimes, and another six *de facto* abolitionists, meaning that they had not carried out an execution in more than ten years. Nigel Rodley, "World-Wide Moves towards Abolition of the Death Penalty: A Seminar Held by Amnesty International on the Occasion of the Eighth United Nations Congress on the Prevention of Crime and the Treatment of Offenders," Havana, 3 September 1990, 17, internal file, AICS(ES), Ottawa.

76 See "12th Conference of European Ministers of Justice, Luxembourg, 20-21 May 1980, Resolution No. 4 on the Death Penalty," and "Resolution on the Abolition of the Death Penalty in the European Community Adopted on 18 June 1981," both of which can be found in Amnesty International International Secretariat, "Death Penalty Handbook," ACT 05/17/82, London, 6 October 1982, LAC, R8298, vol. 66, file "Action 051; 511 Death Penalty."

77 *Ibid.*, 19.

78 Article 2 of the *Second Optional Protocol* to the *ICCPR* states:

> 1. No reservation is admissible to the present Protocol, except for a reservation made at the time of ratification or accession that provides for the application of the death penalty in time of war pursuant to a conviction for a most serious crime of a military nature committed during wartime. 2. The State Party making such a reservation shall at the time of ratification or accession communicate to the Secretary-General of the United Nations the relevant provisions of its national legislation applicable during wartime. 3. The State Party having made such a reservation shall notify the Secretary-General of the United Nations of any beginning or ending of a state of war applicable to its territory.

Second Optional Protocol to the International Covenant on Civil and Political Rights Aiming at the Abolition of the Death Penalty, GA Res. 44/128, open for signature 15 December 1989.

Articles 1 and 2 of the *Protocol to the American Convention* state:

> Article 1: The States Parties to this Protocol shall not apply the death penalty in their territory to any person subject to their jurisdiction; Article 2.1: No reservations may be made to this Protocol. However, at the time of ratification or accession, the States Parties to this instrument may declare that they reserve the right to apply the death penalty in wartime in accordance with international law, for extremely serious crimes of a military nature.

Protocol to the American Convention on Human Rights to Abolish the Death Penalty, approved 8 June 1990, OAS Treaty Service, no. 73. *Ibid.*, 9-11.

79 William A. Schabas, *The Death Penalty as Cruel Treatment and Torture: Capital Punishment Challenged in the World's Courts* (Boston: Northeastern University Press, 1996), 11, 29, 88; see also William A. Schabas, "International Law and the Death Penalty: Reflecting or Promoting Change," in *Capital Punishment: Strategies for Abolition*, ed. Peter Hodgkinson and William A. Schabas (Cambridge: Cambridge University Press, 2004), 36-62; and Nigel S. Rodley, *The Treatment of Prisoners under International Law*, 2nd ed. (Oxford: Oxford University Press, 1999), specifically Chapter 7 on the death penalty in international law.
80 Amnesty International, "The Death Penalty: List of Abolitionist and Retentionist Countries," AI Index: Act 50/01/91, London, 30 January 1991, 6.
81 For an account of the emergence of a norm equating capital punishment with the "right to life," see William A. Schabas, *The Abolition of the Death Penalty in International Law*, 3rd ed. (Cambridge: Cambridge University Press, 2002).
82 Ibid., 7-8.
83 Ibid., 11, 14.
84 Judgment (Sopinka), *Kindler v. Canada (Minister of Justice)*, [1991] 2 S.C.R. 779, 26 September 1991, 5.
85 In their assessment of Cory's judgment in *Kindler*, John M. Evans and Trevor Knight suggest that "where fundamental human rights were concerned, Cory J. generally took a broad view of the role of the law. For example, he tended to support the more expansive and 'purposive' interpretation of human rights legislation, and to insist on minimal procedural safeguards for those facing surrender to a foreign criminal justice system that was likely to put them to death." John M. Evans and Trevor Knight, "Cory on Administrative Law: A Contextual Study," in *Peter Cory at the Supreme Court of Canada, 1989-1999*, ed. Patrick J. Monahan and Sandra A. Forbes (Winnipeg: Published for the Supreme Court of Canada Historical Society, Canadian Legal History Project, Faculty of Law, University of Manitoba, 2001), 111.
86 Judgment (Cory J.), *Kindler v. Canada (Minister of Justice)*, [1991] 2 S.C.R. 779, 26 September 1991, 21-24.
87 Ibid., 10, 28, 30, 46.
88 Schabas, *The Death Penalty as Cruel Treatment and Torture*, 117.
89 Ibid., 5-6, 11.
90 Ibid., 4.
91 See James B. Kelly, *Governing with the Charter: Legislative and Judicial Activism and Framers' Intent* (Vancouver: UBC Press, 2005), 132.
92 See B.M. McLachlin, "The Charter: A New Role for the Judiciary?" *Alberta Law Review* 29, 3 (1991): 540-59.
93 The case that she was referring to was *Canada v. Schmidt*, [1987] 1 S.C.R. 500, 522-23. See Judgment (McLachlin), *Kindler v. Canada (Minister of Justice)*, [1991] 2 S.C.R. 779, 26 September 1991, 10, 12, 13.
94 See Minister of Justice and Attorney General of Canada, "Supreme Court Decision Regarding Ng and Kindler," communiqué, Ottawa, 26 September 1991, LAC, MG32-C93, vol. 16, file 1, "Speeches on Extradition – News Releases, Background Clippings, 1989-1991."

95 Roger Clark, transcripts of television interviews regarding Supreme Court decision in *Kindler*, 26 September 1991, LAC, MG32-C93, vol. 15, Bill Domm Papers, file "Return of Ng and Kindler."
96 *Ibid.*
97 "Our Borders, Their Death Penalty," *Globe and Mail*, 28 September 1991, D6.
98 David Shoalts, "Fugitives Returned to U.S. after Ruling," *Globe and Mail*, 27 September 1991, A1; David Shoalts, "Campbell Defends Extradition," *Globe and Mail*, 7 October 1991, A4; transcript of interview with Dana Lewis of CTV News, Edmonton, 26 September 1991.
99 Transcript of interview with Laura Lynch, CBC News, Ottawa, 26 September 1991; transcript of interview with Chez Television, Peterborough, 26 September 1991.
100 Hugo Adam Bedau, "Abolishing the Death Penalty in the United States: An Analysis of Institutional Obstacles and Future Prospects," in *Capital Punishment: Strategies for Abolition*, ed. Peter Hodgkinson and William A. Schabas (Cambridge: Cambridge University Press, 2004), 200; Schabas, *The Abolition of the Death Penalty in International Law*, 287.
101 Interview with Bob Goodfellow, Executive Director, Amnesty International Canadian Section (English Speaking), Ottawa, 7 January 2003.
102 There was also some speculation that neither Bill C-209 nor Bill C-210 was constitutional. See Kim Campbell, "Letter to Bill Domm re: C-209 and C-210," n.d., LAC, MG32-C93, vol. 15, file 17, "Private Member's Bill C-210 – Briefing Notes, 1989-1990." See also *Hansard*, 6 December 1990, 16407-18.
103 Minister of Justice and Attorney General of Canada, "Extradition Process Streamlined," communiqué, Ottawa, 17 September 1991, LAC, MG32-C93, vol. 15, file 22, "Reform of Extradition Act, 1991."
104 "Minutes and Proceedings and Evidence of the Standing Committee on Justice and the Solicitor General Respecting Bill C-31, An Act to Amend the Extradition Act," vol. 21, Ottawa, 3 December 1991, 21, LAC, MG32-C93, vol. 16, file 2, "Standing Committee on Justice and the Solicitor General – minutes of proceedings concerning Bill C-31, to amend the *Extradition Act*."

There was also the outstanding issue of the UN Human Rights Committee. Shortly after Ng's extradition, both McLeod and the Canadian government had presented their cases to the committee. In his submission, McLeod had contended that Canada had violated Articles 6 and 7 of the *ICCPR* since the death penalty violated an individual's "right to life" and California's use of gas asphyxiation constituted "cruel and inhuman" punishment. The Government of Canada had countered that the covenant did not oblige it to "impose responsibility upon a State for eventualities over which it has no jurisdiction." Moreover, it had downplayed the cruelty of the method of execution and had submitted that the covenant neither offered a "right not to be extradited" nor explicitly prohibited the imposition of the death penalty. Raising the issue of national security, it had argued that, if the Canadian government were not allowed discretion in seeking assurances, Canada ran the risk of becoming a safe haven for American fugitives seeking to escape a death sentence. UN/CCPR/C/49/D/469/1991, 7 January 1994, 2-4.

On 5 November 1993, more than two years after Ng's surrender, the committee issued its ruling. Like the Supreme Court of Canada, it too was divided. The majority sided with the Canadian government – at least in part. It ruled that a violation of Article 6 had not taken place, given that paragraph 2 allowed states to use the death penalty for what constituted the "most serious crimes," of which Ng's qualified. Motivated in part by a desire to prevent the establishment of precedents that might impede the efficacy of the international system, it also ruled that Canada, despite being abolitionist, had a duty to honour its extradition treaties and that a violation of Article 6 would only have occurred had its decision not to seek assurances been made "summarily or arbitrarily." On the question of whether Canada had violated Article 7, the committee ruled that cyanide gas asphyxiation did constitute "cruel and inhuman" treatment. Perhaps simply for the record, the justices called on the Canadian government to "make such representations as might still be possible to avoid the imposition of the death penalty." Surely, it must have known that, for Canada, the *Ng* case was closed. *Ibid.*, 19, 20, 22. See also Schabas, *The Death Penalty as Cruel Treatment and Torture*, 32.

Ng remained contentious following Ng's extradition. In October 1992, Ng sued to remove his two court-appointed attorneys, thereby delaying the proceedings even further. Only in 1999 was he sentenced to death. At the time of writing, he was still on death row, his case having dragged on for nearly twenty years.

105 The cases were *Suresh v. Canada (Minister of Citizenship and Immigration)*, 2002 SCC 1; *United States v. Burns*, 2001 SCC 7; *Schreiber v. Canada (Attorney General)*, 2002 SCC 62; and *Charkaoui v. Canada (Citizenship and Immigration)*, 2007 SCC 9, [2007] 1 S.C.R. 350; *Canada (Prime Minister) v. Khadr*, 2010 SCC 3 Date: 29 January 2010.

106 Article 77 of the *Rome Statute*, "Applicable Penalties," states

1. Subject to article 110, the Court may impose one of the following penalties on a person convicted of a crime referred to in article 5 of this Statute:
   (a) Imprisonment for a specified number of years, which may not exceed a maximum of 30 years; or
   (b) A term of life imprisonment when justified by the extreme gravity of the crime and the individual circumstances of the convicted person.

2. In addition to imprisonment, the Court may order:
   (a) A fine under the criteria provided for in the Rules of Procedure and Evidence;
   (b) A forfeiture of proceeds, property and assets derived directly or indirectly from that crime, without prejudice to the rights of bona fide third parties.

Rome Statute for the International Criminal Court, UN Doc A/CONF.183/9, 17 July 1998.

107 Thomas M.J. Bateman, "The New Globalism in Canadian Charter of Rights Interpretation: Extradition, the Death Penalty, and the Courts," *International Journal of Human Rights* 7, 3 (2003): 49-71. Schabas has also referred to the process of blocking extradition in cases involving the death penalty "indirect abolition." See William A. Schabas, "Indirect Abolition: Capital Punishment's Role in Extradition Law and

Practice," *Loyola of Los Angeles International and Comparative Law Review* 25 (2003): 581-604.
108 The six new Supreme Court justices were Frank Iacobucci, John C. Major, Michel Bastarache, William Ian Corneil Binnie, Louise Arbour, and Louis LeBel. The four remaining were Beverley McLachlin, Claire L'Heureux-Dubé, and Charles Doherty Gonthier.
109 Kelly, *Governing with the Charter*, 250-53.
110 Interview with David Matas, 1 April 2005.
111 Judgment, *United States v. Burns*, 2001 SCC 7.
112 *Ibid.*, para. 10.4.
113 At the international level, the UN Human Rights Committee has also changed its mind on *Kindler*. In August 2003, it heard the case of Roger Judge, a Philadelphia man who had escaped from prison and in June of that year fled to Ste-Anne-des-Plaines in Quebec. He had been convicted of "two counts of first degree murder and possession of an instrument of crime." Here too the Canadian government had agreed to extradition without assurances. This time the Human Rights Committee ruled that Canada had violated Article 6, paragraph 1, of the *ICCPR*. The rationale for its decision was based on developments in the international community since *Kindler*. Over the past ten years, it wrote, "there has been a broadening international consensus in favour of abolition of the death penalty, and in states which have retained the death penalty, a broadening consensus not to carry it out." Citing the Supreme Court of Canada's ruling in *Burns* and a number of other precedents for seeking assurances in capital cases, it contended that any interpretation of the *ICCPR* must be seen in the context of recent views of the death penalty as an unsuitable punishment, both in Canada and in the international community. Like the Supreme Court, it ruled that "they may not remove, either by deportation or extradition, individuals from their jurisdiction if it may be reasonably anticipated that they will be sentenced to death, without ensuring that the death sentence would not be carried out." By deporting Judge, Canada would, in effect, be complicit in his potential execution and in violation of international human rights law. United Nations Human Rights Committee, *Judge v. Canada*, CCPR/C/78/D/829/1998, 13 August 2003, para. 10.3.
114 Canada, Department of Foreign Affairs and International Trade, "Canada Supports International Efforts toward Abolition of the Death Penalty," press release no. 238, Ottawa, 25 November 2005.
115 Aubrey Harris, "Stop Subcontracting the Death Penalty," *Ottawa Citizen*, 18 February 2008.
116 *Smith v. Canada (Attorney General)* (T-2067-07, 2009 FC 228), 4 March 2009; "Government Won't Appeal Ruling Forcing It to Help Albertan on Death Row," *CBC News.ca*, 3 April 2009, http://www.cbc.ca/.

CONCLUSION

1 Norberto Bobbio, *The Age of Rights*, trans. Allan Cameron (Cambridge, MA: Polity Press, 1996), 45, 64. Other scholars have made similarly grand claims about the transformative potential of the idea of "human rights." See Jack Donnelly, "Human

Rights: A New Standard of Civilization?" *International Affairs* 74, 1 (1998): 1-23.
2 Brian Orend, *Human Rights: Concept and Context* (Peterborough: Broadview Press, 2002), 15; Alison Brysk, "Conclusion: From Rights to Realities," in *Globalization and Human Rights*, ed. Alison Brysk (Berkeley: University of California Press, 2002), 297; Michael Ignatieff, *The Rights Revolution* (Toronto: Anansi, 2000), 2, 32, 43.
3 Bobbio, *The Age of Rights*, 47.
4 Rhoda Howard, *Human Rights and the Search for Community* (Boulder, CO: Westview Press, 1995), 12-13.
5 Abdul Aziz Said, "Pursuing Human Dignity," in *Human Rights and World Order*, ed. Abdul Aziz Said (New Brunswick, NJ: Transaction Books, 1978), 2.
6 Robert F. Drinan, *The Mobilization of Shame: A World View of Human Rights* (New Haven: Yale University Press, 2001), xi.
7 Todd Landman, *Protecting Human Rights: A Comparative Study* (Washington, DC: Georgetown University Press, 2005), 4.
8 Since the attacks of 9/11, a vibrant debate among scholars, activists, and government officials about the relationship between individual human rights and national security has focused on devising laws and policies that forge a balance or middle ground between the two. The rationale is that, on the one hand, too strict an adherence to human rights norms could compromise Canadian national security and the physical safety of citizens, while on the other, augmenting the powers available to law enforcement officials without sufficient oversight mechanisms could invite abuses and even authoritarianism. Although some have suggested that, in light of the threat posed by international terrorism, this refocusing of the primacy of rights has been necessary, others have lamented that many of the advances in human rights since the end of the Second World War have been erased. See Howard Adelman, "Canada's Balancing Act: Protecting Human Rights and Countering Terrorist Threats," in *National Insecurity and Human Rights: Democracies Debate Counterterrorism*, ed. Alison Brysk and Gershon Shafir (Berkeley: University of California Press, 2007), 137-56; Colleen Bell, "Subject to Exception: Security Certificates, National Security, and Canada's Role in the 'War on Terror,'" *Canadian Journal of Law and Society* 21, 1 (2006): 63-83; A. Alan Borovoy, *Categorically Incorrect: Ethical Fallacies in Canada's War on Terror* (Toronto: Dundurn Group, 2006); Jack Donnelly, *International Human Rights*, 3rd ed. (Cambridge, MA: Westview Press, 2007), 212-13; Michael Ignatieff, *The Lesser Evil: Political Ethics in the Age of Terror* (Princeton: Princeton University Press, 2004); Erna Paris, *The Sun Climbs Slow: Justice in the Age of Imperial America* (Toronto: Alfred A. Knopf Canada, 2008); Mary Robinson, "Human Rights in the Shadow of 11 September," Fifth Commonwealth Lecture, London, UK, 6 June 2002, in *A Voice for Human Rights*, ed. Kevin Boyle (Philadelphia: University of Pennsylvania Press, 2006); Kenneth Roth, "Review Essay: Getting Away with Torture," *Global Governance* 11 (2005): 389-406; and William Schulz, *Tainted Legacy: 9/11 and the Ruin of Human Rights* (New York: Thunder's Mouth Press, 2003).
9 Martha Finnemore and Kathryn Sikkink, "International Norm Dynamics and Political Change," *International Organization* 52, 4 (1998): 895.

Selected Bibliography

ARCHIVAL COLLECTIONS

Library and Archives Canada, Ottawa

Amnesty International Canadian Section	R8298
Bill Domm	MG32-C93
B'nai Brith Canada	MG28 V133
Canadian Civil Liberties Association	R9833
Canadian Council of Churches	MG28-I327
Department of Citizenship and Immigration	RG 26
Supreme Court of Canada	RG 125

International Institute for Social History, Amsterdam, The Netherlands
The Archives of the International Secretariat of Amnesty International

Supreme Court Records Office, Supreme Court of Canada, Ottawa
Kindler v. Canada (Minister of Justice), [1991] 2 S.C.R. 779.
Singh et al. v. MEI, [1985] 1 S.C.R. 177, file nos. 18209, 17997, 17952, 17898, 18207, 18235, 17904.

Amnesty International Canadian Section (English Speaking), Ottawa
Internal files on Charles Ng and Joseph Kindler

CASES CITED
Ahani v. Canada (Minister of Citizenship and Immigration), [2002] 1 S.C.R. 72.
Baker v. Canada (Minister of Citizenship and Immigration), [1999] 2 S.C.R. 817.

Bliss v. A.-G. Canada, [1979] 1 S.C.R. 183.
Boucher v. The King, [1951] 1 S.C.R. 265.
Canadian Council of Churches v. The Queen and the MEI, Federal Court (Trial-Division), 3 January 1989.
Canadian Council of Churches v. Canada (Minister of Employment and Immigration), [1990] Federal Court of Appeal, A-223-89, 12 March 1990.
Canadian Council of Churches v. Canada (Minister of Employment and Immigration), [1992] 1 S.C.R. 236.
Chieu v. Canada (Minister of Citizenship and Immigration), [2002] 1 S.C.R. 84.
Furman v. Georgia 408 U.S. 238 (1972).
Her Majesty the Queen in the Right of Canada and the Attorney-General for Canada, Representing the United States of America v. Charles Chitat Ng, in the Court of Appeal of Alberta, (1989), 97 A.R. 241, appeal #8903-0169-A, 5 May 1989.
Kindler v. Canada (Minister of Justice), Federal Court of Appeal, no. A-81-87, 20 December 1988.
Kindler v. Canada (Minister of Justice), [1991] 2 S.C.R. 779.
Lavell v. A.-G. Canada, 23 C.R.N.S. 197, 11 R.F.L. 333, [1974] S.C.R. 1349.
Miller and Cockriell v. R., [1977] 2 S.C.R. 680.
Minister of Justice v. Borowski, [1981] 2 S.C.R. 575.
Morgentaler v. The Queen, [1976] 1 S.C.R. 616.
R. v. Andrews and Smith, [1988] 28 O.A.C. 161.
R. v. Andrews, [1990] 3 S.C.R. 870.
R. v. Butler, [1992] 1 S.C.R. 452.
R. v. Drybones, [1970] 9 D.L.R. (3d) 473.
R. v. Finta, [1993] 1 S.C.R. 1138.
R. v. Finta, [1994] 1 S.C.R. 701.
R. v. Keegstra, [1984] 19 CCC (3d) 254.
R. v. Keegstra, [1988] 43 CCC (3d) 150.
R. v. Keegstra, [1990] 3 S.C.R. 697.
R. v. Keegstra, [1995] 2 S.C.R. 381.
R. v. Keegstra, [1996] 1 S.C.R. 458.
R. v. Krymowski, [2005] 1 S.C.R. 101, 2005 SCC 7.
R. v. Morgentaler et al., [1988] 1 S.C.R. 30.
R. v. Oakes, [1986] 1 S.C.R. 103.
R. v. Ruzic, [2001] 1 S.C.R. 687.
R. v. Zundel, [1987] 18 O.A.C. 161.
R. v. Zundel, [1992] 2 S.C.R. 731.
Roper v. Simmons 543 U.S. 551 (2005).
Schreiber v. Canada (Attorney General), 2002 SCC 62.
Singh et al. v. MEI, [1985] 1 S.C.R. 177.
Smith v. Canada (Attorney General) (T-2067-07, 2009 FC 228), 4 March 2009.
Suresh v. Canada (Minister of Citizenship and Immigration), [2002] 1 S.C.R. 3.
United States v. Burns, 2001 SCC 7.

CANADIAN GOVERNMENT BILLS AND TREATIES

Act to Amend the Criminal Code, S.C. 1967, c. 15.

An Act to Amend the Immigration Act, 1976, and to Amend Other Acts in Consequence Thereof, 35-36-37 Elizabeth II, 1988, c. 35.

An Act to Amend the Immigration Act, 1976, and the Criminal Code in Consequence Thereof, 35-36-37 Elizabeth II, 1988, c. 35.

An Act to amend the Immigration Act and other Acts in Consequence Thereof, R.S. 1992, c. 49.

Anti-terrorism Act (2001, c. 41)

Canadian Bill of Rights (1960, c. 44)

Criminal Code of Canada, R.S.C. 1970, c. C-34.

Criminal Code, R.S.C. 1985, c. C-46, s. 181.

Criminal Law Amendment Act, S.C. 1973-74, c. 38.

Criminal Law Amendment Act (No. 2), S.C. 1976, c. 105.

Extradition Act, R.S.C. 1985, c. E-23.

Immigration Act, S.C. 1976, c. 52, s. 46.

Immigration Appeal Board Act, S.C. 1966-67, c. 90, s. 15.

Immigration and Refugee Protection Act (2001, c. 27)

Indian Act, R.S.C. 1952, c. 149.

Human Rights Act, R.S. 1985, c. H-6, s. 13; 2001, c. 41, s. 88.

Bill C-28, *An Act to Amend the Criminal Code (Capital Punishment, Form of Sentence)*, Second Session, Twenty-Seventh Parliament, first reading, Ottawa, 11 May 1967.

Bill C-93, *An Act to Amend the Criminal Code (Punishment for Murder)*, Second Session, Twenty-Seventh Parliament, first reading, Ottawa, 11 May 1967.

Bill C-141, *An Act to Amend the Criminal Code (Abolition of Capital Punishment) and the Parole Act (Persons Convicted of Murder or Treason)*, Second Session, Twenty-Seventh Parliament, first reading, Ottawa, 28 June 1967.

Bill C-209, *An Act to Amend the Extradition Act (Appeal)*, Second Session, Thirty-Fourth Parliament, first reading, Ottawa, 10 April 1989.

Bill C-210, *An Act to Amend the Criminal Code and the Supreme Court Act (Habeas Corpus)*, Second Session, Thirty-Fourth Parliament, first reading, Ottawa, 10 April 1989.

Bill S-5, *An Act to Amend the Criminal Code*, Second Session, Twenty-Seventh Parliament, Ottawa, 9 May 1967.

Bill S-21, *An Act to Amend the Criminal Code*, First Session, Twenty-Eighth Parliament, Ottawa, 22 April 1969.

CANADIAN GOVERNMENT DOCUMENTS

Canada. Department of Manpower and Immigration. *Annual Report, 1966-1967*. Ottawa: Government of Canada, 1967.

–. *Annual Report, 1975-1976*. Ottawa: Government of Canada, 1976.

–. *Green Paper on Immigration: Immigration Policy Perspectives*. Ottawa: Queen's Printer, 1974.

–. *White Paper on Immigration*, Ottawa: Queen's Printer, 1966.

–. House of Commons. *The First Report to the House of the Special Committee on Participation of Visible Minorities in Canadian Society*. Second Session of the Thirty-Second Parliament, 1983-84. March 1984.

Plaut, W. Gunther. *Refugee Determination in Canada: Proposal for a New System, Report to the Honourable Flora MacDonald, Minister of Employment and Immigration*. Ottawa: Government of Canada, 1985.

Ratushny, Ed. *A New Refugee Status Determination Process for Canada*. Report to the Honourable John Roberts. Ottawa: Government of Canada, 1983.

Report to the Minister of Justice of the Special Committee on Hate Propaganda in Canada. Ottawa: Queen's Printer, 1966.

Robinson, W.G. *The Refugee Status Determination Process: A Report of the Task Force on Immigration Practices and Procedures to the Honourable Lloyd Axworthy*. Ottawa: Government of Canada, 1982.

DOCUMENTS IN INTERNATIONAL LAW

American Convention on Human Rights. OAS Official Records, OEA/Ser.K/XVII.1, Doc. 65 Rev./Con.1 (1970).

Convention Relating to the Status of Refugees. GA Res. 429(V), 14 December 1950. Adopted 28 July 1951.

International Covenant on Civil and Political Rights. GA Res. 2200A(XXI), 16 December 1966. Entry into force 23 March 1976, in accordance with Article 49.

International Convention on the Elimination of All Forms of Racial Discrimination. GA Res. 2106 (XX), 21 December 1965. Entry into force 4 January 1969.

Protocol Relating to the Status of Refugees. GA Res. 1186(XLI), 18 November 1966.

Protocol to the American Convention on Human Rights to Abolish the Death Penalty. Approved 8 June 1990. OAS Treaty Service, no. 73.

Second Optional Protocol to the International Covenant on Civil and Political Rights Aiming at the Abolition of the Death Penalty. GA Res. 44/128, 15 December 1989.

Universal Declaration of Human Rights. GA Res. 217 A(III), 10 December 1948.

UN AND OAS DOCUMENTS

Organization of American States. Inter-American Commission on Human Rights. "Press Communiqué" no. 14/97. Washington, DC, 17 October 1997.

–. "Report on the Situation of Human Rights of Asylum Seekers within the Canadian Refugee Determination System." OEA/Ser.L/V/II.106, Doc. 40 rev. Washington, DC, 28 February 2000.

Rome Statute for the International Criminal Court. UN Doc. A/CONF.183/9. 17 July 1998.

UN High Commission for Refugees Branch Office, Canada. "Submission to the Task Force on Immigration Practices and Procedures." February 1981.

UN Human Rights Committee. UN/CCPR/C/49/D/469/1991. 7 January 1994.

–. *Judge v. Canada*, CCPR/C/78/D/829/1998. 13 August 2003.

Selected Bibliography

INTERVIEWS AND CORRESPONDENCE
Harry Arthurs (correspondence), 5 March 2005.
A. Alan Borovoy, Toronto, 8 February 2005.
Tom Clark (telephone), United Church of Canada, 17 June 2004.
Bob Goodfellow, Ottawa, 7 January 2003.
David Matas (telephone), 1 April 2005.
Walter McLean (telephone), 24 August 2004.
Nigel Rodley (telephone), 23 September 2003.
Michael Schelew, Toronto, 19 August 2004.

NEWSPAPERS AND PERIODICALS
Canadian Jewish News
Canadian Lawyer
Law Times
Maclean's
Calgary Herald
Calgary Sun
Canadian Forum
Daily Star
Edmonton Journal
Edmonton Sun
Gallup Report
Globe and Mail
Lethbridge Herald
New York Times
Ottawa Citizen
Ottawa Sunday Sun
Peterborough Examiner
Red Deer Advocate
Sacramento Bee Magazine
Saint John Telegraph Journal
Toronto Star
Toronto Sun
Winnipeg Free Press
Weekend Magazine

SECONDARY SOURCES
Abella, Irving. *A Coat of Many Colours: Two Centuries of Jewish Life in Canada.* Toronto: Lester and Orpen Dennys, 1990.

Abella, Irving, and Harold Troper. *None Is Too Many: Canada and the Jews of Europe, 1933-1948.* Toronto: Lester and Orpen Dennys, 1982.

Adelman, Howard. "An Immigration Dream: Hungarian Refugees Come to Canada – An Analysis." In *Breaking Ground: The 1956 Hungarian Refugee Movement to Canada*, ed. Robert H. Keyserlingk, 25-44. Toronto: York Lanes Press, 1993.

–. "Canada's Balancing Act: Protecting Human Rights and Countering Terrorist Threats." In *National Insecurity and Human Rights: Democracies Debate Counterterrorism*, ed. Alison Brysk and Gershon Shafir, 137-56. Berkeley: University of California Press, 2007.

–. "Canadian Refugee Policy in the Postwar Period: An Analysis." In *Refugee Policy: Canada and the United States*, ed. Howard Adelman, 172-223. Toronto: York Lanes Press, 1991.

–. "Rabbi W. Gunther Plaut's Contribution to Canadian Refugee Law and Practice." In *A Rabbi of Words and Deeds: Essays in Honour of the 90th Birthday of W. Gunther Plaut*, ed. John Moscowitz and Natalie Fingerhut, 67-76. Toronto: Holy Blossom Temple, 2002.

–. "Refugee and Border Security Post-September 11." *Refuge* 20, 4 (2002): 5-14.

Ages, Arnold. "Antisemitism: The Uneasy Calm." In *The Canadian Jewish Mosaic*, ed. M. Weinfeld, W. Shaffir, and I. Cotler, 383-95. Toronto: John Wiley and Sons, 1981.

Alfredsson, G., and Asbjorn Eide. *The Universal Declaration of Human Rights: A Common Standard of Achievement*. The Hague: Martinus Nijhoff, 1999.

Amnesty International. *The Death Penalty*. London: Amnesty International Publications, 1979.

–. *When the State Kills ... The Death Penalty v. Human Rights*. London: Amnesty International Publications, 1989.

Anderson, Ellen. *Judging Bertha Wilson: Law as Large as Life*. Toronto: University of Toronto Press for the Osgoode Society for Canadian Legal History, 2001.

Arthurs, H.W. "Hate Propaganda – An Argument against Attempts to Stop It by Legislation." *Chitty's Law Journal* 18, 1 (1970): 1-5.

Avery, Donald H. *Reluctant Host: Canada's Response to Immigrant Workers, 1896-1994*. Toronto: McClelland and Stewart, 1995.

Backhouse, Constance. *Colour-Coded: A Legal History of Racism in Canada, 1900-1950*. Toronto: University of Toronto Press for the Osgoode Society for Canadian Legal History, 1999.

Baehr, Peter R. "Amnesty International and Its Self-Imposed Limited Mandate." *Netherlands Quarterly of Human Rights* 12, 1 (1994): 5-21.

Bakan, Joel. *Just Words: Constitutional Rights and Social Wrongs*. Toronto: University of Toronto Press, 1997.

Bangarth, Stephanie. *Voices Raised in Protest: Defending North American Citizens of Japanese Ancestry, 1942-49*. Vancouver: UBC Press, 2008.

Bateman, Thomas M.J. "The New Globalism in Canadian Charter of Rights Interpretation: Extradition, the Death Penalty, and the Courts." *International Journal of Human Rights* 7, 3 (2003): 49-71.

Bedau, Hugo Adam. "Abolishing the Death Penalty in the United States: An Analysis of Institutional Obstacles and Future Prospects." In *Capital Punishment: Strategies for Abolition*, ed. Peter Hodgkinson and William A. Schabas, 187-207. Cambridge: Cambridge University Press, 2004.

Bell, Colleen. "Subject to Exception: Security Certificates, National Security, and Canada's Role in the 'War on Terror.'" *Canadian Journal of Law and Society* 21, 1 (2006): 63-83.

Bercuson, David, and Douglas Wertheimer. *A Trust Betrayed: The Keegstra Affair.* Toronto: Doubleday Canada, 1985.
Bialystok, Franklin. *Delayed Impact: The Holocaust and the Canadian Jewish Community.* Montreal/Kingston: McGill-Queen's University Press, 2000.
–. "Neo-Nazis in Toronto: The Allan Gardens Riot." In "New Perspectives on Canada, the Holocaust, and Survivors," special issue, *Canadian Jewish Studies* 4-5 (1996-97): 1-38.
Bobbio, Norberto. *The Age of Rights.* Trans. Allan Cameron. Cambridge, MA: Polity Press, 1996.
Borovoy, A. Alan. *Categorically Incorrect: Ethical Fallacies in Canada's War on Terror.* Toronto: Dundurn Group, 2006.
–. *The New Anti-Liberals.* Toronto: Canadian Scholars Press, 1999.
–. "Rebuilding a Free Society." *Canadian Forum* (January 1971): 349-55.
–. *When Freedoms Collide: The Case for Our Civil Liberties.* Toronto: Lester and Orpen Dennys, 1988.
–. "The Zundel Appeal." *Criminal Reports* 56 C.R. (3d): 77-81.
Bossin, Michael. "Bill C-31: Limited Access to Refugee Determination and Protection." *Refuge* 19, 4 (2001): 55-61.
Bothwell, Robert, Ian Drummond, and John English. *Canada since 1945.* Rev. ed. Toronto: University of Toronto Press, 1989.
Braun, Stefan. *Democracy Off Balance: Freedom of Expression and Hate Propaganda Law in Canada.* Toronto: University of Toronto Press, 2004.
Brodie, Ian. *The Friends of the Court: The Privileging of Interest Group Litigants in Canada.* New York: SUNY Press, 2002.
–. "Interest Group Litigation and the Embedded State: Canada's Court Challenges Program." *Canadian Journal of Political Science* 34, 2 (2001): 357-76.
Brysk, Alison. "Conclusion: From Rights to Realities." In *Globalization and Human Rights*, ed. Alison Brysk, 242-56. Berkeley: University of California Press, 2002.
Buchanan, Tom. "'The Truth Will Set You Free': The Making of Amnesty International." *Journal of Contemporary History* 37, 4 (2002): 575-97.
Burgers, Jan Herman. "The Road to San Francisco: The Revival of Human Rights Ideas in the 20th Century." *Human Rights Quarterly* 14 (1992): 447-77.
Bushnell, Ian. *The Captive Court: A Study of the Supreme Court of Canada.* Montreal/Kingston: McGill-Queen's University Press, 1992.
Cairns, Alan C. "The Charter: A Political Science Perspective," *Osgoode Hall Law Journal* 30, 3 (1992): 615-25.
–. "International Influences on the Charter." In *Charter versus Federalism: The Dilemmas of Constitutional Reform.* Montreal/Kingston: McGill-Queen's University Press, 1992.
Campbell, Charles M. *Betrayal and Deceit: The Politics of Canadian Immigration.* Vancouver: Jasmine Books, 2000.
Canadian Jewish Congress. *Fifty Years of Service, 1919-1969.* Montreal: Canadian Jewish Congress, 1970.
Cassin, René. *La Declaration universelle et la mise en oeuvre des droits de l'homme.* Paris: Librarie du Recueil Sirey, 1951.

Chandler, David Ballantine. "Capital Punishment and the Canadian Parliament: A Test of Durkheim's Hypothesis on Repressive Law." PhD diss., Cornell University, 1970.
Clark, Ann Marie. *Diplomacy of Conscience: Amnesty International and Changing Human Rights Norms.* Princeton: Princeton University Press, 2001.
–. "Non-Governmental Organizations and Their Influence on International Society." *Journal of International Affairs* 48, 2 (1995): 507-25.
Clément, Dominique. *Canada's Rights Revolution.* Vancouver: UBC Press, 2009.
Corbett, David C. *Canada's Immigration Policy: A Critique.* Toronto: University of Toronto Press, 1957.
Davies, Alan, ed. *Antisemitism in Canada: History and Interpretation.* Waterloo: Wilfrid Laurier University Press, 1992.
–. "The Keegstra Affair." In *Antisemitism in Canada: History and Interpretation,* ed. Alan Davies, 227-47. Waterloo: Wilfrid Laurier University Press, 1992.
Dawson, Mary. "The Impact of the Charter on the Public Policy Process and the Department of Justice." *Osgoode Hall Law Journal* 30, 3 (1992): 595-603.
Dirks, Gerald E. "Canada and Immigration: International and Domestic Considerations in the Decade Preceding the 1956 Hungarian Exodus." In *Breaking Ground: The 1956 Hungarian Refugee Movement to Canada,* ed. Robert H. Keyserlingk, 3-11. Toronto: York Lanes Press, 1993.
–. *Canada's Refugee Policy: Indifference or Opportunism?* Montreal/Kingston: McGill-Queen's University Press, 1977.
–. *Controversy and Complexity: Canadian Immigration Policy during the 1980s.* Montreal/Kingston: McGill-Queen's University Press, 1995.
–. "A Policy within a Policy: The Identification and Admission of Refugees to Canada." *Canadian Journal of Political Science* 17, 2 (1984): 279-307.
Donnelly, Jack. "Human Rights: A New Standard of Civilization?" *International Affairs* 74, 1 (1998): 1-23.
–. *International Human Rights.* 3rd ed. Cambridge, MA: Westview Press, 2007.
Drinan, Robert F. *The Mobilization of Shame: A World View of Human Rights.* New Haven: Yale University Press, 2001.
Eide, Asbjorn. "The Historical Significance of the Universal Declaration." *International Social Science Journal* 50, 4 (1998): 475-97.
Endelman, Todd M. "Antisemitism in Western Europe Today." In *Contemporary Antisemitism: Canada and the World,* ed. Derek J. Penslar, Michael R. Marrus, and Janice Gross Stein, 64-79. Toronto: University of Toronto Press, 2005.
English, John. *Citizen of the World: The Life of Pierre Elliott Trudeau.* Vol. 1, *1919-1968.* Toronto: Alfred A. Knopf Canada, 2006.
–. *Just Watch Me: The Life of Pierre Elliott Trudeau, 1968-2000.* Toronto: Random House, 2009.
–. *The Worldly Years: The Life of Lester Pearson.* Vol. 2, *1949-1972.* Toronto: Alfred A. Knopf Canada, 1992.
English, John, Richard Gwyn, and P. Whitney Lackenbauer, eds. *The Hidden Pierre Elliott Trudeau: The Faith behind the Politics.* Ottawa: Novalis, 2004.

Fairburn, Bill. "The Inter-Church Committee on Human Rights in Latin America." In *Coalitions for Justice,* ed. Christopher Lind and Joe Mihevc, 169-84. Ottawa: Novalis, 1994.
Finnemore, Martha, and Kathryn Sikkink. "International Norm Dynamics and Political Change." *International Organization* 52, 4 (1998): 887-917.
Girard, Philip. *Bora Laskin: Bringing Law to Life.* Toronto: University of Toronto Press, 2005.
Goering, Curt. "Amnesty International and Economic, Social, and Cultural Rights." In *Ethics in Action: The Ethical Challenges of International Human Rights Nongovernmental Organizations,* ed. Daniel A. Bell and Jean-Marc Coicaud, 204-17. New York: Cambridge University Press, 2007.
Gold, Marc. "The Rhetoric of Rights: The Supreme Court and the Charter." *Osgoode Hall Law Journal* 25, 2 (1987): 375-410.
Granatstein, Jack L. *Canada, 1957-1967: The Years of Uncertainty and Innovation.* Toronto: McClelland and Stewart, 1986.
Grey, Julius H. *Immigration Law in Canada.* Toronto: Butterworths, 1984.
Hathaway, James C. *The Law of Refugee Status.* Markham, ON: Butterworths Canada, 1991.
–. "Selective Concern: An Overview of Refugee Law in Canada." *McGill Law Review* 33, 4 (1987-88): 676-715.
Hathaway, James C., and R. Alexander Neve. "Fundamental Justice and the Deflection of Refugees in Canada." *Osgoode Hall Law Journal* 34, 2 (1996): 213-71.
Hawkins, Freda. *Canada and Immigration: Public Policy and Public Concern.* Montreal/Kingston: McGill-Queen's University Press, 1972.
Hopf, Ted. "The Promise of Constructivism in International Relations Theory." *International Security* 23, 1 (1998): 171-200.
Hopgood, Stephen. *Keepers of the Flame: Understanding Amnesty International.* Ithaca: Cornell University Press, 2006.
Howard, Rhoda. "The Canadian Government Response to Africa's Refugee Crisis." *Canadian Journal of African Studies* 15, 1 (1981): 95-116.
–. "Contemporary Canadian Refugee Policy: A Critical Assessment." *Canadian Public Policy* 6, 2 (1980): 361-73.
–. *Human Rights and the Search for Community.* Boulder: Westview Press, 1995.
Humphrey, John P. *Human Rights and the United Nations: A Great Adventure.* Dobbs Ferry, NY: Transnational, 1984.
–. "The United Nations Charter and the Universal Declaration of Human Rights." In *The International Protection of Human Rights,* ed. Evan Luard, 39-58. New York: Frederick A. Praeger, 1967.
–. "The Universal Declaration of Human Rights: Its History, Impact, and Juridical Character." In *Human Rights: Thirty Years after the Universal Declaration,* ed. B.G. Ramcharan, 21-37. The Hague: Martinus Nijhoff, 1979.
Ignatieff, Michael. *The Lesser Evil: Political Ethics in the Age of Terror.* Princeton: Princeton University Press, 2004.
–. *The Rights Revolution.* Toronto: Anansi, 2000.

Iriye, Akira. "A Century of NGOs." *Diplomatic History* 23, 3 (1999): 421-35.
Ishay, Micheline R. *The History of Human Rights: From Ancient Times to the Globalization Era.* Berkeley: University of California Press, 2004.
Kallen, Evelyn, and Lawrence Lam. "Target for Hate: The Impact of the Zundel and Keegstra Trials on a Jewish-Canadian Audience." *Canadian Ethnic Studies* 25, 1 (1993): 9-24.
Kaplan, William. "Maxwell Cohen and the Report of the Special Committee on Hate Propaganda." In *Law, Policy, and International Justice: Essays in Honour of Maxwell Cohen,* ed. William Kaplan and Donald McRae, 243-74. Montreal/Kingston: McGill-Queen's University Press, 1993.
Kaufman, Edy. "Prisoners of Conscience: The Shaping of a New Human Rights Concept." *Human Rights Quarterly* 13, 3 (1991): 339-67.
Kelly, James B. *Governing with the Charter: Legislative and Judicial Activism and Framers' Intent.* Vancouver: UBC Press, 2005.
–. "Reconciling Rights and Federalism during Review of the Charter of Rights and Freedoms: The Supreme Court of Canada and the Centralization Thesis, 1982-1999." *Canadian Journal of Political Science* 34, 2 (2001): 321-55.
Keyserlingk, Robert H., ed. *Breaking Ground: The 1956 Hungarian Refugee Movement to Canada.* Toronto: York Lanes Press, 1993.
Kinsella, Warren. *Web of Hate: Inside Canada's Far Right Network.* Toronto: HarperCollins, 2001.
Knopff, Rainer, and F.L. Morton. *Charter Politics.* Scarborough: Nelson Canada, 1992.
Korey, William. *NGOs and the Universal Declaration of Human Rights: "A Curious Grapevine."* New York: St. Martin's Press, 1998.
Lambertson, Ross. *Repression and Resistance: Canadian Human Rights Activists, 1930-1960.* Toronto: University of Toronto Press, 2005.
Landman, Todd. *Protecting Human Rights: A Comparative Study.* Washington, DC: Georgetown University Press, 2005.
Lanphier, C. Michael. "Canada's Response to Refugees." *International Migration Review* 15, 1-2 (1981): 113-30.
Lauren, Paul Gordon. "First Principles of Racial Equality: History and the Politics and Diplomacy of Human Rights Provisions in the United Nations Charter." *Human Rights Quarterly* 5, 1 (1983): 1-26.
–. "Human Rights in History: Diplomacy and Racial Equality at the Paris Peace Conference." *Diplomatic History* 2 (1978): 257-78.
Lederman, W.R. "Democratic Parliaments, Independent Courts, and the Canadian Charter of Rights and Freedoms." *Queen's Law Journal* 11, 1 (1985): 1-25.
Lipsitz, Edmond Y., ed. *Who's Who in Canadian Jewry: Canadian Jewry at Year 2000 and Beyond.* 3rd ed. Toronto: JESL Educational Products, 2000.
Lowry, Michelle. "Creating Human Insecurity: The National Security Focus in Canada's Immigration System." *Refuge* 21, 1 (2002): 28-40.
Macartney, C.A. "The League of Nations' Protection of Minority Rights." In *The International Protection of Human Rights,* ed. Evan Luard, 22-38. New York: Frederick A. Praeger, 1967.

MacFadyen, Joshua D. "'Nip the Noxious Growth in the Bud': *Ortenberg v. Plamondon* and the Roots of Canadian Anti-Hate Activism." *Canadian Jewish Studies* 12 (2004): 73-96.
MacGuigan, Mark R. "Proposed Anti-Hate Legislation." *Chitty's Law Journal* 15, 9 (1967): 302-6.
Macklin, Audrey. "Mr. Suresh and the Evil Twin." *Refuge* 20, 4 (2002): 15-22.
Magnet, Joseph. "Hate Propaganda in Canada." In *Free Expression: Essays in Law and Philosophy*, ed. W.J. Waluchow, 223-50. Oxford: Oxford University Press, 1994.
Malarek, Victor. *Haven's Gate: Canada's Immigration Fiasco.* Toronto: Macmillan, 1987.
Mandel, Michael. *The Charter of Rights and Freedoms and the Legalization of Politics in Canada.* Toronto: Wall and Thompson, 1989.
Manfredi, Christopher P. *Feminist Activism in the Supreme Court: Legal Mobilization and the Women's Legal Education and Action Fund.* Vancouver: UBC Press, 2004.
–. *Judicial Power and the Charter: Canada and the Paradox of Liberal Constitutionalism.* New York: Oxford University Press, 2000.
Martin, Robert Ivan. *The Most Dangerous Branch: How the Supreme Court of Canada Has Undermined Our Law and Our Democracy.* Montreal/Kingston: McGill-Queen's University Press, 2003.
Matas, David. *Aftershock: Anti-Zionism and Antisemitism.* Toronto: Dundurn Group, 2005.
Matas, David, and Ilana Simon. *Closing the Doors: The Failure of Refugee Protection.* Toronto: Summerhill Press, 1989.
McCall, Christina, and Stephen Clarkson. *Trudeau and Our Times.* Vol. 1, *The Magnificent Obsession.* Toronto: McClelland and Stewart, 1990.
McCormick, Peter. *Canada's Courts: A Social Scientist's Ground-Breaking Account of the Canadian Judicial System.* Toronto: James Lorimer, 1994.
McLachlin, Beverley M. "The Charter: A New Role for the Judiciary?" *Alberta Law Review* 29, 3 (1991): 540-59.
McMurty, Roy. "Law and Antisemitism: The Role of the State in Responding to Hatred." In *Contemporary Antisemitism: Canada and the World*, ed. Derek J. Penslar, Michael R. Marrus, and Janice Gross Stein, 26-32. Toronto: University of Toronto Press, 2005.
Megivern, James J. *The Death Penalty: An Historical and Theological Survey.* New York: Paulist Press, 1997.
Mertl, Steve, and John Ward. *Keegstra: The Trial, the Issues, the Consequences.* Saskatoon: Western Producer Prairie Books, 1985.
Monahan, Patrick J., and Marie Finkelstein. "The Charter of Rights and Public Policy in Canada." *Osgoode Hall Law Journal* 30, 3 (1992): 501-46.
Monshipouri, Mahmood, Neil Englehart, Andrew J. Nathan, and Kavita Philip, eds. *Constructing Human Rights in the Age of Globalization.* New York: M.E. Sharpe, 2003.
Morsink, Johannes. "Cultural Genocide, the Universal Declaration, and Minority Rights." *Human Rights Quarterly* 21, 4 (1999): 1009-60.

Morton, F.L., and Avril Allen. "Feminists and the Courts: Measuring Success in Interest Group Litigation in Canada." *Canadian Journal of Political Science* 34, 1 (2001): 55-84.

Morton, F.L., and Rainer Knopff. *Charter Politics.* Toronto: Nelson Canada, 1992.

–. *The Charter Revolution and the Court Party.* Peterborough: Broadview Press, 2000.

Morton, F.L., G. Solomon, I. McNish, and D.W. Poulton. "Judicial Nullification of Statutes under the Charter of Rights and Freedoms, 1982-1988." *Alberta Law Review* 28, 2 (1990): 396-426.

Mulroney, Brian. "Antisemitism: An Enduring Reality." In *Contemporary Antisemitism: Canada and the World,* ed. Derek J. Penslar, Michael R. Marrus, and Janice Gross Stein, 15-25. Toronto: University of Toronto Press, 2005.

–. *Memoirs.* Toronto: McClelland and Stewart, 2007.

Orend, Brian. *Human Rights: Concept and Context.* Peterborough: Broadview Press, 2002.

Owram, Doug. *Born at the Right Time: A History of the Baby Boom Generation.* Toronto: University of Toronto Press, 1997.

Paris, Erna. *The Sun Climbs Slow: Justice in the Age of Imperial America.* Toronto: Alfred A. Knopf Canada, 2008.

Pearson, Lester B. *Mike: The Memoirs of the Rt. Hon. Lester B. Pearson.* Vol. 3, *1957-1968.* Toronto: University of Toronto Press, 1975.

Penslar, Derek J. "Antisemitism and Anti-Zionism: A Historical Approach." In *Contemporary Antisemitism: Canada and the World,* ed. Derek J. Penslar, Michael R. Marrus, and Janice Gross Stein, 80-95. Toronto: University of Toronto Press, 2005.

–. "Introduction." In *Contemporary Antisemitism: Canada and the World,* ed. Derek J. Penslar, Michael R. Marrus, and Janice Gross Stein, 3-12. Toronto: University of Toronto Press, 2005.

Pickersgill, J.W. *Seeing Canada Whole: A Memoir.* Markham, ON: Fitzhenry and Whiteside, 1994.

Plaut, W. Gunther. *Asylum: A Moral Dilemma.* Westport, CT: Praeger, 1995.

–. *Refugee Determination in Canada: Proposal for a New System, Report to the Honourable Flora MacDonald, Minister of Employment and Immigration.* Ottawa: Government of Canada, 1985.

Power, Jonathan. *Amnesty International: The Human Rights Story.* Oxford: Pergamon Press, 1981.

–. *Like Water on Stone: The Story of Amnesty International.* Boston: Northeastern University Press, 2001.

Pratt, Anna. *Securing Borders: Detention and Deportation in Canada.* Vancouver: UBC Press, 2005.

Pritchett, C. Herman. *The Roosevelt Court: A Study in Judicial Politics and Values, 1937-1947.* New York: Octagon Books, 1963.

Prutschi, Manuel. "The Zündel Affair." In *Antisemitism in Canada: History and Interpretation,* ed. Alan Davies, 249-77. Waterloo: Wilfrid Laurier University Press, 1992.

Ptolemy, Kathleen. "From Oppression to Promise: Journeying Together with the Refugee." In *Canadian Churches and Foreign Policy*, ed. Bonnie Greene, 143-60. Toronto: James Lorimer 1990.

Radwanski, George. *Trudeau*. Toronto: Macmillan, 1978.

Ratushny, Ed. *A New Refugee Status Determination Process for Canada*. Report to the Honourable John Roberts. Ottawa: Government of Canada, 1983.

Risse, Thomas, and Kathryn Sikkink. "The Socialization of International Human Rights Norms into Domestic Practices: Introduction." In *The Power of Human Rights: International Norms and Domestic Change*, ed. Thomas Risse, Stephen C. Ropp, and Kathryn Sikkink, 1-38. Cambridge: Cambridge University Press, 1999.

Robinson, Mary. *A Voice for Human Rights*. Ed. Kevin Boyle. Philadelphia: University of Pennsylvania Press, 2006.

Robinson, W.G. *The Refugee Status Determination Process: A Report of the Task Force on Immigration Practices and Procedures to the Honourable Lloyd Axworthy*. Ottawa: Government of Canada, 1982.

Rodley, Nigel S. *The Treatment of Prisoners under International Law*. 2nd ed. Oxford: Oxford University Press, 1999.

Roth, Kenneth. "Review Essay: Getting Away with Torture." *Global Governance* 11 (2005): 389-406.

Russell, Peter H. *The Judiciary in Canada: The Third Branch of Government*. Toronto: McGraw-Hill Ryerson, 1987.

Said, Abdul Aziz. "Pursuing Human Dignity." In *Human Rights and World Order*, ed. Abdul Aziz Said, 1-21. New Brunswick, NJ: Transaction Books, 1978.

Saywell, John T. *The Lawmakers: Judicial Power and the Shaping of Canadian Federalism*. Toronto: University of Toronto Press for the Osgoode Society for Canadian Legal History, 2002.

Schabas, William A. *The Abolition of the Death Penalty in International Law*. 3rd ed. Cambridge: Cambridge University Press, 2002.

–. *The Death Penalty as Cruel Treatment and Torture: Capital Punishment Challenged in the World's Courts*. Boston: Northeastern University Press, 1996.

–. "Indirect Abolition: Capital Punishment's Role in Extradition Law and Practice." *Loyola of Los Angeles International and Comparative Law Review* 25 (2003): 581-604.

–. "International Law and the Death Penalty: Reflecting or Promoting Change." In *Capital Punishment: Strategies for Abolition*, ed. Peter Hodgkinson and William A. Schabas, 36-62. Cambridge: Cambridge University Press, 2004.

Schneider, Wendie Ellen. "Past Imperfect: *Irving v. Penguin Books Ltd*." *Yale Law Journal* 110 (2001): 1531-45.

Schulz, William. *Tainted Legacy: 9/11 and the Ruin of Human Rights*. New York: Thunder's Mouth Press, 2003.

Sharp, Mitchell. *Which Reminds Me ... A Memoir*. Toronto: University of Toronto Press, 1994.

Sharpe, Robert J., and Kent Roach. *Brian Dickson: A Judge's Journey*. Toronto: University of Toronto Press for the Osgoode Society for Canadian Legal History, 2003.

Shefman, Alan. *The Review of Anti-Semitism 1983.* Downsview, ON: League for Human Rights of B'nai Brith Canada, 1984.

Shilton, Elizabeth J. "Charter Litigation and the Policy Process of Government: A Public Interest Perspective." *Osgoode Hall Law Journal* 30, 3 (1992): 653-60.

Smith, Miriam. "Ghosts of the Judicial Committee of the Privy Council: Group Politics and Charter Litigation in Canadian Political Science." *Canadian Journal of Political Science* 35, 1 (2002): 3-29.

–. *Lesbian and Gay Rights in Canada: Social Movements and Equality-Seeking, 1971-1995.* Toronto: University of Toronto Press, 1999.

–. "Social Movements and Equality Seeking: The Case of Gay Liberation in Canada." *Canadian Journal of Political Science* 31, 2 (1998): 285-309.

Smithey, Shannon Ishiyama. "Cooperation and Conflict: Group Activity in *R. v. Keegstra.*" In *The Myth of the Sacred: The Charter, the Courts, and the Politics of the Constitution in Canada,* ed. Patrick James, Donald E. Abelson, and Michael Lusztig, 189-204. Montreal/Kingston: McGill-Queen's University Press, 2002.

Snell, James G., and Frederick Vaughan. *The Supreme Court of Canada: History of the Institution.* Toronto: University of Toronto Press, 1985.

Stingel, Janine. *Social Discredit: Anti-Semitism, Social Credit, and the Jewish Response.* Montreal/Kingston: McGill-Queen's University Press, 2000.

Stoffman, Daniel. *Who Gets In: What's Wrong with Canada's Immigration Program – and How to Fix It.* Toronto: Macfarlane Walter and Ross, 2002.

Sumner, L.W. *The Hateful and the Obscene: Studies in the Limits of Free Expression.* Toronto: University of Toronto Press, 2004.

Tessler, Mark. "The Nature and Determinants of Arab Attitudes towards Israel." In *Contemporary Antisemitism: Canada and the World,* ed. Derek J. Penslar, Michael R. Marrus, and Janice Gross Stein, 96-119. Toronto: University of Toronto Press, 2005.

Thakur, Ramesh. "Human Rights: Amnesty International and the United Nations." *Journal of Peace Research* 31, 2 (1994): 143-60.

Thompson, Andrew S. "Beyond Expression: Amnesty International's Decision to Oppose Capital Punishment, 1973." *Journal of Human Rights* 7, 4 (2008): 327-40.

–. "Slow to Leave the Bedrooms of the Nation: Trudeau and the Modernizing of Canadian Law, 1967-1969." In *The Hidden Pierre Elliott Trudeau: The Faith behind the Politics,* ed. John English, Richard Gwyn, and P. Whitney Lackenbauer, 117-33. Ottawa: Novalis, 2004.

Thompson, Andrew S., and Stephanie Bangarth. "Transnational Christian Charity: The Canadian Council of Churches, the World Council of Churches, and the Hungarian Refugee Crisis, 1956-1957." *American Review of Canadian Studies* 38, 3 (2008): 295-317.

Thompson, Henriette. "The Inter-Church Committee for Refugees." In *Coalitions for Justice,* ed. Christopher Lind and Joe Mihevc, 203-18. Ottawa: Novalis, 1994.

Tolley, Howard Jr. *The UN Commission on Human Rights.* Boulder, CO: Westview Press, 1987.

Trudeau, Pierre Elliott. *Federalism and the French Canadians.* Toronto: Macmillan, 1968.

–. *Memoirs*. Toronto: McClelland and Stewart, 1993.
–. "The Values of a Just Society." In *Towards a Just Society: The Trudeau Years*, ed. Thomas S. Axworthy and Pierre Elliott Trudeau, 357-85. Markham, ON: Viking, 1990.
United Nations. *Capital Punishment*. New York: UN Department of Economic and Social Affairs, 1962.
Walker, James W.St.G. "The 'Jewish Phase' in the Movement for Racial Equality in Canada." *Canadian Ethnic Studies* 34, 1 (2000): 1-29.
–. *"Race," Rights, and the Law in the Supreme Court of Canada: Historical Case Studies*. Waterloo: Wilfrid Laurier University Press for the Osgoode Society for Canadian Legal History, 1998.
Weimann, Gabriel, and Conrad Winn. *Hate on Trial: The Zundel Affair, the Media, Public Opinion in Canada*. Oakville, ON: Mosaic Press, 1986.
Weinfeld, Morton. "The Changing Dimensions of Contemporary Canadian Antisemitism." In *Contemporary Antisemitism: Canada and the World*, ed. Derek J. Penslar, Michael R. Marrus, and Janice Gross Stein, 35-51. Toronto: University of Toronto Press, 2005.
Welch, Claude E. "Amnesty International and Human Rights Watch: A Comparison." In *NGOs and Human Rights: Promise and Performance*, ed. Claude E. Welch Jr., 85-118. Philadelphia: University of Pennsylvania Press, 2001.
Welch, Jillian. "No Room at the Top: Interest Group Interveners and Charter Litigation in the Supreme Court of Canada." *University of Toronto Faculty of Law Review* 43, 2 (1985): 204-31.
Whitaker, Reg. *Double Standard: The Secret History of Canadian Immigration*. Toronto: Lester and Orpen Dennys, 1987.
–. "Refugee Policy after September 11: Not Much New." *Refuge* 20, 4 (2002): 29-33.
Whitaker, Reg, and Gary Marcuse. *Cold War Canada: The Making of a National Insecurity State, 1945-1957*. Toronto: University of Toronto Press, 1995.
Whyte, John D. "Legality and Legitimacy: The Problem of Judicial Review of Legislation." *Queen's Law Journal* 12, 1 (1987): 1-20.
Winston, Morton E. "Assessing the Effectiveness of International Human Rights NGOs." In *NGOs and Human Rights: Promise and Performance*, ed. Claude E. Welch Jr., 25-54. Philadelphia: University of Pennsylvania Press, 2001.
Wydrzynski, Christopher J. *Canadian Immigration Law and Procedure*. Aurora: Canada Law Book, 1983.
–. "Refugees and the Immigration Act." *McGill Law Journal* 25, 2 (1979): 154-92.
Zipperstein, Steven J. "Historical Reflections on Contemporary Antisemitism." In *Contemporary Antisemitism: Canada and the World*, ed. Derek J. Penslar, Michael R. Marrus, and Janice Gross Stein, 52-63. Toronto: University of Toronto Press, 2005.

Index

A New Refugee Status Determination Process for Canada, 27
Abella, Irving, 75
abolition of capital punishment. *See* capital punishment
abolitionist movement, 90-91, 106-7, 115-16
ACLU. *See* American Civil Liberties Union
Act to Amend the Criminal Code and the Supreme Court Act (Habeas Corpus), 102, 112
Act to Amend the Criminal Code (Hate Propaganda): application of, 69-72, 74, 156n102; constitutionality of, 12-13, 69, 74, 76-86; controversies surrounding, 54; hearings relating to, 64-69; opposition to, 59; support for, 60, 64
Act to Amend the Criminal Code in Relation to the Punishment for Murder and Certain Other Serious Offences, 92-95, 164n20
Act to Amend the Extradition Act (Appeal), 102, 112

Act to Amend the Immigration Act, 1976 and the Criminal Code in Consequence Thereof: constitutionality of, 44-46; criticisms of, 42-43; introduction of, 41-42
Act to Establish a New Refugee Determination Process: constitutionality of, 44-46; criticism of 43, 49; introduction of, 40-41
AI. *See* Amnesty International and Amnesty International Canada
Alberta Court of Appeal, 76, 84-85, 100
Alberta Court of Queen's Bench, 99
Alberta Teachers' Association, 70
Allan Gardens Riot, 59-61, 146n30, 147nn34-35
Allende government, 23, 133n36
Allmand, Warren, 13, 92-95
American Civil Liberties Union (ACLU), 58
amendments to the *Extradition Act,* 112-13
American Declaration of the Rights and Duties of Man, 47

Index

Amnesty International (AI), 89-91, 97, 103, 106, 162n1, 163n7, 164nn9-10, 173nn74-75
Amnesty International (AI) Canada: backlash against, 103-4, 170nn62-63; on capital punishment, 88, 97, 99, 113, 116, 167n36; intervention in *Burns*, 114; intervention in *Kindler*, 9, 13, 105-6, 109, 111, 114, 171-72nn70-71, 172-73nn73-74; on refugee rights, 24, 29, 52; origins of, 166n32
Andras, Robert, 20, 23
Andrews, Donald Clarke, 76, 83, 152n78
antisemitism, 55, 57, 59-60, 69, 82, 85-87, 143n3, 150n56, 161-62nn180-83
Approved Church Program, 18
Arcand, Adrian, 55, 70
Argentina's "Dirty Wars," 25
Armstrong, Jill, 67
Arthurs, Harry, 67, 146n24
Ashburton-Webster Treaty, 95
asylum, rights of, 15
Axworthy, Lloyd, 26-28, 35

Backlog(s), 22, 27, 31, 38, 46, 49
Baker, George, 98
Beattie, William John, 59-60, 67, 146-47nn29-30, 147n34, 149n51
Beetz, Jean, 6-7, 36
Benenson, Peter, 89, 162n1, 163n7
Berton, Pierre, 64, 150n54
Bill C-3. *See Act to Amend the Criminal Code (Hate Propaganda)*
Bill C-11. *See Immigration and Refugee Protection Act*
Bill C-21. *See Act to Amend the Criminal Code and the Supreme Court Act (Habeas Corpus)*
Bill C-31. *See* amendments to the *Extradition Act*
Bill C-55. *See Act to Establish a New Refugee Determination Process*
Bill C-84 (capital punishment). *See Act to Amend the Criminal Code in Relation to the Punishment for Murder and Certain Other Serious Offences*
Bill C-84 (refugees). *See Act to Amend the Immigration Act, 1976 and the Criminal Code in Consequence Thereof*
Bill C-209. *See Act to Amend the Extradition Act (Appeal)*
Bill S-5. *See Act to Amend the Criminal Code (Hate Propaganda)*
Bill S-21. *See Act to Amend the Criminal Code (Hate Propaganda)*
Bill S-49. *See Act to Amend the Criminal Code (Hate Propaganda)*
Bill of Rights, 1960: in *CCC v. MEI*, 44-47; on hate propaganda law, 69; infringements of, 4; passing of, 3; quasi-constitutional status of, 5; in *Singh*, 11, 29, 34-36, 136n77
Bliss v. A.-G. Canada, 5
B'nai Brith, 60, 76, 78-79, 81, 85, 143n1, 155n98
Bobbio, Norberto, 1, 14, 117
Borovoy, A. Alan: feud with Christie, 75-76, 157n123; on hate propaganda law, 69-72, 76, 81, 86-87, 153n85, 162n184; on interest-group interventions, 6; on James Keegstra, 72, 74, 84, 160n167; on Ernst Zündel, 73-74, 160n173
Bouchard, Benoît, 39, 41
Bowie, Eric, 30-31, 34, 35
British Empire, 5
Broadcasting Act, 61
Burns, Glen Sebastian, 113-15

Campbell, Kim, 100, 111
Canada Post Corporation Act, 70
Canada-US Extradition Treaty, 13, 88, 95-96, 100-1, 105-6, 114-15
Canadian Bar Association, 6, 138n109
Canadian bill of rights. *See Bill of Rights, 1960*
Canadian Broadcasting Corporation, 63-64, 149n52, 150n54

Canadian Christian Council for the Resettlement of Refugees, 18
Canadian Civil Liberties Association (CCLA): intervention in *Keegstra*, 9, 12, 54, 75-78, 80-81, 83-84; on Cohen Committee, 62-63; on freedom of expression, 58-59, 63, 86-87; on hate propaganda law, 12, 74; on interest-group interventions, 6, 124n24; origins, 58; Senate hearings, 67-68; on Zündel trials, 73, 75-76, 85, 154nn88-89
Canadian Conference of Catholic Bishops, 24
Canadian Council for Refugees, 39, 52
Canadian Council of Churches (CCC): advocacy, 16, 40, 53, 129n10; *CCC v. MEI*, 44-46, 50, 139n116; Commission on World Concerns, 37; contributions to WCC, 17; criticisms of *Immigration Act, 1976*, 21, 24-27; intervention in *Singh*, 9, 11, 28-29; origins of, 15-17, 127n1; relationship with Government of Canada, 17-19, 22-24, 51-52; theological changes in, 22, 132n33
Canadian Council of Churches v. The Queen and the MEI (CCC v. MEI), 44-46, 50
Canadian government. *See* Government of Canada
Canadian Holocaust Remembrance Association, 72
Canadian Jewish Congress (CJC): Allan Gardens Riot, 60; on Cohen Committee recommendations, 62, 66, 70; on confronting antisemitism, 55-57, 59-60, 63-64, 72, 75, 86-87, 144n9; feud with CBC, 63-64; on hate propaganda law, 12, 60, 63, 74, 87, 150n58, 162n184; intervention in *Keegstra*, 9, 12, 54, 78-79, 81, 84; origins of, 55, 143n1; refugees, 18, 128n8; Senate hearings, 65-66; Zündel trials, 70-73, 76, 85, 154n89

Canadian Labour Congress, 97
Canadian Nationalist Socialist Party. *See* Nationalist Socialist Party of Canada
Canadian Security Intelligence Service (CSIS), 50
Canadian University Students Overseas (CUSO), 37
capital punishment: abolition of, 1, 13, 90-95, 97-99, 110; and crimes of Charles Chitat Ng, 100; Joseph Kindler, 100; norms relating to, 14, 92, 105, 112, 114-16; support for, 92-94, 98, 119, 164n11
Cartwright, John Robert, 105
CCC. *See* Canadian Council of Churches
CCLA. *See* Canadian Civil Liberties Association
Charter of Rights and Freedoms: effects of, 6-8, 49, 53, 117-19, 124n32; in *CCC v. MEI*, 44-47; introduction of, 3, 5; in *Keegstra*, 12, 76-85; in *Kindler*, 13-14, 104-11; relating to capital punishment, 89, 116; relating to extradition, 99-101, 114-15; in *Singh*, 11, 29-33, 35-36, 50, 136n77
Chilean refugee crisis, 20, 23, 133n39
"chilling effect," 81, 84
Chrétien government, 48
Christie, Doug: in *Keegstra*, 81-85; politics of, 71, 75-76, 157-58nn123-24; and Zündel trial, 73, 157-58nn123-24
Church Council on Justice and Corrections, 97
civil libertarianism, 2, 4, 7-8, 86
civil society actors. *See* non-governmental organizations
CJC. *See* Canadian Jewish Congress
Clark, Roger, 111-13
Clark, Tom, 39-40
Coalition against the Return of the Death Penalty (CARDP), 97
Coderre, Denis, 48-49

Index

Cohen Committee. *See* Special Committee on Hate Propaganda in Canada
Cohen, Maxwell, 58-62, 145n18, 145n21, 146n28, 149n47, 151n60
Commission on Reconstruction and Inter-Church Aid, Refugee Division, 16-17
Conference of the Canadian Institute for the Administration of Justice, 71
Conference of European Ministers of Justice, 106
Constitution. *See Charter of Rights and Freedoms*
constructivism, 9
Convention Refugee Determination Division, 40
Corry, J.A., 58
Cory, Peter, 45-46, 77, 109, 174n85
Costello, Jack, 48
Cotler, Irwin, 78, 115
Council of Europe, 106
Coveney, C. David, 31, 34
"Court Party," 8
courts. *See* judiciary
Cram, George, 23-24, 39
"credible basis," 40, 43
crimes against humanity, 57
crimes against the Jewish people, 57
Criminal Code of Canada: and capital punishment, 13, 91-97; and hate propaganda, 12, 56-57, 61, 70, 76-85; liberalization of, 4; and "spreading of false news," 72-73, 85
Criminal Lawyers Association of Ontario, 114
Crosbie, John, 100, 106, 108, 110, 168n48
CSIS. *See* Canadian Security Intelligence Service
Cullen, Bud, 20, 25-26
CUSO. *See* Canadian University Students Overseas

death penalty. *See* capital punishment
death row phenomenon, 108, 115

Delegation of Concerned Church, Legal, Medical, Labour, and Humanitarian Organizations, 24-26, 133-34n43
Department of Citizenship and Immigration. *See* Department of Immigration
Department of Employment and Immigration. *See* Department of Immigration
Department of Immigration 18, 19, 26, 28, 49
Department of Manpower and Immigration. *See* Department of Immigration
Dickson, Brian, 6-7, 35, 83, 123n18
Diefenbaker, John, 94, 130n22
Dion, Gérard, 58
displaced persons, 16
divorce, 3
Domm, Bill: and capital punishment, 13, 96-97, 102, 165n30; and extradition reforms, 101-2, 112; on Joseph Kindler and Charles Chitat Ng, 13, 102, 111, 169n54
Drew, Jan, 48
Duplessis, Maurice, 3

ecumenical movement, 16
ecumenism, 22
egalitarianism, 2, 4, 7-8
Eichmann, Adolf, 57
Estey, Willard, 6-7, 36
European Council, 106
Extradition Act, 105, 109, 111, 171n67

fascism. *See* Nazism
Factums, 7
Falsehoods law. *See* spreading false news
Favreau, Guy, 58
FCSS. *See* Federation of Canadian Sikh Societies
Federal Court of Appeal: and extradition, 100-1, 113, 168n48; and refugee rights, 22, 25, 28, 33, 37-38, 40-43, 50

Federal Court, Trial Division, 44, 49, 52, 100-1, 116
federal government. *See* Government of Canada
Federation of Canadian Sikh Societies (FCSS), 11, 29, 135n61
"Four Freedoms" speech, 2
Fraser, Bruce, 79-80
freedom of expression: limits to, 1, 54, 56-58, 62-63, 76-85, 118-19, 161n176; martyrs for, 70, 74; misuse of, 12, 56, 87; right to, 12, 54-55, 58-59, 69, 74, 76-85, 89-90; safeguards protecting, 66, 70-72
freedom of speech. *See* freedom of expression
Front de libération du Québec, 93, 153n84
Front Page Challenge, 63-64, 150n54

Gallagher, W.J., 16
Garber, Michael, 57-58
gay and lesbian rights, 8
genocide, 61-62, 118
Genocide Convention, 2
German ultranationalist National Democratic Party (NPD), 63
Globe and Mail: on capital punishment, 98; on hate propaganda law, 59, 62, 68-69, 76, 147n32, 150n59
Goebbels, Joseph, 65
Gonthier, Charles Doherty, 109
Goodfellow, Bob, 97
Government of Alberta, 76, 78
Government of Canada: authority of, 88; on capital punishment, 91, 93, 97; and *Kindler*, 14, 107-8, 111; relationship with CCC, 17-19, 22-24, 51-52, 129n11; and *Singh*, 11; and *Suresh*, 50-51
Green, Mendel, 29, 32, 34
Green Paper on Immigration, 20
Greenspan, Edward, 114
Grey, Julius, 105, 110, 171n70
group defamation, 12, 56, 61

habeas corpus, 99, 101-02, 113
Hague Agreement on Refugee Seaman, 19
Harper government, 116
Harris, Sydney, 57, 60, 65-66
hate-mongering, 56, 59, 62-63, 67-68, 72, 83, 117
hate propaganda: confronting problem of, 1, 54-55, 57, 59, 61-63, 83, 118; effects of 13, 65, 79; promotion of 12, 57, 61-65, 70, 73, 78-79, 82-83
hate propaganda law. *See Act to Amend the Criminal Code (Hate Propaganda)*
hate speech. *See* hate propaganda
Hayes, Saul, 57-59, 65, 144n15, 149n47, 151n60
Head, Wilson, 67
Hitler, Adolf, 55, 57, 147n37
Hocké, Jean-Pierre, 42
Holocaust: denial of, 70-73, 75, 86; event of, 55, 57, 65, 74, 79, 82; survivors of, 57, 60, 73
Honey, Floyd, 23
House of Commons. *See* Parliament
human rights: abuses, 23; advancement of, 14, 54, 117, 178n8; age of, 1-2, 5, 8, 19, 117, 120; consciousness, 1, 5; culture of, 4; discourse of, 2, 3, 5; individual, 15, 91, 178n8; international, 3, 9; jurisprudence on, 1; modern era of, 2; movement, 2; norms, 1, 2, 10, 14, 52, 119-20, 178n8; principled ideas about, 9, 54, 88, 117-18, 120; revolution, 3, 7
Hungarian refugee crisis, 17-18

IAB. *See* Immigration Appeal Board
IACHR. *See* Inter-American Commission on Human Rights
Iacobucci, Frank, 85
ICCHRLA. *See* Inter-Church Committee on Human Rights in Latin America

ICCPR. *See* International Covenant on Civil and Political Rights
ICCR. *See* Inter-Church Committee for Refugees
ICEFRD. *See* International Convention on the Elimination of All Forms of Racial Discrimination
ICESCR. *See* International Covenant on Economic Social and Cultural Rights
Immigration Act (1952), 18, 19, 32
Immigration Act, 1976: abuse of, 38-39; criticisms of, 24-27, 141n125; constitutionality of, 28-36, 44-46, 50-52; terms of, 20-22, 50, 130-32n26; reforms to, 11, 39-41, 46-49, 140nn122-23
Immigration and Refugee Protection Act (IRPA), 48, 141n126. *See also* amendments to the *Extradition Act*
Immigration Appeal Board (IAB): constitutionality of, 28, 31-32, 34-36; functions of, 19-22, 38; problems with, 25;
immigration policies, 19
Immigration Refugee Board (IRB), 38, 40, 46
Indian Act, 4, 34
Inter-American Commission on Human Rights (IACHR), 47-48
InterAmicus, 78-79, 81
Inter-Church Committee for Refugees (ICCR), 23-24, 29, 42-43, 48, 137n106, 138n109
Inter-Church Committee on Chile, 23
Inter-Church Committee on Human Rights in Latin America (ICCHRLA), 23-24
interest groups. *See* non-governmental organizations
interest-group interventions. *See* intervener status
international abolitionist movement. *See* abolitionist movement
International Centre for Criminal Law and Human Rights, 114

international community, 14
International Convention on the Elimination of All Forms of Racial Discrimination (ICEFRD), 78-79, 159n140
International Covenant on Civil and Political Rights (ICCPR), 3, 172n73, 175n104, 177n113
International Covenant on Economic Social and Cultural Rights (ICESCR), 3
international law: advancement of, 3, 5, 118; and capital punishment, 14, 105-6, 109-10, 113-16; and hate propaganda, 82-84; and refugees, 47-48
International Refugee Organization, 17
international Zionist conspiracy. *See* Jewish conspiracies
intervener status, 5, 6
IRB. *See* Immigration Refugee Board
IRPA. *See* Immigration and Refugee Protection Act

Jackman, Barbara: advocacy of, 40, 138n109, 142n144; and *CCC v. MEI,* 44-46, 138n111; and *Singh,* 29, 31-32, 34, 136n79; and *Suresh,* 50-51
JCRC. *See* Joint Community Relations Committee
Jewish community: on James Keegstra, 74; reactions to neo-Nazis, 57, 60, 63-64, 147n33; vulnerability of, 12, 54-55, 69, 75, 81-82; on Zündel, 70, 74
Jewish conspiracies, 57, 65, 74-75, 82, 86
Joint Community Relations Committee (JCRC), 60, 63, 69-70, 143n1
judicial activism. *See* judicial review
judicial review, 7, 22, 49, 53, 119, 124n32, 125nn34-35
judiciary, 1, 6, 8, 12, 14, 44, 53, 57, 92, 115, 120

Kayfetz, Benjamin, 60, 151n60
Keegstra, James: charges against, 12, 71, 74, 84-85, 155n92, 160n167; politics of, 70-73, 77, 81-83, 85, 154n90, 156n100, 157n115
Kindler, Joseph, 99-106, 108, 111-12, 114, 168n48
Kindler v. Canada (Minister of Justice), 9, 12, 104-13, 115, 119, 177n113
King government, 55
Knox Presbyterian Church, 37

La Forest, Gérard V., 109-11
Lake, Leonard Thomas, 99
LaMarsh, Judy, 64
Lamer, Antonio, 35, 45, 109
Laporte, Pierre, 93, 153n84
Laskin, Bora, 4, 56, 58
Lavell v. A.-G. Canada, 5, 123-n24
LEAF. *See* Women's Legal Education and Action Fund
Legends of Our Time, 82
League of Human Rights for B'nai Brith. *See* B'nai Brith
legal mobilization. *See* strategic litigation
Lewis, Doug, 100, 110
L'Heureux-Dubé, Claire, 109
liberal democracies. *See* liberal parliamentary democracies
liberal parliamentary democracies, 1, 2, 9, 53, 55, 116, 119-20
Liberation Tigers of Tamil Eelam (LTTE), 50
Lockyear, James, 114
Lougheed government, 71
LTTE. *See* Liberation Tigers of Tamil Eelam

MacDonald, Flora, 37, 39
MacGuigan, Mark, 58, 62, 67, 149n47, 152n70, 155-56n98
MacKay, Shane, 58
MacLeod, Donald, 99-100, 175n104
Mandela, Nelson, 104
manifestly unfounded claims, 26

marketplace of ideas, 59, 83
marriage breakdown, 3
Martin, Paul, 64
Matas, David, 105-6, 110-12, 171-72nn70-71, 172n73
Mazankowski, Don, 96
McCarthy, Joseph, 62, 148-49n45
McDougall, Barbara, 43-44
McIntyre, William Rogers, 36
McLachlin, Beverley, 8, 45, 83-85, 110-11, 160n164
McLean, Walter, 37-39
Meech Lake Accord, 7
ministerial discretion, 51
minorities: protection from hate, 3, 12, 54, 58, 61-62, 65, 78, 83, 85, 118-19
moratorium, 92-93, 95
Morgentaler v. The Queen, 5, 124n24
Mosley, Oswald, 64, 67, 150n54
Mulroney, Brian: on capital punishment 97-98, 167n37; election victory of, 27, 96
Mulroney government: *CCC v. MEI*, 44-46; and *Ng* and *Kindler*, 112; reforms to *Immigration Act*, 11, 36-44, 46-47; responses to refugee arrivals, 38-40, 49

Nansen Medal, 37
Nathan Phillips Square, 63
National Defence Act, 94
national security, 47, 51, 116, 120, 178n8
Nationalist Socialist Party of Canada, 59, 76
Nazism, 55, 58, 61, 63, 65
neo-Nazism, 54, 60, 62-64, 68-69, 76
Ng, Charles Chitat: crimes of, 99, 101-5, 111-12, 114-15, 175n104
Nineteen Eighty-Four, 72
non-governmental organizations, 1, 3, 6, 9, 14, 117-20
norm entrepreneurs, 10
norms: and capital punishment, 88-89, 106-7, 109-11, 113-16; and freedom

of expression, 79, 87; human rights, 1, 2, 10, 14, 116, 120; and refugees, 15-16, 19, 22, 24, 27, 52-53; and state sovereignty, 19, 88; theories about, 9-10, 14, 119
NPD. *See* German ultranationalist National Democratic Party

Oakes test, 77, 79-84
OAS. *See* Organization of American States
October Crisis, 93, 153n84
Olson, Clifford, 102
Olympic Games, 94
Ontario Court of Appeal, 75-77, 79-80
Ontario Federation of Labour, 24
oral hearing: calls for, 21-22, 26-28; in *Singh*, 11, 30-36; reforms, 37-40
Organization of American States (OAS), 47-48, 107, 141n125
Orwell, George, 72
Ottawa. *See* Government of Canada
Ouellet, André, 70

Park, Eamon, 67
Parker, Graham, 67
Parliament: on capital punishment, 91-98, 110; on hate propaganda law, 64, 68, 71; on refugee rights, 20, 40-44, 48; on rights, 120
parliamentary supremacy, 2, 4, 5, 36
Participation of Visible Minorities in Canadian Society, 71
Pearson, Lester B., 62, 92, 148n45
Pearson government, 57, 91-92
Pennell, Lawrence, 64
Pettigrew, Pierre, 115
Pickersgill, Jack, 17
Pinochet, Augusto, 20, 23
Plaut, W. Gunther, 27, 37, 40, 73
POC. *See* prisoners of conscience
political and civil rights, 10
Pontius Pilate, 109
Postal Review Board, 70
postmaster general, 57

public interest litigation. *See* strategic litigation
Presbyterian Church, 22
principles of fundamental justice: relating to capital punishment, 105, 107, 109-10; relating to refugee rights, 32-36, 51
prisoners of conscience (POC), 89, 104, 162n1, 163n7
Protocol to the American Convention on Human Rights to Abolish the Death Penalty, 107, 172n73, 173n78
Protocol to the Convention Relating to the Status of Refugees, 19-20, 32
Prutschi, Manuel, 84
public interest groups. *See* non-governmental organizations
public interest standing, 44-46

Quebec, 2, 3
Quiet Revolution, 3

R. v. Andrews and Smith, 77, 79
R. v. Drybones, 4, 34, 69, 153n81
R. v. Keegstra, 9, 12, 77-85, 119, 157n121
Rafay, Atif Ahmad, 113-15
Ratushny, Ed, 27
refoulement, 33-34, 40, 42, 47, 50-53, 135n71, 139n116
Refugees: advocates of, 11, 21, 24, 27-29, 39, 47, 51-52; assistance to, 16; attitudes toward, 12; Canadian policies toward, 18, 19; claimants, 11, 21, 30, 32, 34-35, 38, 46-47; Convention, 20-22, 28, 33, 35, 40-41, 45, 47-48, 50; fear of persecution, 33; inland and port-of-entry claims, 47; Jewish, 55; Latin American, 24; Portuguese, 38; rights of, 1, 11, 15, 19, 22, 28-36, 44-45, 52-53, 118; Sikh, 41; Tamil, 39-40
Refugee Appeal Division, 48-49
Refugee Concerns Project, 23
Refugee Determination in Canada: Proposals for a New System, 37-38

Refugee Determination Division, 40
refugee determination system. See *Immigration Act, 1976*
Refugee Review Board, 25
Refugee Status Advisory Committee (RSAC): constitutionality of, 32, 34-36; criticisms of, 24-28; establishment of, 21
religious conspiracy. See Jewish conspiracies
Rhinoceros Party, 72
Roberts, John, 27
Robillard, Lucienne, 50
Robinson, W.G., 26
Rock, Allan, 114
Rome Statute of the International Criminal Court, 114, 176n106
Roosevelt, Franklin Delano, 2
Rosenberg, Marc, 80-81, 84
Rosenfeldt, Gary, 102-4, 111
Rosenfeldt, Sharon, 102
Ross, Andrew, 23, 133n36
RSAC. See Refugee Status Advisory Committee
Ruby, Clayton, 114

safe haven, 101, 105, 109, 115
Safe Third Country Agreement, 49, 52
safe third countries, 40, 43, 46, 138-39n111, 139n116
Samidsdat Publishers, 70, 72-73
Schelew, Michael, 29, 32, 34
scientific racism, 2
Scott, Ian, 31-32, 34-36, 136n75
search for equality. See egalitarianism
Second Optional Protocol to the ICCPR Aiming at Abolition of the Death Penalty, 107, 115, 172n73, 173n78
Second World War: event of, 2, 55, 60, 89; and postwar era, 5, 11, 15, 52, 118
security certificates, 41, 50
Senate Human Rights Committee, 48
Senate of the Republic of Italy, 114
senior immigration officer, 21, 24

Sgro, Judy, 51-52
Sharp, Mitchell, 23, 132n34
shock the conscience, 14, 105, 110, 115-16
Singh et al. v. MEI: impact of, 37, 39, 40, 44, 49-50, 53, 106; trial, 9, 11, 28-36, 119
Six Day War, 69
Smith, Robert Wayne, 76, 83
Smith, Ronald, 116
Social Credit Party, 55, 72, 156n100
Sopinka, John, 45, 109
Special Committee on Hate Propaganda in Canada: establishment of, 58; in *Keegstra*, 77, 79-81, 83; reaction to, 62-63, 67; recommendations of, 60-62, 64-65, 86, 148nn42-43
Special Review Committee, 22
spreading false news, 56, 72-73, 85
Standing Committee on Justice and the Solicitor General, 96, 113
Standing Conference of Canadian Organizations Concerned for Refugees, 39
state sovereignty, 15, 52
strategic litigation, 6-8
Suez Canal Crisis, 5
Sunday, 63
Supreme Court of Canada: backlash against, 7-8, 124n32; and *Burns*, 113-15, 177n113; and *CCC v. MEI*, 45-46; conservatism of, 5; constitutionality of hate propaganda law, 69, 74, 86-87; constitutionality of spreading false news law, 85; extradition, 101-2, 113; and *Keegstra*, 12-13, 54, 76-85; and *Kindler*, 14, 104-11, 170-71nn66-67; origins of, 4; refugee rights, 16, 52; and *Singh*, 11, 28-36, 49-50; and *Suresh*, 50-51; third party interventions, 1, 2, 6-7, 10-11, 117-18
Suresh v. Minister (Citizenship and Immigration), 50-51, 142n142
Suresh, Manickavasagam, 50-51

Tait, John C., 107-8, 139n116
Task Force on Immigration Practices and Procedures on the Refugee Status Determination Process, 26, 35
terrorism, 23, 47-51, 93-94, 120, 178n8
third-party interventions. *See* intervener status
Toronto City Council, 59
torture, 50-51, 106, 110, 115
Trudeau government, 19-20, 94, 133n39
Trudeau, Pierre Elliott: on capital punishment, 92-95, 97; and Cohen Committee, 58, 66, 145n21, 151-52nn67-68; on hate propaganda, 66; and Laskin appointment, 4; and patriation of Constitution 5; reforms to *Criminal Code*, 3-4, 122n13; on refugees, 132n34

*U*DHR. See *Universal Declaration of Human Rights*
UN *Charter*, 2
UN *Convention against Torture* 52, 172n73
UN *Convention Relating to the Status of Refugees*, 19-20, 32, 52, 128n3, 130n23, 135n71
UN *Genocide Convention. See Genocide Convention*
UN high commissioner for human rights, 26
UN Human Rights Committee, 111, 175n104, 177n113
United Church, 16, 22, 47
United Nations Relief and Rehabilitation Agency (UNNRA), 17
United States v. Burns, 113-16, 177n113
United States v. Charles Chitat Ng, 99-101, 109, 115
Universal Declaration of Human Rights (UDHR), 2, 172n73
UNNRA. *See* United Nations Relief and Rehabilitation Agency

Victims of Violence Society (VOV), 102-3, 111
Vietnamese boat people, 37
von Thadden, Adolf, 63-64, 67, 149n52
vulnerable groups. *See* minorities

war crimes, 57
Washington Association of Criminal Defence Lawyers, 114
WCC. World Council of Churches (WCC)
Weiner, Gerry, 39-40
Western Canada Concept, 71, 155n94
Westminster parliamentary system. *See* liberal parliamentary democracies
Westphalian international system, 16
White Paper on Immigration, 19
white supremacy. *See* neo-Nazism
Wiesel, Elie, 82
Wilson, Bertha, 6-7, 29, 35-36, 106, 136n79
Women's Legal Education and Action Fund (LEAF), 78-79, 81, 159n141
World Council of Churches (WCC) 16-17, 128n9, 132n34

Yom Kippur War, 69
Yorkminster Baptist Church, 16

Zündel, Ernst: false news trials, 72-76, 81, 84-85, 154nn88-89, 156n102, 157n122, 160n173; postal hearings, 70-71

LAW AND SOCIETY

Andrew S. Thompson
In Defence of Principles: NGOs and Human Rights in Canada (2010)

Aaron Doyle and Dawn Moore (eds.)
Critical Criminology in Canada: New Voices, New Directions (2010)

Joanna R. Quinn
The Politics of Acknowledgement: Truth Commissions in Uganda and Haiti (2010)

Patrick James
Constitutional Politics in Canada after the Charter: Liberalism, Communitarianism, and Systemism (2010)

Louis A. Knafla and Haijo Westra (eds.)
Aboriginal Title and Indigenous Peoples: Canada, Australia, and New Zealand (2010)

Janet Mosher and Joan Brockman (eds.)
Constructing Crime: Contemporary Processes of Criminalization (2010)

Stephen Clarkson and Stepan Wood
A Perilous Imbalance: The Globalization of Canadian Law and Governance (2009)

Amanda Glasbeek
Feminized Justice: The Toronto Women's Court, 1913-34 (2009)

Kimberley Brooks (ed.)
Justice Bertha Wilson: One Woman's Difference (2009)

Wayne V. McIntosh and Cynthia L. Cates
Multi-Party Litigation: The Strategic Context (2009)

Renisa Mawani
Colonial Proximities: Crossracial Encounters and Juridical Truths in British Columbia, 1871-1921 (2009)

James B. Kelly and Christopher P. Manfredi (eds.)
Contested Constitutionalism: Reflections on the Canadian Charter of Rights and Freedoms (2009)

Catherine E. Bell and Robert K. Paterson (eds.)
Protection of First Nations Cultural Heritage: Laws, Policy, and Reform (2008)

Catherine E. Bell and Val Napoleon (eds.)
First Nations Cultural Heritage and Law: Case Studies, Voices, and Perspectives (2008)

Hamar Foster, Benjamin L. Berger, and A.R. Buck (eds.)
The Grand Experiment: Law and Legal Culture in British Settler Societies (2008)

Richard J. Moon (ed.)
Law and Religious Pluralism in Canada (2008)

Douglas C. Harris
Landing Native Fisheries: Indian Reserves and Fishing Rights in British Columbia, 1849-1925 (2008)

Peggy J. Blair
Lament for a First Nation: The Williams Treaties in Southern Ontario (2008)

Lori G. Beaman
Defining Harm: Religious Freedom and the Limits of the Law (2007)

Stephen Tierney (ed.)
Multiculturalism and the Canadian Constitution (2007)

Julie Macfarlane
The New Lawyer: How Settlement Is Transforming the Practice of Law (2007)

Kimberley White
Negotiating Responsibility: Law, Murder, and States of Mind (2007)

Dawn Moore
Criminal Artefacts: Governing Drugs and Users (2007)

Hamar Foster, Heather Raven, and Jeremy Webber (eds.)
Let Right Be Done: Aboriginal Title, the Calder *Case, and the Future of Indigenous Rights* (2007)

Dorothy E. Chunn, Susan B. Boyd, and Hester Lessard (eds.)
Reaction and Resistance: Feminism, Law, and Social Change (2007)

Margot Young, Susan B. Boyd, Gwen Brodsky, and Shelagh Day (eds.)
Poverty: Rights, Social Citizenship, and Legal Activism (2007)

Rosanna L. Langer
Defining Rights and Wrongs: Bureaucracy, Human Rights, and Public Accountability (2007)

C.L. Ostberg and Matthew E. Wetstein
Attitudinal Decision Making in the Supreme Court of Canada (2007)

Chris Clarkson
Domestic Reforms: Political Visions and Family Regulation in British Columbia, 1862-1940 (2007)

Jean McKenzie Leiper
Bar Codes: Women in the Legal Profession (2006)

Gerald Baier
Courts and Federalism: Judicial Doctrine in the United States, Australia, and Canada (2006)

Avigail Eisenberg (ed.)
Diversity and Equality: The Changing Framework of Freedom in Canada (2006)

Randy K. Lippert
Sanctuary, Sovereignty, Sacrifice: Canadian Sanctuary Incidents, Power, and Law (2005)

James B. Kelly
Governing with the Charter: Legislative and Judicial Activism and Framers' Intent (2005)

Dianne Pothier and Richard Devlin (eds.)
Critical Disability Theory: Essays in Philosophy, Politics, Policy, and Law (2005)

Susan G. Drummond
Mapping Marriage Law in Spanish Gitano Communities (2005)

Louis A. Knafla and Jonathan Swainger (eds.)
Laws and Societies in the Canadian Prairie West, 1670-1940 (2005)

Ikechi Mgbeoji
Global Biopiracy: Patents, Plants, and Indigenous Knowledge (2005)

Florian Sauvageau, David Schneiderman, and David Taras, with Ruth Klinkhammer and Pierre Trudel
The Last Word: Media Coverage of the Supreme Court of Canada (2005)

Gerald Kernerman
Multicultural Nationalism: Civilizing Difference, Constituting Community (2005)

Pamela A. Jordan
Defending Rights in Russia: Lawyers, the State, and Legal Reform in the Post-Soviet Era (2005)

Anna Pratt
Securing Borders: Detention and Deportation in Canada (2005)

Kirsten Johnson Kramar
Unwilling Mothers, Unwanted Babies: Infanticide in Canada (2005)

W.A. Bogart
Good Government? Good Citizens? Courts, Politics, and Markets in a Changing Canada (2005)

Catherine Dauvergne
Humanitarianism, Identity, and Nation: Migration Laws in Canada and Australia (2005)

Michael Lee Ross
First Nations Sacred Sites in Canada's Courts (2005)

Andrew Woolford
Between Justice and Certainty: Treaty Making in British Columbia (2005)

John McLaren, Andrew Buck, and Nancy Wright (eds.)
Despotic Dominion: Property Rights in British Settler Societies (2004)

Georges Campeau
From UI to EI: Waging War on the Welfare State (2004)

Alvin J. Esau
The Courts and the Colonies: The Litigation of Hutterite Church Disputes (2004)

Christopher N. Kendall
Gay Male Pornography: An Issue of Sex Discrimination (2004)

Roy B. Flemming
Tournament of Appeals: Granting Judicial Review in Canada (2004)

Constance Backhouse and Nancy L. Backhouse
The Heiress vs the Establishment: Mrs. Campbell's Campaign for Legal Justice (2004)

Christopher P. Manfredi
Feminist Activism in the Supreme Court: Legal Mobilization and the Women's Legal Education and Action Fund (2004)

Annalise Acorn
Compulsory Compassion: A Critique of Restorative Justice (2004)

Jonathan Swainger and Constance Backhouse (eds.)
People and Place: Historical Influences on Legal Culture (2003)

Jim Phillips and Rosemary Gartner
Murdering Holiness: The Trials of Franz Creffield and George Mitchell (2003)

David R. Boyd
Unnatural Law: Rethinking Canadian Environmental Law and Policy (2003)

Ikechi Mgbeoji
Collective Insecurity: The Liberian Crisis, Unilateralism, and Global Order (2003)

Rebecca Johnson
Taxing Choices: The Intersection of Class, Gender, Parenthood, and the Law (2002)

John McLaren, Robert Menzies, and Dorothy E. Chunn (eds.)
Regulating Lives: Historical Essays on the State, Society, the Individual, and the Law (2002)

Joan Brockman
Gender in the Legal Profession: Fitting or Breaking the Mould (2001)